BECOMING
ISRAEL

Eli Lizorkin-Eyzenberg, Ph.D.

JEWISH STUDIES
FOR CHRISTIANS
Tel-Aviv, Israel

ISBN: 9781792822872

Becoming Israel, Copyright © 2019 by Eliyahu Lizorkin-Eyzenberg. This book contains material protected under International and Federal Copyright Laws and Treaties. Any unauthorized reprint or use of this material is prohibited. No part of this book may be reproduced or transmitted in any form or by any means, electronic or mechanical, including photocopying, recording, or by any information storage and retrieval system without express written permission from the author (dr.eli.israel@gmail.com).

To my wonderful daughter Lana
with much love and care.

Contents

INTRODUCTION AND DISCLAIMER 1

CHAPTER ONE: THE LIFE OF ADAM 4

CHAPTER TWO: THE LIFE OF NOAH 22

CHAPTER THREE: THE LIFE OF ABRAHAM 37

CHAPTER FOUR: THE LIFE OF ISAAC 68

CHAPTER FIVE: THE LIFE OF JACOB 82

CHAPTER SIX: THE LIFE OF JOSEPH 136

BIBLIOGRAPHY 175

INTRODUCTION AND DISCLAIMER

I wrote this book for someone who is willing to come along with me on an exciting journey of deeper reflection; someone who is willing to pull back the layers of translation traditions by looking at the original Hebrew of the Book of Genesis itself. I intend to go slowly, rethinking some very familiar texts that describe the lives of key Biblical characters. By slowly reading this book you will discover for yourself the riches of the Ancient Hebrew stories that were first written to provide a guide for the emerging people of Israel. Whether you are part of today's "Jewish people" or what many have come to call a "Jewish coalition" – the members of the nations of the world that worship Israel's God in Christ Jesus along with the people of Israel – this book is for you, because these great Torah stories are your heritage as well. Without them you, too, just like an Israelite of old, do not know where you came from and where it is that you are going.

As the former slaves left Egypt, they took with them on their journey the ideology of their former Egyptian owners. It has been said many times and by many people that it took a relatively short time to get Israel out of Egypt, but it took at least 40 years to get Egypt out of Israel. That is to say that Moses had a tough task before him. He needed to provide for the people of Israel, who were about to covenant with their God (this is what the Book of Exodus is all about), the fundamental narrative that explained their current struggles and set a clear trajectory of hope for their future. Moses, and any others who took part in the composition and editing of the book of Genesis, did so by retelling unbelievably honest and awe-inspiring stories of human origins. They got as quickly as they could to the central story of the Book of Genesis – the formation of the family of Israel. It is primarily these stories about Abraham, Isaac and Jacob (and his children) that serve as the foundation of the Torah. Think about it, while we often concentrate on the story of the creation of the world and human origins, that takes only eleven chapters – while the story of "becoming Israel" takes the rest of the thirty-nine.

Translation as Interpretation

Those of you who know me know that I am not someone who decries the very idea of translation or believes that all translations are wrong or not useful. Far from it. I believe that translation work into the vernacular languages of various people groups is, in fact, extremely important; but I am also persuaded that no matter how good any given translation is and no matter by what group of people or individual/s it is accomplished, it is still an interpretation of the original text we call the Word of God and not the Word of God itself. Most people think that because the majority of Bible translators are committed to God that they would never introduce anything of "their own" into the text of translation. But, truth be told, objective translation is impossible, because any text is understood through the worldview of the translator. Translation is in some way an act of interpretation of the original Scriptures; knowing the original languages does not give you the ability to know exactly what the original words and sentences meant but, instead, gives the ability to determine the range of possible meanings. My point is simple: Everyone involved in translation of the Bible must make translation decisions when various meaning possibilities present themselves in the text. That happens more often than you realize. That, in and of itself, should not discourage you or scare you in anyway; instead it should encourage you to learn how to use simple tools such as an Interlinear Bible, dictionaries, or perhaps, Bible study software to be able to see for yourself what other translation options are in the text (sometimes you will be amazed and puzzled as to why the translators opted out of better ways to say it and, at other times, you will see their logic quite clearly).

Another thing is important to state at the start. Sometimes the issue is not that the translators have followed a "wrong" trail, pursuing an erroneous trajectory of meaning, but that something said in Hebrew sometimes simply cannot be translated into other languages clearly. So, by learning how to read in Hebrew and use Bible study tools, you will be able to delve into the original Hebrew text and discover for yourself the rich treasure that lies beneath translation. You will be able in some way to experience and feel the language in which these sacred texts were penned.

I approached writing this book in a particular way. I first worked with text as I always do – alone. This is of no surprise to those of you who read my book *The Jewish Gospel of John: Discovering Jesus, King of All Israel*. You know my style and my approach. But then I invited into this conversation several Jewish and Christian scholars. In particular, on the Jewish side I used the works of Jonathan Sacks and Robert Alter, while on the Christian side I stayed mostly with the commentary on Genesis by Walter Brueggemann. I fully realize that this is an extremely limited list of works, and if I were writing a complete commentary on the Book of Genesis I would have had to consult and interact with many more Jewish and Christian thinkers. However, for my purposes I decided not to clutter my mind with too much but only to supplement my own insights with the insights of these great men from which I felt you, my readers, would surely benefit.

When presenting parallel Hebrew and English texts of Genesis, I have used the New Jewish Publication Society translation. Note that sometimes verse numbers differ in Hebrew and in English (the two sets of numbers appear separated by slashes when relevant).

CHAPTER ONE: THE LIFE OF ADAM

Adam and his life partner Eve are undoubtedly the most well-known couple in the history of the world. They are the parents of all humankind. Their story is how it all began. Adam and Eve are the subjects not only of countless sermons and Bible studies, but also of classical and modern art. Although their story is one of the most familiar and discussed stories in the Western world, our understanding is usually based on translations and not on the original Hebrew text. Therefore, important nuances of the story are often overlooked. Even though many other Biblical characters had spouses, Adam and Eve are unique and cannot be discussed or examined separately from each other. Therefore, this study will look at them together.

The Hebrew word אָדָם *(adam)*, which is translated as "Adam," simply means "human." There are other words for "man" in Hebrew, such as אִישׁ *(ish)* and גֶּבֶר *(gever)*, but אָדָם *(adam)* best signifies the idea of "humanity." The word אָדָם *(adam)* is connected with several other Hebrew words. This connection clarified its meaning for the original readership of the book of Genesis – the ancient Hebrews understood something we generally do not. Two words connected with *Adam* are אָדֹם *(adom)* "red" and אֲדָמָה *(adamah)* "ground, earth," which show us that the basic meaning of Adam's name was somehow associated with both "redness" and "ground." Another word, דָּם *(dam)* "blood," comes from a different root but has similar sounds and thus may have sprung to mind via association.

The First Account of Human Creation

The first account of Adam's origin is found in Genesis 1:26-31. However, it is important to read this account in the context of the whole creation story. Having presented the creation of light (Day 1), sky (Day 2), land and plants (Day 3), stars (Day 4), and fish and birds (Day 5), the stage was set for the most important work of creation on Day 6. On the sixth day, God created land animals and humans. It is striking to see that, while the human race is created last, it is nevertheless created within the same day as the animal kingdom. The moral of the story here is not that humans are animals, but that humans and land animals have a much closer relationship than anything else in creation. This will become abundantly clear later when we examine the story of the next hero of the Hebrew Bible – Noah. It all began in Genesis 1:26 when God, speaking either to Himself or to His heavenly council, said:

וַיֹּאמֶר אֱלֹהִים נַעֲשֶׂה אָדָם בְּצַלְמֵנוּ כִּדְמוּתֵנוּ וְיִרְדּוּ בִדְגַת הַיָּם וּבְעוֹף הַשָּׁמַיִם וּבַבְּהֵמָה וּבְכָל־הָאָרֶץ וּבְכָל־הָרֶמֶשׂ הָרֹמֵשׂ עַל־הָאָרֶץ:

"Let us make man in our image, after our likeness. They shall rule the fish of the sea, the birds of the sky, the cattle, the whole earth, and all the creeping things that creep on earth." (Gen. 1:26)

Adam (and, as we will see in the next verse, this includes Eve) was created not only to be connected with redness (perhaps from blood) and the ground, but also as the author of Genesis described it בְּצַלְמֵנוּ כִּדְמוּתֵנוּ (*be-tsalmenu ki-dmutenu*), which is commonly and faithfully translated "in our image and likeness." The two concepts of צֶלֶם (*tselem*) and דְּמוּת (*demut*) are very similar and, in fact, function as parallelism. The ending "נוּ-" (*-nu*) makes both "image" and "likeness" qualified by the possessive "our."

Like many other languages of the world, Hebrew is a poetic language. It has its own poetic conventions and constructions. One such construction is Hebrew parallelism. This is a literary device whereby the second line (or in this case, word) says something synonymous or complementary to the first, thus expanding the meaning of the first concept. As we will see in later discussions, צֶלֶם (*tselem*) is connected with the idea of a "shadow" צֵל (*tsel*), an imperfect image resembling that which casts it. דְּמוּת (*demut*) is parallel to צֶלֶם (*tselem*) and is connected with the ideas of "similarity" and "imagination." The Hebrew words for "image" and "likeness" use different prefixes, "into" -בְּ (*be-*) and "as/according to" -כְּ (*ke-*), but this is normal for Hebrew. They could be translated differently but do not necessarily need to be.

Thus the Torah begins its story-telling, seeking to persuade former Egyptian slaves – the Israelites – that not only the Pharaoh of Egypt, but they, too, have great divine origins. All humans were created in the image and the likeness of God. Together their father Adam and mother Eve were powerful rulers of all God's creation. They were to exercise redemptive dominion over the fish, birds, cattle, the earth and every creeping thing.

The verb יִרְדּוּ *(yirdu)* "they shall rule" in the abovementioned Genesis 1:26 is not the normal verb for the simple idea of "ruling"; rather, in many contexts its underlying root connotes "dominating" or even "subjugating." God's creation needed a boots-on-the-ground manager, or better yet, a "dominant" "king" who would nonetheless be loving and selfless.

Incidentally, the idea of the "son of God" in the Hebrew Bible essentially denotes "kingship," meaning "being appointed by God to rule" (Ps. 2). This is probably why when Luke describes the genealogy of Jesus going back to Adam, we read that he was not only "the son of Shem, the son of Noah, the son of Lamech, the son of Methuselah, the son of Enoch, the son of Jared, the son of Mahalaleel, the son of Cainan, the son of Enosh, the son of Seth, the son of Adam…," but also that Adam was "the son of God" (3:36b-38). The New Testament Scriptures will later develop this connection in very significant ways, showing how Christ the King becomes the last Adam who will eventually bring fallen humanity into a new, redemptive relationship with God in a way that is much greater than it once was at the time of creation (1 Cor. 15:35-58). We read in Genesis 1:28:

וַיְבָרֶךְ אֹתָם אֱלֹהִים וַיֹּאמֶר לָהֶם אֱלֹהִים פְּרוּ וּרְבוּ וּמִלְאוּ אֶת־הָאָרֶץ וְכִבְשֻׁהָ וּרְדוּ בִּדְגַת הַיָּם וּבְעוֹף הַשָּׁמַיִם וּבְכָל־חַיָּה הָרֹמֶשֶׂת עַל־הָאָרֶץ:

God blessed them, and God said to them, "Be fertile and increase, fill the earth and master it; and rule the fish of the sea, the birds of the sky, and all the living things that creep on the earth." (Gen. 1:28)

As we read about the blessing that God placed upon Adam and Eve, we must understand the basic meaning of this highly important ancient concept. The Hebrew word בָּרַךְ *(barakh)* may literally mean either "to bless" or "to kneel." In Hebrew the related word בֶּרֶךְ *(berekh)* means "knee." It's not clear which of the two meanings of the verb came first. It is interesting that in the Hebrew Bible the verb בָּרַךְ *(barakh)* "bless" is often juxtaposed with the verb אָרַר *(arar)* "curse." The latter verb may be connected to the idea of "binding" and "limitation" or "restriction." For that reason we may speculate that בָּרַךְ *(barakh)* perhaps had an opposite connotation, namely "gaining freedom" or "being set free." This concept is very hard for us to visualize because to the modern mind it remains just a concept. But for the ancients "the blessing" was something very real, possessing the enormous creative power of God that was meant to be released in His final creation – humanity. The Israelites that had just left Egypt needed to understand that they worshiped the God of all humanity, especially since this very God had singled them out for a special covenantal relationship through their forefathers Abraham, Isaac and Jacob. What would be the relationship between them and the nations of the world? What is the difference between the blessings of Israel and the blessings of the world? All these questions the Torah will yet raise and answer in the minds of Israelites in the stories that await us.

There are other linguistic treasures that could be pointed out here, but we will continue with our story of Adam and Eve. In blessing Adam and Eve, God set their trajectory for growth and expansion. It is customary to call "be fruitful and multiply" a commandment, but the natural flow of the text rather seems to point to this being a description of the blessing given. Now that Adam and Eve are blessed by God, they are "set free" to fulfill their magnificent purpose to exercise loving and caring dominion over the created order by being fertile and increasing numerically, thereby filling the earth and mastering it. There comes a time in life when we as humanity must realize that the desire of our God's heart is to release us to the joy of freedom. The desire of God is set for all humanity. Humanity must grow, must possess the earth, and reflect the praise of God who called it into being; and yet, as we will see in the future stories of the Torah, the family and people of Israel will be called to play a very special role in leading all other nations in their worship of God. Apostle Peter wrote in one of his letters:

> "You are a chosen race, a royal priesthood, a holy nation, a people for His own possession, that you may proclaim the excellencies of him who called you out of darkness into His marvelous light... Keep your conduct among the Gentiles honorable, so that when they speak against you as evildoers, they may see your good deeds and glorify God on the day of visitation." (1 Peter 2:9, 12)

As modern children of Adam, especially the last Adam (Christ/Messiah), we realize the importance of engaging with the world around us, not simply escaping it. This cultural mandate forces us to think through how we can press the crown-rights of Christ Jesus as we continue to pray, "Your kingdom come on Earth as it is in heaven," and seek to expand His rule in every area of human existence and in every geographical inch of the planet Earth.

God's Provision for Humans and Animals

As soon as the blessing is declared, God's provision for both humans and animals is announced in Genesis 1:29-31:

וַיֹּאמֶר אֱלֹהִים הִנֵּה נָתַתִּי לָכֶם אֶת־כָּל־עֵשֶׂב זֹרֵעַ זֶרַע אֲשֶׁר עַל־פְּנֵי כָל־הָאָרֶץ וְאֶת־כָּל־הָעֵץ אֲשֶׁר־בּוֹ פְרִי־עֵץ זֹרֵעַ זָרַע לָכֶם יִהְיֶה לְאָכְלָה:

God said, "See, I give you every seed-bearing plant that is upon all the earth, and every tree that has seed-bearing fruit; they shall be yours for food. (Gen. 1:29)

וּלְכָל־חַיַּת הָאָרֶץ וּלְכָל־עוֹף הַשָּׁמַיִם וּלְכֹל רוֹמֵשׂ עַל־הָאָרֶץ אֲשֶׁר־בּוֹ נֶפֶשׁ חַיָּה אֶת־כָּל־יֶרֶק עֵשֶׂב לְאָכְלָה וַיְהִי־כֵן:

And to all the animals on land, to all the birds of the sky, and to everything that creeps on earth, in which there is the breath of life, [I give] all the green plants for food." And it was so. (Gen. 1:30)

וַיַּרְא אֱלֹהִים אֶת־כָּל־אֲשֶׁר עָשָׂה וְהִנֵּה־טוֹב מְאֹד וַיְהִי־עֶרֶב וַיְהִי־בֹקֶר יוֹם הַשִּׁשִּׁי:

And God saw all that He had made, and found it very good. And there was evening and there was morning, the sixth day. (Gen. 1:31)

In this Biblical version, the Hebrew word for "day" is יוֹם *(yom)* and for "sixth" is שִׁשִּׁי *(shishi)*, or together with the definite article ה- *(ha-)*: יוֹם הַשִּׁשִּׁי *(yom ha-shishi)* "the sixth day." In Hebrew the word "six" is שֵׁשׁ *(shesh)*; the addition of the letter י *(yod)* at the end of this word turns it into an adjective שִׁשִּׁי *(shishi)* "sixth." The word שַׁבָּת *(shabbat)*, which is the Hebrew name for the seventh day, is grammatically related to such words as "ceasing," "resting" and "sitting." For instance, Exodus 31:17 tells us that God "rested" שָׁבַת *(shavat)* on the seventh day and "was refreshed."

The Israelite week was thus established at the time of creation as a seven-day cycle. Today we take this for granted, but the idea that humans should organize and track their time around periods of seven days was not always universally accepted. Periods of six- and ten-day weeks can be found in a number of ancient cultures. Moreover, in the Israelite/Jewish week, the days – instead of being named – are simply numbered. None of the days receive lofty names associated, for example, with ancient deities or heavenly bodies, as in other calendar systems. Only the seventh day has been privileged to have its own name שַׁבָּת *(shabbat)* "the Sabbath."

Today people are often preoccupied with the question of which day should be set aside for God's worship, Sunday or Saturday. The biblical injunction in the Torah naturally is not seeking to affect this modern issue. Instead it sought to set as law the most generous rhythm of work and rest known to man, protecting both man and animal (one day in seven). Today we, too, should be chiefly concerned not with which day is the correct one for worship (Saturday or Sunday), but rather that this one-in-seven Israelite rhythm of rest and work be ensured. The Sabbath is not the Sabbath of business unto the Lord (as Sunday most often is for modern Christians), but the Sabbath of rest (Hebrews 4:9). Certainly not overriding, but endorsing the true goal for the giving of the Sabbath, Jesus states: "The Sabbath was made for man, not man for the Sabbath." (Mark 2:27) This one-in-seven, rest-work ratio is God's blueprint for human productivity, success and growth.

What is interesting is that only when humanity is created and the blessings upon humans and animals confirmed does God evaluate His entire work of creation. While He evaluated the creation of each previous part as טוֹב *(tov)* "good," it is only upon the sixth day that He looked over His *entire* creation ("all that he had made") and declared that it was not simply טוֹב *(tov)* "good," but טוֹב מְאֹד *(tov meod)* "very good." We tend to think that humanity is God's most important creation, but the Torah seems to assume a communal nature of creation instead. The creation of man is something important, but it is not complete without the rest of creation.

The Second Account of Human Creation

Genesis 2 begins by focusing on day "seven." God has ceased from all his creation work and, as with previous blessings upon animals and humans, he now blesses this seventh day and sets it apart from the other six. The introductory section which began in Genesis 1:1 ends in Genesis 2:4 with the words, "Such is the story of heaven and earth when they were created."

Piece by piece, albeit in a somewhat truncated fashion, the Torah goes on to provide the ancient Israelites (and us modern readers by extension) with more information about the origins of Adam. After a brief explanation about creation prior to the first rain, the chapter expands on the story of the creation of Adam. We read in Genesis 2:7:

וַיִּיצֶר יהוה אֱלֹהִים אֶת־הָאָדָם עָפָר מִן־הָאֲדָמָה וַיִּפַּח בְּאַפָּיו נִשְׁמַת חַיִּים וַיְהִי הָאָדָם לְנֶפֶשׁ חַיָּה:

The LORD God formed man from the dust of the earth. He blew into his nostrils the breath of life, and man became a living being. (Gen. 2:7)

We have already briefly mentioned that the word for "Adam" or "human" אָדָם *(adam)* is connected to the word for "ground" or "earth" אֲדָמָה *(adamah)*. But here in the text we are given a small bit of important qualification: Adam is not simply formed from the "ground" אֲדָמָה *(adamah)*, but from the עָפָר *(afar)* of the ground. The simplest meaning of this Hebrew word עָפָר *(afar)* is "dust" or "dry earth." It can be associated via sound similarity (alliteration) and juxtaposition with אֵפֶר *(efer)* "ashes," as when Job says "I repent in dust and ashes" (Job 42:6; see also on Gen. 18:27 below).

If the two accounts of Adam's creation are compared (Gen. 1:26-28 and Gen. 2:4-25), some interesting differences emerge. Incidentally, just like in other Near Eastern works of literature, there are many pairs in the book of Genesis. In this case, two separate accounts of creation are provided, without any seeming tension in the text itself as to their significant differences. The first account refers to the Creator as "God," or אֱלֹהִים (*Elohim*) in Hebrew, while the second refers to the Creator as the "LORD God," or יהוה אֱלֹהִים (*YHWH Elohim*).

Secondly, the two accounts describe different ways of bringing about the creation. In the first account, God creates through speaking. In the second, He takes physical actions. Thirdly, the world is created in a different order. In the first account, mankind is presented as the climax of creation, with Adam and Eve created together. In the second account, God first creates man; He then plants vegetation in the Garden of Eden, forms the animals and birds and, finally, He brings forth a woman.

There are two fundamentally different approaches to understanding these divergent stories. The first approach seeks to harmonize the material and basically sees the second account of creation as an expansion of the first. The second approach seeks to differentiate between the various source traditions from which the book of Genesis (and Torah as a whole) eventually emerged.

Life in the Garden

After some specifications of the original location of the Garden of Eden in relation to rivers and other lands (vs. 10-14), we read in Genesis 2:15-17:

וַיִּקַּח יהוה אֱלֹהִים אֶת־הָאָדָם וַיַּנִּחֵהוּ בְגַן־עֵדֶן לְעָבְדָהּ וּלְשָׁמְרָהּ:

The LORD God took the man and placed him in the Garden of Eden, to till it and tend it. (Gen. 2:15)

Note that the word used for "placing" יָנַח *(yanach)* Adam in the Garden has a root connection to the name of the next great hero we will consider – "Noah" נֹחַ *(Noach)*. The Hebrew word for "Eden" עֵדֶן *(eden)* carries within itself the idea of "pleasure," "fertility," "delight," "luxury" and "refinement." Therefore, the Garden of Eden should be understood in these terms. Moreover, here we are told that Adam was placed in the Garden of delight literally "to work it" לְעָבְדָהּ *(le-avdah)* and "to guard it" לְשָׁמְרָהּ *(le-shamrah)*. The noun form corresponding to this working of the soil would be עֲבֹדָה *(avodah)*. While there are several different words in Hebrew that communicate the idea of worship (especially when it comes to the aspect of "service before God"), this same basic word for "work" עֲבֹדָה *(avodah)* is one that definitely applies to the service and worship of God עֲבֹדָה *(avodah)*. The commission "to work," which we associate today with struggle and toil, was given to Adam before the fall of humanity took place, not after. In other words, when God tasked Adam with working the ground in the Garden of Eden, it was still "very good," not yet affected by sin, death and misery.

וַיְצַו יהוה אֱלֹהִים עַל־הָאָדָם לֵאמֹר מִכֹּל עֵץ־הַגָּן אָכֹל תֹּאכֵל:

And the LORD God commanded the man, saying, "Of every tree of the Garden you are free to eat. (Gen. 2:16)

וּמֵעֵץ הַדַּעַת טוֹב וָרָע לֹא תֹאכַל מִמֶּנּוּ כִּי בְּיוֹם אֲכָלְךָ מִמֶּנּוּ מוֹת תָּמוּת:

But as for the tree of knowledge of good and bad, you must not eat of it; for as soon as you eat of it, you shall die." (Gen. 2:17)

What is translated into English at the end of verse 17 as simply "you shall die" actually carries a much stronger effect in Hebrew. The phrase מוֹת תָּמוּת *(mot tamot)* is more accurately translated as "dying you shall die" or "doomed to die." This is a typical Hebraic grammatical structure that repeats the root. Another example of Hebrew emphasis (of a different kind, but with a similar repetition of sound) is found in Genesis 12:1. There God commands Abram to leave his native country and go to a land He will show him. He says not simply "go," but something like "get going" or "go for yourself" לֶךְ־לְךָ *(lekh lekha)*.

This verse records the first actual commandment given to Adam. Perhaps to differentiate it from other imperatives within blessings, such as we have seen before ("Be fertile and increase [in number]"), here the Hebrew word specifically denoting the idea of a "commandment" is used: וַיְצַו *(va-yetsav)* "and He commanded." The Hebrew noun for "commandment" is מִצְוָה *(mitsvah),* which originates from the same root as the word used here in verse 16.

The Creation of Eve

Once Adam's placement and duties in the Garden have been specified, together with just one very important limitation, the author continues on to the origins of Eve. We read in Genesis 2:18-24:

וַיֹּאמֶר יהוה אֱלֹהִים לֹא־טוֹב הֱיוֹת הָאָדָם לְבַדּוֹ אֶעֱשֶׂה־לּוֹ עֵזֶר כְּנֶגְדּוֹ:

The LORD God said, "It is not good for man to be alone; I will make a fitting helper for him." (Gen. 2:18)

וַיִּצֶר יהוה אֱלֹהִים מִן־הָאֲדָמָה כָּל־חַיַּת הַשָּׂדֶה וְאֵת כָּל־עוֹף הַשָּׁמַיִם וַיָּבֵא אֶל־הָאָדָם לִרְאוֹת מַה־יִּקְרָא־לוֹ וְכֹל אֲשֶׁר יִקְרָא־לוֹ הָאָדָם נֶפֶשׁ חַיָּה הוּא שְׁמוֹ׃

And the LORD God formed out of the earth all the wild beasts and all the birds of the sky, and brought them to the man to see what he would call them; and whatever the man called each living creature, that would be its name. (Gen. 2:19)

וַיִּקְרָא הָאָדָם שֵׁמוֹת לְכָל־הַבְּהֵמָה וּלְעוֹף הַשָּׁמַיִם וּלְכֹל חַיַּת הַשָּׂדֶה וּלְאָדָם לֹא־מָצָא עֵזֶר כְּנֶגְדּוֹ׃

And the man gave names to all the cattle and to the birds of the sky and to all the wild beasts; but for Adam no fitting helper was found. (Gen. 2:20)

The majority of English translations describe Adam's life-partner, Eve, as something akin to a "fitting helper." However, the Hebrew phrase עֵזֶר כְּנֶגְדּוֹ *(ezer ke-negdo)*, if translated more literally, carries an intriguing meaning. Adam's wife Eve is described in oppositional terms; that is, as "a helper [who is] opposite to him." However, even the word "helper" is a weak translation. The use of עֵזֶר *(ezer)* connotes an active intervention on behalf of someone, often in a military context. It is no secret that good marriages are those unions in which each spouse complements the other and fulfills that which is lacking in the other. For example, a good wife stands fully behind her husband, but she does not just go along with everything he puts forth. Instead she freely speaks her mind, often in oppositional terms. The husband's ideas are thereby tested, tried and at times tempered by the wisdom of this oppositional, but loving interventional agent (helper).

וַיַּפֵּל יהוה אֱלֹהִים תַּרְדֵּמָה עַל־הָאָדָם וַיִּישָׁן וַיִּקַּח אַחַת מִצַּלְעֹתָיו וַיִּסְגֹּר בָּשָׂר תַּחְתֶּנָּה׃

So the LORD God cast a deep sleep upon the man; and, while he slept, He took one of his ribs and closed up the flesh at that spot. (Gen. 2:21)

וַיִּבֶן יהוה אֱלֹהִים אֶת־הַצֵּלָע אֲשֶׁר־לָקַח מִן־הָאָדָם לְאִשָּׁה וַיְבִאֶהָ אֶל־הָאָדָם׃

And the LORD God fashioned the rib that He had taken from the man into a woman; and He brought her to the man. (Gen. 2:22)

וַיֹּאמֶר הָאָדָם זֹאת הַפַּעַם עֶצֶם מֵעֲצָמַי וּבָשָׂר מִבְּשָׂרִי לְזֹאת יִקָּרֵא אִשָּׁה כִּי מֵאִישׁ לֻקֳחָה־זֹּאת:

Then the man said, "This one at last is bone of my bones and flesh of my flesh. This one shall be called Woman, for from man was she taken." (Gen. 2:23)

עַל־כֵּן יַעֲזָב־אִישׁ אֶת־אָבִיו וְאֶת־אִמּוֹ וְדָבַק בְּאִשְׁתּוֹ וְהָיוּ לְבָשָׂר אֶחָד:

Hence a man leaves his father and mother and clings to his wife, so that they become one flesh. (Gen. 2:24)

וַיִּהְיוּ שְׁנֵיהֶם עֲרוּמִּים הָאָדָם וְאִשְׁתּוֹ וְלֹא יִתְבֹּשָׁשׁוּ:

The two of them were naked, the man and his wife, yet they felt no shame. (Gen. 2:25)

The Hebrew word for "woman" is אִשָּׁה *(isha)*, which sounds very much like the word used in this section for "man" אִישׁ *(ish)*. Both also sound like the word for "fire" אֵשׁ *(esh)*. It is, of course, possible that the connection with "fire" is coincidental and only the connection between man and woman should be seriously considered (after all, only that connection is explicitly stated in the text). What is interesting, however, is that these two words, "man" אִישׁ *(ish)* and "woman" אִשָּׁה *(isha)* might not even be etymologically related. One theory is that the word אִישׁ *(ish)* "man" comes from the root אוש, connoting "strength" or "existence," while the word אִשָּׁה *(isha)* "woman" comes from the root אנש, meaning "mortal." Yet even if there is no actual root connection between the Hebrew words for "man" and "woman," the auditory connection is still there. This is an excellent example of what sometimes happens in Hebrew. Connections of sound may be used to point to an underlying principle or broader issue.

In verse 22 "the LORD God built a woman": וַיִּבֶן יהוה אֱלֹהִים... לְאִשָּׁה *(va-yiven YHWH Elohim... le-ishah)*. Though it seems strange to speak this way about the creation of Eve, it is certainly consistent with the grammar and the context. Here God works or "builds" with some hard material. The word for צֵלָע *(tsela)* is often translated "rib" but properly means "side" or "edge." It can be used to designate an architectural element. The plural word for "naked" is עֲרוּמִים *(arumim)*. As a result, human disobedience is connected via sound association and word play with the cunning nature of the serpent. The word for "cunning," "crafty" or "wise" in Genesis 3:1 is similarly עָרוּם *(arum)*.

As modern-day people who also believe the Bible to be the Word of God, many of us find it difficult to accept stories such as this uncritically. The creation of Eve from Adam arguably tops the list of hard-to-believe Biblical stories. However, I think there is a simple way out of this conundrum. What we need to understand is that we tend to read these ancient texts as modern, science-oriented people, and not as ancients who often had very limited interest in or exposure to scientific inquiry. Unless we are willing to put ourselves in the shoes of those for whom this section of Torah was originally intended, we will continually "major on the minors, and minor on the majors." You see, the questions we are asking of the text are modern questions; to interpret the Bible faithfully we must first learn how to ask "ancient questions." Only when we have grasped the ancient meaning of these holy texts can we move towards legitimate and accurate application to our modern times and lives.

The Fall of Adam and Eve

Once the creation of Eve and the specifics of her relationship to Adam have been clearly set forth, the narrative will lay the foundation for a presentation of all the troubles that will beset both the emerging Israelite community and the largely hostile people groups around them. We read in Genesis 2:25-3:5 about the fateful conversation between Eve and the serpent in the Garden of Eden. Through a series of unfortunate interactions with the serpent, Eve comes to violate the only commandment that God had given to the new humanity. However, all of this took place because of Adam's silence. After all, he appeared to be nearby:

וַתֵּרֶא הָאִשָּׁה כִּי טוֹב הָעֵץ לְמַאֲכָל וְכִי תַאֲוָה־הוּא לָעֵינַיִם וְנֶחְמָד הָעֵץ לְהַשְׂכִּיל וַתִּקַּח מִפִּרְיוֹ וַתֹּאכַל וַתִּתֵּן גַּם־לְאִישָׁהּ עִמָּהּ וַיֹּאכַל׃

When the woman saw that the tree was good for eating and a delight to the eyes, and that the tree was desirable as a source of wisdom, she took of its fruit and ate. She also gave some to her husband, and he ate. (Gen. 3:6)

After the Fall

Only after they disobey God's commandment does the dissonance of shame and insecurity begin to characterize the first couple. We read about a new relationship with their Maker characterized by disconnect, fear and shame.

וַיִּשְׁמְעוּ אֶת־קוֹל יהוה אֱלֹהִים מִתְהַלֵּךְ בַּגָּן לְרוּחַ הַיּוֹם וַיִּתְחַבֵּא הָאָדָם וְאִשְׁתּוֹ מִפְּנֵי יהוה אֱלֹהִים בְּתוֹךְ עֵץ הַגָּן׃

They heard the sound of the LORD God moving about in the Garden at the breezy time of day; and the man and his wife hid from the LORD God among the trees of the Garden. (Gen. 3:8)

וַיִּקְרָא יהוה אֱלֹהִים אֶל־הָאָדָם וַיֹּאמֶר לוֹ אַיֶּכָּה׃

The LORD God called out to the man and said to him, "Where are you?" (Gen. 3:9)

וַיֹּאמֶר אֶת־קֹלְךָ שָׁמַעְתִּי בַּגָּן וָאִירָא כִּי־עֵירֹם אָנֹכִי וָאֵחָבֵא׃

He replied, "I heard the sound of You in the Garden, and I was afraid because I was naked, so I hid." (Gen. 3:10)

וַיֹּאמֶר מִי הִגִּיד לְךָ כִּי עֵירֹם אָתָּה הֲמִן־הָעֵץ אֲשֶׁר צִוִּיתִיךָ לְבִלְתִּי אֲכָל־מִמֶּנּוּ אָכָלְתָּ׃

Then He asked, "Who told you that you were naked? Did you eat of the tree from which I had forbidden you to eat?" (Gen. 3:11)

וַיֹּאמֶר הָאָדָם הָאִשָּׁה אֲשֶׁר נָתַתָּה עִמָּדִי הִוא נָתְנָה־לִּי מִן־הָעֵץ וָאֹכֵל׃

The man said, "The woman You put at my side—she gave me of the tree, and I ate." (Gen. 3:12)

Part of the reasoning behind this book is to give you a simple way to grasp the basics of how Hebrew words function in a sentence. These insights are meant to provoke in you a commitment and desire for more serious study. So in this section I am going to show you how Hebrew attaches suffixes and prefixes to expand the meanings of words. For example, in verse 6 quoted above, we see that Eve, after violating God's command, gave the forbidden fruit to her husband to eat. The phrase "also to her husband" גַּם־לְאִישָׁהּ *(gam le-ishah)* has the letter ה *(hey)* after the word אִישׁ *(ish)* "man, husband," making the meaning "her husband." The word also begins with a preposition, לְ *(le)* "to." So we see that just one word in Hebrew לְאִישָׁהּ *(le-ishah)* translates into English as no fewer than three words, "to her husband." In fact, this is a normal occurrence in the family of ancient Semitic languages such as Arabic, Aramaic and Hebrew.

When God enters the Garden in order to spend time with His final creation, He encounters something "unexpected." (Because the Biblical story is told in fully anthropomorphic terms, we should continue reading and talking about it in the same terms). Suddenly Adam and Eve feel uncomfortable in God's presence. It is very interesting to observe how the author describes this encounter. Giving a literal translation to the beginning of the sentence וַיִּשְׁמְעוּ אֶת־קוֹל יהוה אֱלֹהִים מִתְהַלֵּךְ בַּגָּן *(va-yishmeu et kol YHWH Elohim mithalekh ba-gan)* brings out this fascinating phrase: "and they heard the voice of the LORD God walking around the Garden" (vs. 8). It is usual to speak of hearing people walking around, or of hearing someone's voice; but to speak of the *voice* walking around (as the text may imply here) is most unusual. How could they hear "the voice walking around"?

Without addressing the blame-shifting games of Adam (who said Eve was to blame), God questions Eve, only to get a similar response from her (the Serpent was to blame). Upon hearing this, the LORD pronounces a permanent curse upon the serpent and then proceeds with additional statements in reverse order of the progression of blame-shifting He just heard from the humans.

כִּי עָשִׂיתָ זֹּאת אָרוּר אַתָּה מִכָּל־הַבְּהֵמָה וּמִכֹּל חַיַּת הַשָּׂדֶה עַל־גְּחֹנְךָ תֵלֵךְ וְעָפָר תֹּאכַל כָּל־יְמֵי חַיֶּיךָ:

"Because you did this, more cursed shall you be than all cattle and all the wild beasts: on your belly shall you crawl and dirt [or, dust] shall you eat all the days of your life. (Gen. 3:14)

וְאֵיבָה אָשִׁית בֵּינְךָ וּבֵין הָאִשָּׁה וּבֵין זַרְעֲךָ וּבֵין זַרְעָהּ הוּא יְשׁוּפְךָ רֹאשׁ וְאַתָּה תְּשׁוּפֶנּוּ עָקֵב:

I will put enmity between you and the woman, and between your offspring and hers; they shall strike at your head, and you shall strike at their heel." (Gen. 3:15)

The Hebrew word אָרַר *(arar)* is usually translated as "to curse" and hence, in our mind, it carries an uncertain though certainly negative meaning. Some usages indicate that it could be defined along the lines of "binding," "thwarting" or "restricting" someone or something. (See Gen. 3:14; Ex. 22:28; Job 3:8.) This matches the content of the serpent's curse – being limited and restricted more than other animal life. The Hebrew Bible never actually identifies this serpent with Satan. The well-known story that is thought to place Satan in the Garden of Eden (Ezek. 28:13-15) does not place him there in the form of a serpent, but rather in the form of an archangel. It was not until the late first century that a Jewish anti-Roman document, which we call the Book of Revelation, clearly identified "the ancient serpent" with the presumed head of the demonic powers: ὁ ὄφις ὁ ἀρχαῖος *(ho ofis ho archaios)* "the ancient serpent" – ὅς ἐστιν διάβολος καὶ Ὁ Σατανᾶς *(hos estin diabolos kai ho Satanas)* "who is the devil and Satan" (Rev. 20:2).

As for Eve, the Lord did not truly curse her but instead issued a strong disciplinary measure. We read in Genesis 3:16:

אֶל־הָאִשָּׁה אָמַר הַרְבָּה אַרְבֶּה עִצְּבוֹנֵךְ וְהֵרֹנֵךְ בְּעֶצֶב תֵּלְדִי בָנִים וְאֶל־אִישֵׁךְ תְּשׁוּקָתֵךְ וְהוּא יִמְשָׁל־בָּךְ:

And to the woman He said, "I will make most severe your pangs in childbearing; in pain shall you bear children. Yet your urge shall be for your husband, and he shall rule over you." (Gen. 3:16)

This verse describes two things that will significantly affect the woman. First, she "will suffer greatly in childbirth" הַרְבָּה אַרְבֶּה עִצְּבוֹנֵךְ *(harbah arbeh itsvonekh)*. Second, she will have a special longing for her husband (presumably one that he will not have for her), and "he will rule over her" יִמְשָׁל־בָּךְ *(yimshal bakh)*. This is a confusing text, which few have made much sense of, especially if one tries to understand it from the standpoint of our modern egalitarian values.

Adam did not receive the same kind of personal disciplinary action as did Eve. However, he also did not escape the painful consequences of his disobedience. God announces that He is cursing the ground because of Adam. It is clear that God holds Adam accountable for everything that took place. The fall of humanity from God's full favor is caused ultimately not by the serpent, nor by Eve, but by Adam himself.

וּלְאָדָם אָמַר כִּי־שָׁמַעְתָּ לְקוֹל אִשְׁתֶּךָ וַתֹּאכַל מִן־הָעֵץ אֲשֶׁר צִוִּיתִיךָ לֵאמֹר לֹא תֹאכַל מִמֶּנּוּ אֲרוּרָה הָאֲדָמָה בַּעֲבוּרֶךָ בְּעִצָּבוֹן תֹּאכֲלֶנָּה כֹּל יְמֵי חַיֶּיךָ:

To Adam He said, "Because you did as your wife said and ate of the tree about which I commanded you, 'You shall not eat of it,' cursed be the ground because of you; by toil shall you eat of it all the days of your life... (Gen. 3:17)

וַיִּקְרָא הָאָדָם שֵׁם אִשְׁתּוֹ חַוָּה כִּי הִוא הָיְתָה אֵם כָּל־חָי:

The man named his wife Eve, because she was the mother of all the living. (Gen. 3:20)

The English word "Eve" is of course not the original name of the first human female. Her name in Hebrew is חַוָּה *(Chavah)*, which has a Hebrew root connection with the verb חָיָה *(chayah)* "to live," as well as noun forms such as חַי *(chai)* and חַיִּים *(chayim)* that communicate the idea of "life." In Hebrew, therefore, it makes perfect sense to call Adam's woman חַוָּה *(Chavah)*, because she would one day become the mother of "all the living" כָּל־חָי *(kol chai)*.

God's accusation against Adam has to do with his preference for the voice of God's beautiful and gracious creation (his wife) over the voice of his Creator, in spite of the explicit commandment not to eat of the forbidden tree. However, in great mercy to his final creation, God does not curse Adam himself, but only the ground: אֲרוּרָה הָאֲדָמָה *(arurah ha-adamah)* "cursed be the ground." This curse will later be mitigated because of the faith and sacrifice of Adam's descendant, Noah – but more about that later. The LORD's further actions were far from a whimsical judgment.

Instead, they were already directed towards the restoration of humanity and all that humanity was supposed to nurture and protect.

וַיַּעַשׂ יהוה אֱלֹהִים לְאָדָם וּלְאִשְׁתּוֹ כָּתְנוֹת עוֹר וַיַּלְבִּשֵׁם:

And the LORD God made garments of skins for Adam and his wife, and clothed them. (Gen. 3:21)

The Hebrew word כָּתְנוֹת *(katnot)* for the garments that God made for Adam and Eve should probably be translated "tunics." In this case they were not tunics made of fabric, but rather of "skin" or "fur" עוֹר *(or)*. This verse seems to imply that once the first human (Adam) had disobeyed God's only commandment, thus thwarting His purposes for creation and humanity's role in the world, animals had to die: blood needed to be shed. We understand this because we read that God "clothed" Adam and Eve יַּלְבִּשֵׁם *(yalbishem)* with tunics made of animal skin, thus laying the foundation for the future animal sacrifice practices of Israel.

וַיֹּאמֶר יהוה אֱלֹהִים הֵן הָאָדָם הָיָה כְּאַחַד מִמֶּנּוּ לָדַעַת טוֹב וָרָע וְעַתָּה פֶּן־יִשְׁלַח יָדוֹ וְלָקַח גַּם מֵעֵץ הַחַיִּים וְאָכַל וָחַי לְעֹלָם:

And the LORD God said, "Now that the man has become like one of us, knowing good and bad, what if he should stretch out his hand and take also from the tree of life and eat, and live forever!" (Gen. 3:22)

וַיְשַׁלְּחֵהוּ יהוה אֱלֹהִים מִגַּן־עֵדֶן לַעֲבֹד אֶת־הָאֲדָמָה אֲשֶׁר לֻקַּח מִשָּׁם:

So the LORD God banished him from the Garden of Eden, to till the soil from which he was taken. (Gen. 3:23)

וַיְגָרֶשׁ אֶת־הָאָדָם וַיַּשְׁכֵּן מִקֶּדֶם לְגַן־עֵדֶן אֶת־הַכְּרֻבִים וְאֵת לַהַט הַחֶרֶב הַמִּתְהַפֶּכֶת לִשְׁמֹר אֶת־דֶּרֶךְ עֵץ הַחַיִּים:

He drove the man out, and stationed east of the Garden of Eden the cherubim and the fiery ever-turning sword, to guard the way to the tree of life. (Gen. 3:24)

The Hebrew word translated as "banished" is גָּרַשׁ *(garash)*. In Modern Hebrew, the same root is used to form a variety of Hebrew words connected to the idea of divorce. In a very real sense, the LORD God "divorced" Adam and Eve from the Garden of Eden (and in a way from Himself), because of the clear and immediate danger that the Tree of Life now presented to them. In spite of what is traditionally thought, God did not judge Adam and Eve by sending them away from the Garden of Eden. Exiling them from the garden of delight was not disciplinary but protective and merciful. Now that they were exposed to the knowledge of good and evil, the well-founded fear of God was that humanity might remain in that state of misery and death forever if they also ate of the "tree of everlasting life" עֵץ הַחַיִּים *(ets ha-chayim)* which was also located in the Garden. Thus it was for their own safety, hope and redemption that God now barred them from the Garden.

MY REQUEST

Dear reader, may I ask you for a favor? Would you take three minutes of your time and provide an encouraging feedback to other people shopping on Amazon.com about this book (assuming you like it of course!)?

Here is how: 1. Go to Amazon.com and search for the title of this book – "Becoming Israel". 2. Click on the title, click on the "ratings" link (right under the author's name) and click "Write a customer review" button. 3. Rate the book and leave a few words.

This will really help me a lot, especially if you genuinely love this book! After writing a review please drop me a personal note and let me know - dr.eli.israel@gmail.com. I would appreciate your help with this.

Dr. Eli Lizorkin-Eyzenberg

CHAPTER TWO: THE LIFE OF NOAH

One of the most significant characters in the Bible is the man by the name of Noah. Although "the Noah brand" seems to be present everywhere (from religious stores to secular Hollywood productions), most people remain unaware of many crucial nuances that are present in the original Hebrew text. We will seek to remedy the situation by paying careful attention to the original Hebrew in order to grasp more fully this rich Biblical character and the events associated with him. The Hebrew name נֹחַ *(Noach)* is derived from the verb נוּחַ *(nuach)*, which has a wide range of meanings, most of which convey the idea of rest and relief. The kind of rest that the Hebrew implies here is not merely relaxation from exertion, but rather stationary rest – the absence of activity and movement.

The Generations of Noah

We first hear about Noah in תּוֹלְדֹת אָדָם *(toldot adam)* "the book of generations of Adam" in Genesis 5. The entire chapter traces the line of Seth (one of Adam's sons). This text, among other things, shows Noah's familial connection not only to אָדָם *(Adam)* "Adam," but also to three other important biblical characters – שֵׁת *(Shet)* "Seth," אֱנוֹשׁ *(Enosh)* "Enosh" and חֲנוֹךְ *(Chanokh)* "Enoch." While other people mentioned in the genealogy of Noah are also important, the story will be told in such a way that Noah's connection with these four seems to be emphasized.

1. אָדָם *(Adam)* "Adam"
2. שֵׁת *(Shet)* "Seth"
3. אֱנוֹשׁ *(Enosh)* "Enosh"
4. קֵינָן *(Kenan)* "Kenan"
5. מַהֲלַלְאֵל *(Mahalalel)* "Mahalalel"
6. יֶרֶד *(Yered)* "Jared"
7. חֲנוֹךְ *(Chanokh)* "Enoch"
8. מְתוּשֶׁלַח *(Metushelach)* "Methuselah"
9. לֶמֶךְ *(Lemekh)* "Lamech"
10. נֹחַ *(Noach)* "Noah"

The name "Enosh" in Hebrew אֱנוֹשׁ *(Enosh)* means something like "man" or "human." It relates to the idea of mortality. It can also be associated by sound with the Hebrew word נְשָׁמָה *(neshamah)*, one of the words that captures the Jewish concept of "the soul." In Modern Hebrew when we speak of someone behaving in a humane way we use the adjective אֱנוֹשִׁי *(enoshi)*, which could also be interpreted literally as meaning "of Enosh."

All the Biblical authors were very selective in the kind of material they chose to present. They tell their readers only what they want them to know. It is noteworthy that the Torah lists Noah as the tenth son of Adam. Similarly, Enosh is descendent number 3 and Enoch is number 7. Thee three numbers may be markers of something significant, as elsewhere they have symbolic meanings.

Cain's line will not survive the flood, and post-flood humanity will re-emerge from Noah, the son of Seth. We first read about Adam and Eve's giving birth to שֵׁת *(Shet)* "Seth" in Genesis 4:25-26:

וַיֵּדַע אָדָם עוֹד אֶת־אִשְׁתּוֹ וַתֵּלֶד בֵּן וַתִּקְרָא אֶת־שְׁמוֹ שֵׁת כִּי שָׁת־לִי אֱלֹהִים זֶרַע אַחֵר תַּחַת הֶבֶל כִּי הֲרָגוֹ קָיִן:

Adam knew his wife again, and she bore a son and named him Seth, meaning, "God has provided me with another offspring in place of Abel," for Cain had killed him. (Gen. 4:25)

וּלְשֵׁת גַּם־הוּא יֻלַּד־בֵּן וַיִּקְרָא אֶת־שְׁמוֹ אֱנוֹשׁ אָז הוּחַל לִקְרֹא בְּשֵׁם יהוה:

And to Seth, in turn, a son was born, and he named him Enosh. It was then that men began to invoke the LORD by name. (Gen. 4:26)

We read about Enoch in Genesis 5:24:

וַיִּתְהַלֵּךְ חֲנוֹךְ אֶת־הָאֱלֹהִים וְאֵינֶנּוּ כִּי־לָקַח אֹתוֹ אֱלֹהִים:

Enoch walked with God; then he was no more, for God took him. (Gen. 5:24)

In Hebrew the name Cain קַיִן *(Kayin)* carries the meaning of something "acquired." Eve called Cain this because she thought that she had "acquired" him from or with the help of the LORD (Gen. 4:1). The name Seth in Hebrew שֵׁת *(Shet)* means something like "appointed"; the Hebrew verb שִׁית *(shit)* means "to set" or "to appoint" (by extension, perhaps, "to provide"). One of the biggest problems with reading the Bible always and only in translation is the problem of losing the original meaning of names. Translations and adaptations do not simply change the original meaning, but also render the names meaningless. Unless we take time to go back into the Hebrew, the Biblical names of people and places in translation will continue to have no connection with the original reference points and ideas buried within the text itself. That is our great loss, and a loss that we need to make every effort to minimize. This is our treasure that needs to be reclaimed.

The list of Adam's descendants through the line of Seth is indeed interesting for several reasons. For example, look at who is listed and the lifespan assigned to each:

1. אָדָם *(Adam)* Adam – 930 years
2. שֵׁת *(Shet)* Seth – 912 years
3. אֱנוֹשׁ *(Enosh)* Enosh – 905 years
4. קֵינָן *(Kenan)* Kenan – 910 years
5. מַהֲלַלְאֵל *(Mahalalel)* Mahalalel – 895 years
6. יֶרֶד *(Yered)* Jared – 962 years
7. חֲנוֹךְ *(Chanokh)* Enoch – 365 years
8. מְתוּשֶׁלַח *(Metushelach)* Methuselah – 969 years
9. לֶמֶךְ *(Lemekh)* Lamech – 777 years
10. נֹחַ *(Noach)* Noah – 950 years

Such expansive pre-flood lifespans will be significantly diminished after the flood. These seemingly enormous numbers, however, are actually very small in comparison to those given in the pre-flood stories of the Mesopotamian and Sumerian Kings. There the longest-ruling king is said to have ruled over 65,000 years.

Enoch lived 365 years before the LORD took him (365 years probably correspond to the fullness of the solar calendar, 365 days). The years of Lamech's life (the father of Noah) seem to be particularly noteworthy (777 years). It is Lamech who would bring into the dying world a son, Noah, who would save the world through his faith-filled obedience.

Noah as a New Adam

When we finally get to Noah, we hear about the prophetic words of his father Lamech. In Genesis 5:28-29 we read:

וַיְחִי־לֶמֶךְ שְׁתַּיִם וּשְׁמֹנִים שָׁנָה וּמְאַת שָׁנָה וַיּוֹלֶד בֵּן:

When Lamech had lived 182 years, he begot a son. (Gen. 5:28)

וַיִּקְרָא אֶת־שְׁמוֹ נֹחַ לֵאמֹר זֶה יְנַחֲמֵנוּ מִמַּעֲשֵׂנוּ וּמֵעִצְּבוֹן יָדֵינוּ מִן־הָאֲדָמָה אֲשֶׁר אֵרְרָהּ יהוה:

And he named him Noah, saying, "This one will provide us relief from our work and from the toil of our hands, out of the very soil which the LORD placed under a curse." (Gen. 5:29)

Here again is what God had told Adam when the great Fall occurred (Gen. 3:17):

וּלְאָדָם אָמַר כִּי־שָׁמַעְתָּ לְקוֹל אִשְׁתֶּךָ וַתֹּאכַל מִן־הָעֵץ אֲשֶׁר צִוִּיתִיךָ לֵאמֹר לֹא תֹאכַל מִמֶּנּוּ אֲרוּרָה הָאֲדָמָה בַּעֲבוּרֶךָ בְּעִצָּבוֹן תֹּאכֲלֶנָּה כֹּל יְמֵי חַיֶּיךָ:

To Adam He said, "Because you did as your wife said and ate of the tree about which I commanded you, 'You shall not eat of it,' cursed be the ground because of you; by toil shall you eat of it all the days of your life" (Gen. 3:17)

The Hebrew phrase אֲרוּרָה הָאֲדָמָה *(arurah ha-adamah)* means something like "the ground is cursed." The Hebrew verb אָרַר *(arar)* is usually translated as "to curse" but (as mentioned above) its uses in Biblical Hebrew may include "binding," "thwarting" or "restricting" someone or something. The allusion in Genesis 5:29 to Genesis 3:17 is one of several indications in this narrative that Noah is presented as a "new Adam" – a righteous antidote to the failure of Adam, the father of universal mankind. Adam's action thrust all his posterity into hard work to get produce from the ground, which had been cursed by God. Noah is born to Lamech as someone who will bring relief and rest to the tired worker of the cursed land.

The Growing Evil of Humanity

In time the total moral failure of the human race became absolutely clear to its Maker. The judgment of God was just, according to Genesis 6:5:

וַיַּרְא יהוה כִּי רַבָּה רָעַת הָאָדָם בָּאָרֶץ וְכָל־יֵצֶר מַחְשְׁבֹת לִבּוֹ רַק רַע כָּל־הַיּוֹם:

The LORD saw how great was man's wickedness on earth, and how every plan devised by his mind was nothing but evil all the time. (Gen. 6:5)

The Hebrew word יֵצֶר *(yetser)* in the phrase יֵצֶר מַחְשְׁבֹת לִבּוֹ *(yetzer machshevot libo)* connects with the idea of something being "produced" or "formed." The phrase can be translated as "the intent/plan/produce/result of the thoughts of his heart." The totality of humanity's fall is unmistakable and striking. Because of the linguistic identity in the text between "Adam" and "man," we can understand more clearly how Adam's failure affected his human offspring to the utmost degree. This text, in particular, emphasizes the totality of the fall – "every plan/intent" was "nothing but evil all the time." Although God then determines to pass judgment on the world through the flood, Noah finds favor in His eyes. We read about this in Genesis 6:7-8:

וַיֹּאמֶר יהוה אֶמְחֶה אֶת־הָאָדָם אֲשֶׁר־בָּרָאתִי מֵעַל פְּנֵי הָאֲדָמָה מֵאָדָם עַד־בְּהֵמָה עַד־רֶמֶשׂ וְעַד־עוֹף הַשָּׁמָיִם כִּי נִחַמְתִּי כִּי עֲשִׂיתִם:

The LORD said, "I will blot out from the earth the men whom I created – men together with beasts, creeping things, and birds of the sky; for I regret that I made them."(Gen. 6:7)

וְנֹחַ מָצָא חֵן בְּעֵינֵי יהוה:

But Noah found favor with the LORD. (Gen. 6:8).

The Hebrew phrase מָצָא חֵן בְּעֵינֵי יהוה *(matsah chen be-eyne YHWH)* literally means "he [Noah] found grace in the eyes of the LORD." In Modern Hebrew when we ask each other, "Do you like such-and-such?" we might use this ancient biblical phrase: "Did it find grace in your eyes?" It has been pointed out that the word חֵן *(chen)* for "grace/favor" in Hebrew uses the same letters as the name נֹחַ *(Noach)* "Noah," only reversed. (The reason that the letter נ *(nun)* in "Noah" looks different from the same letter ן *(nun)*

in "grace" is because it is one of the letters have a "final form" and therefore look different when they appear at the end of a word).
Humanity is not separated from animal life. The role of Adam as the head of God's creation was not temporary. When Adam failed in his task, this affected not only his human offspring, but animal life as well. We will see shortly that just as judgment comes to the posterity of Adam and all animal life under his dominion, so does the salvation offered through this descendant of Adam. It is not only Noah and his posterity that will be saved from the waters of the flood, but also animal life. Noah is indeed a "new Adam" – the hope of the fallen world.

The Literary Structure of Chiasm

The Torah very often uses a complex and beautiful literary structure known today as *chiasm* (or *chiasmus*). The basic idea is that words, phrases, or other elements can be arranged to mirror each other, so that the text lays out a given set of meanings and then goes back through their parallels in the reverse order. Analyzing the use of chiasmus can reveal a text's intricate design and holistic nature.

Commonly pairs such as A and A', B and B' and so on are used to symbolize these "mirrored" elements. If we analyze the story of Noah in this way, we see a long pattern climaxing in line P (which lacks a parallel and signifies the main point) at the center of the chiasm. Here is an outline to illustrate the thematic chiasm in Genesis 6-9:

A Noah (6:10a)
__B Shem, Ham, and Japheth (6:10b)
___C Ark to be built (6:14-16)
____D Flood announced (6:17)
_____E Covenant with Noah (6:18-20)
_____F Food in the ark (6:21)
_____G Command to enter the ark (7:1-3)
_____H 7 days waiting for flood (7:4-5)
_____I 7 days waiting for flood (7:7-10)
_____J Entry to ark (7:11-15)
_____K The LORD (*YHWH*) shuts Noah in (7:16)
_____L 40 days of flood (7:17a)
_____M Waters increase (7:17b-18)

```
_____N Mountains covered (7:19-20)
_____O 150 days: water prevail (7:21-24)
_____P GOD REMEMBERS NOAH (8:1)
_____O' 150 days: waters abate (8:3)
_____N' Mountain tops visible (8:4-5)
_____M' Waters abate (8:5)
_____L' 40 days (end of) (8:6a)
_____K' Noah opens window of ark (8:6b)
_____J' Raven and dove leave ark (8:7-9)
_____I' 7 days waiting for waters to subside (8:10-11)
_____H' 7 days waiting for waters to subside (8:12-13)
_____G' Command to leave ark (8:15-17 [22])
_____F' Food outside ark (9:1-4)
_____E' Covenant with all flesh (9:8-10)
_____D' No flood in the future (9:11-17)
____C' Ark left (9:18a)
___B' Shem, Ham and Japheth (9:18b)
A' Noah (9:19)
```

The central element of the chiasm in Genesis 8:1 reads as follows:

וַיִּזְכֹּר אֱלֹהִים אֶת־נֹחַ וְאֵת כָּל־הַחַיָּה וְאֶת־כָּל־הַבְּהֵמָה אֲשֶׁר אִתּוֹ בַּתֵּבָה וַיַּעֲבֵר אֱלֹהִים רוּחַ עַל־הָאָרֶץ וַיָּשֹׁכּוּ הַמָּיִם׃

God remembered Noah and all the beasts and all the cattle that were with him in the ark, and God caused a wind to blow across the earth, and the waters subsided. (Gen. 8:1)

Since the central element of the chiasm functions as the focal point of the entire story – the tipping point not to be missed – we must assign it the first importance. Everything else described in the story is also important, but not nearly as important as the message of Genesis 8:1 (God remembering Noah). This "event" marks the triumph of mercy over judgment. God remembered Noah, just as He will later remember Abraham (Gen. 19:29) and other great figures of Israel's redemptive history – and, perhaps most importantly, the people of Israel during the yet-to-come Passover deliverance from Egypt. At that time, we are told, God remembered his covenant with Abraham, Isaac and Jacob (Ex. 2:23-25).

A Note on Hebrew Insights

The Hebrew language, like many other languages, has gender (masculine and feminine) and number (singular and plural). While these specifications are grammatically important, we should be careful not to make too much of them as we look into the original Hebrew text. Sometimes focusing on number and gender can be used to read a desired meaning into the text even when not fully justified. For example, the English word "God" (singular) corresponds to Hebrew אֱלֹהִים *(Elohim)*, which is written in the form of a plural and means "God" or "gods." In other words, in the Hebrew Bible the exact same word אֱלֹהִים *(Elohim)* is used both for the singular "God" and for a plurality of "foreign gods." Hence we must be careful as we seek genuine insights from the language of the original text.

God's Saving Grace to Noah

Most of what we know about the life of Noah comes from Genesis 6:9 on (where the story of the flood begins). We learn that Noah was a righteous man, blameless in his generation, and that he walked with God. One can almost see a progression of spirituality in this description of Noah's life and its juxtaposition with the corruption of all others. Despite the rampant wickedness that was increasing exponentially upon the earth, one man stood out – Noah. The Bible says וְנֹחַ מָצָא חֵן בְּעֵינֵי יהוה *(ve-Noach matsa chen be-eyne YHWH)* "but Noah found grace in the eyes of the Lord." As God was about to send judgment upon the world for its overwhelming wickedness, He extended His grace to Noah and his family, thereby continuing His redemptive program for both fallen humanity and the animal life for which Adam bore responsibility.

Here is the text of Genesis 6:9:

אֵלֶּה תּוֹלְדֹת נֹחַ נֹחַ אִישׁ צַדִּיק תָּמִים הָיָה בְּדֹרֹתָיו אֶת־הָאֱלֹהִים הִתְהַלֶּךְ־נֹחַ׃

This is the line [lit., generations] of Noah. Noah was a righteous man; he was blameless in his generation; Noah walked with God. (Gen. 6:9)

Compare this with what we read in Genesis 3:8 about God walking with Adam:

וַיִּשְׁמְעוּ אֶת־קוֹל יהוה אֱלֹהִים מִתְהַלֵּךְ בַּגָּן לְרוּחַ הַיּוֹם

They heard the sound of the LORD God walking in the garden at the breezy time of day… (Gen. 3:8)

And what is more, we also read in Genesis 5:24:

וַיִּתְהַלֵּךְ חֲנוֹךְ אֶת־הָאֱלֹהִים וְאֵינֶנּוּ כִּי־לָקַח אֹתוֹ אֱלֹהִים:

Enoch walked with God; then he was no more, for God took him. (Gen. 5:24)

A particular Hebrew verb form is used here הִתְהַלֵּךְ *(hithalekh)* "to stroll or walk around." It conveys a nuanced version of the same idea as "to walk." The verb form can imply communion with someone while walking, i.e., "to stroll around (with someone)." In this case the verb refers to communion with God Himself. From the statement that Noah was righteous, we understand that he was obedient to God's commands (as well as he was able according to how he understood them at that time). He was blameless in his generation, meaning that his integrity stood out in the context of the people of his day. All of this is summed up well in the difficult-to-translate phrase אֶת־הָאֱלֹהִים הִתְהַלֶּךְ־נֹחַ *(et ha-Elohim hithalekh Noach)* "Noah walked (around) with God." His life, therefore, was characterized by his ability to enter into this relationship with his Maker. Like Adam and Enoch before him, Noah "walked with God."

Noah's Obedience

In Genesis 6:14-21 we read of all the preparations God tells Noah he must make before the flood. Genesis 6:22 gives us Noah's response:

וַיַּעַשׂ נֹחַ כְּכֹל אֲשֶׁר צִוָּה אֹתוֹ אֱלֹהִים כֵּן עָשָׂה:

Noah did so; just as God commanded him, so he did. (Gen. 6:22)

When everything was ready, God told Noah to execute the plan and enter the ark (Gen. 7:1-4). In the following verse (vs. 5) we read:

וַיַּעַשׂ נֹחַ כְּכֹל אֲשֶׁר־צִוָּהוּ יהוה׃

And Noah did just as the LORD commanded him. (Gen. 7:5)

After the flood had come and gone, we read the following words in Genesis 8:

וַיְדַבֵּר אֱלֹהִים אֶל־נֹחַ לֵאמֹר׃ צֵא מִן־הַתֵּבָה אַתָּה וְאִשְׁתְּךָ וּבָנֶיךָ וּנְשֵׁי־בָנֶיךָ אִתָּךְ׃

God spoke to Noah, saying, "Come out of the ark, together with your wife, your sons, and your sons' wives." (Gen. 8:15-16)

וַיֵּצֵא־נֹחַ וּבָנָיו וְאִשְׁתּוֹ וּנְשֵׁי־בָנָיו אִתּוֹ׃

So Noah came out, together with his sons, his wife, and his sons' wives. (Gen. 8:18)

כָּל־הַחַיָּה כָּל־הָרֶמֶשׂ וְכָל־הָעוֹף כֹּל רוֹמֵשׂ עַל־הָאָרֶץ לְמִשְׁפְּחֹתֵיהֶם יָצְאוּ מִן־הַתֵּבָה׃

Every animal, every creeping thing, and every bird, everything that stirs on earth came out of the ark by families. (Gen. 8:19)

Hebrew is a concise language. Its forms of expression are often shorter and simpler than equivalent expressions in other languages. For example, as we see in Genesis 8:16, suffixes are often used instead of completely separate words. In several places we have two English words in the translation, but only one in Hebrew: אִשְׁתְּךָ *(ishtekha)* "your wife"; בָּנֶיךָ *(vanekha)* "your sons"; אִתָּךְ *(itakh)* "with you." Sometimes what is packaged into a single Hebrew word is even more extensive.

In these verses we can see Noah's trusting obedience to God, as he obeys without hesitation everything that God commands. Noah, unlike the first Adam, simply does everything that God tells him to do. While walking with God, Adam showed himself to be unrighteous and therefore led the entire human race toward misery and death. By contrast, Noah, as the "new Adam," has succeeded in reversing this painful legacy. He will lead his posterity, even if imperfectly, toward new life and a fresh start.

Noah's Redemptive Worship

Like several great men of God after him, Noah built an altar to God and offered sacrifices. We read in the following verse (Gen. 8:20) that:

וַיִּבֶן נֹחַ מִזְבֵּחַ לַיהוה וַיִּקַּח מִכֹּל הַבְּהֵמָה הַטְּהוֹרָה וּמִכֹּל הָעוֹף הַטָּהֹר וַיַּעַל עֹלֹת בַּמִּזְבֵּחַ:

Then Noah built an altar to the LORD and, taking of every clean animal and of every clean bird, he offered burnt offerings on the altar. (Gen. 8:20)

Once sacrifices were offered, we are told:

וַיָּרַח יהוה אֶת־רֵיחַ הַנִּיחֹחַ וַיֹּאמֶר יהוה אֶל־לִבּוֹ לֹא־אֹסִף לְקַלֵּל עוֹד אֶת־הָאֲדָמָה בַּעֲבוּר הָאָדָם כִּי יֵצֶר לֵב הָאָדָם רַע מִנְּעֻרָיו וְלֹא־אֹסִף עוֹד לְהַכּוֹת אֶת־כָּל־חַי כַּאֲשֶׁר עָשִׂיתִי:

The LORD smelled the pleasing odor, and the Lord said to Himself: "Never again will I curse the ground because of man, since the devisings of man's mind are evil from his youth; nor will I ever again destroy every living being, as I have done. (Gen. 8:21)

One of the most important Hebrew words for "sacrifice" or "burnt offering" is עֹלָה (*olah*), which literally communicates the idea of "going up" or "ascent." The burnt offering is thus "something that goes up." Moreover, a related word conveys the action, or the movement of offering or giving. When Noah presented the burnt offering upon the altar, the Hebrew says וַיַּעַל עֹלֹת (*va-yaal olot*) "and he offered the offerings" – or more literally, "he presented upward something [the sacrifice] that goes up." The beauty of the Hebrew language is that it is incredibly tangible, literal and simple.

The wholehearted and proper worship rendered to God by Noah resulted in enduring blessing to all his posterity and animal life. The amazing thing is that, because of Noah's sacrifice, God promised not to curse the ground again. Maybe the text even implies that He was reversing the previous curse that had made life on Earth so unbearable. If so, the human and animal race would no longer work the ground knowing that the LORD had cursed it. Because of Noah's obedience and sacrifice, God's anger was turned into understanding.

The Curse of Canaan and Blessing of Shem and Japheth

We read the following narrative in Genesis 9:20-29:

> Noah, a tiller of the soil, was the first to plant a vineyard. He drank of the wine and became drunk, "and he uncovered himself within his tent" וַיִּתְגַּל בְּתוֹךְ אָהֳלֹה *(va-yitgal be-toch ohaloh)*. "Ham, the father of Canaan, saw his father's nakedness" וַיַּרְא חָם אֲבִי כְנַעַן אֵת עֶרְוַת אָבִיו *(va-yar Cham avi Kenaan et irvat aviv)* and told his two brothers outside. But Shem and Japheth took a cloth, placed it against both their backs and, walking backward, they covered their father's nakedness. Their faces were turned the other way, so that they did not see their father's nakedness. When Noah woke up from his wine "and learned what his youngest son had done to him" וַיֵּדַע אֵת אֲשֶׁר־עָשָׂה־לוֹ בְּנוֹ הַקָּטָן *(va-yada et asher asah lo beno ha-katan)*, he said, "Cursed be Canaan; the lowest of slaves shall he be to his brothers." And he said, "Blessed be the LORD, the God of Shem; 'let Canaan be a slave to them' וִיהִי כְנַעַן עֶבֶד לָמוֹ *(vi-hi Kenaan eved lamo)*. 'May God enlarge Japheth' יַפְתְּ אֱלֹהִים לְיֶפֶת *(yaft Elohim le-Yefet)*, 'and let him dwell in the tents of Shem' וְיִשְׁכֹּן בְּאָהֳלֵי־שֵׁם *(ve-yishkon be-ohale Shem)*; 'and let Canaan be a slave to them.' וִיהִי כְנַעַן עֶבֶד לָמוֹ *(vi-hi Kenaan eved lamo).*" Noah lived after the flood 350 years. And all the days of Noah came to 950 years; then he died.

There are no Biblical names that do not carry some special significance, even when the original meaning of the name has been lost and it is no longer possible to know with any certainty what it originally meant. Let us take, for example, the name *Japheth*. In English it is just Japheth, but in Hebrew it means something: "expanded" or "enlarged." So we read that God יַפְתְּ *(yaft)* "enlarged" the person named יֶפֶת *(yefet)* "enlarged" – Japheth. The flood, while giving humanity a new start, did not eradicate evil entirely. Even though the line of Cain was destroyed, human evil inherited from Adam continued to reside even in the descendants of Seth and Noah. One of the sons of Noah, Ham (father of Canaan), did something that was considered evil to his father while he was sleeping.

It is not clear whether the offense was just seeing his father naked, making fun of him (Ex. 20:12), engaging in a homosexual rape (see Lev. 20:13), or perhaps sleeping with Noah's wife. In Leviticus 20:11 to "uncover the nakedness of one's father" means to sleep with his wife. One thing we do know for certain – Ham's action was to be detested. This perplexing passage might be connected to the sexual perverseness that Israelite culture sometimes thought to be typical of the Canaanites, the descendants of Canaan (see Lev. 18:3-4, 24-30). The curse upon Ham's son Canaan follows the ancient covenantal dynamic of corporate responsibility and explains to contemporary readers of the Torah the animosity that exists between Israelites and Canaanites. It also predicts by implication a bright shared future for Noah's other sons שֵׁם *(Shem)* "Shem" and יֶפֶת *(Yefet)* "Japeth."

The Covenant with Noah

וַיְבָרֶךְ אֱלֹהִים אֶת־נֹחַ וְאֶת־בָּנָיו וַיֹּאמֶר לָהֶם פְּרוּ וּרְבוּ וּמִלְאוּ אֶת־הָאָרֶץ:

God blessed Noah and his sons, and said to them, "Be fertile and increase, and fill the earth. (Gen. 9:1)

וּמוֹרַאֲכֶם וְחִתְּכֶם יִהְיֶה עַל כָּל־חַיַּת הָאָרֶץ וְעַל כָּל־עוֹף הַשָּׁמָיִם בְּכֹל אֲשֶׁר תִּרְמֹשׂ הָאֲדָמָה וּבְכָל־דְּגֵי הַיָּם בְּיֶדְכֶם נִתָּנוּ:

The fear and the dread of you shall be upon all the beasts of the earth and upon all the birds of the sky — everything with which the earth is astir — and upon all the fish of the sea; they are given into your hand. (Gen. 9:2)

כָּל־רֶמֶשׂ אֲשֶׁר הוּא־חַי לָכֶם יִהְיֶה לְאָכְלָה כְּיֶרֶק עֵשֶׂב נָתַתִּי לָכֶם אֶת־כֹּל:

Every creature that lives shall be yours to eat; as with the green grasses, I give you all these. (Gen. 9:3)

אַךְ־בָּשָׂר בְּנַפְשׁוֹ דָמוֹ לֹא תֹאכֵלוּ:

You must not, however, eat flesh with its life-blood in it. (Gen. 9:4)

וְאַךְ אֶת־דִּמְכֶם לְנַפְשֹׁתֵיכֶם אֶדְרֹשׁ מִיַּד כָּל־חַיָּה אֶדְרְשֶׁנּוּ וּמִיַּד הָאָדָם מִיַּד אִישׁ אָחִיו אֶדְרֹשׁ אֶת־נֶפֶשׁ הָאָדָם:

But for your own life-blood I will require a reckoning: I will require it of every beast; of man, too, will I require a reckoning for human life, of every man for that of his fellow man! (Gen. 9:5)

שָׁפֵךְ דַּם הָאָדָם בָּאָדָם דָּמוֹ יִשָּׁפֵךְ כִּי בְּצֶלֶם אֱלֹהִים עָשָׂה אֶת־הָאָדָם:

Whoever sheds the blood of man, by man shall his blood be shed; For in His image Did God make man. (Gen. 9:6)

וַאֲנִי הִנְנִי מֵקִים אֶת־בְּרִיתִי אִתְּכֶם וְאֶת־זַרְעֲכֶם אַחֲרֵיכֶם:

I now establish My covenant with you and your offspring to come, and with every living thing that is with you. (Gen. 9:9-10)

The Hebrew word צֶלֶם *(tselem)* signifies "image" (as in "image of God" in Gen. 9:6). This word is a beautiful example of how Hebrew assonance (sound similarity) often works in the text. The word צֶלֶם *(tselem)* "image" shares some sounds with another Hebrew word, צֵל *(tsel)*, which means "shadow." A shadow always resembles the real thing from which it derives its form. The צֶלֶם אֱלֹהִים *(tselem Elohim)* "image of God" may provoke associations with צֵל אֱלֹהִים *(tsel Elohim)* "God's shadow" – an imperfect copy or image. It is interesting that the person in charge of the decoration of the Tabernacle of Moses was named בְּצַלְאֵל *(Betsalel)* "Bezalel," which in Hebrew literally means "in the shadow of God." (The preposition ב- [be-], in this case, is to be translated as the simple English preposition "in.")

The Covenant that God makes with Noah includes his children and animal life on Earth. Noah and his company are given exactly the same commands as those once given to Noah's ancestor Adam (Gen. 1:28), once again showing Noah to be the "new Adam." Moreover, just as God gave Adam to eat from all the produce of the garden with the exception of one tree located in the middle of the Garden (Gen. 2:16-17), here too Noah is given everything for food. He must, however, honor God by never eating any meat with its blood still in it (Gen. 9:4). Human life is sharply distinguished from animal life; the idea that human beings are created in the image of God (1:26-27) requires a higher degree of respect for human life (Gen. 9:5-6). Will Noah and his posterity keep this simple test? Will they live up to God's gracious and holy expectations? Or will he too, like Adam, tell God that he and his wife know better? What does the future of humanity really hold? Torah has a lot to say about it – but more in the chapters to come.

MY REQUEST

Dear reader, may I ask you for a favor? Would you take three minutes of your time and provide an encouraging feedback to other people shopping on Amazon.com about this book (assuming you like it of course!)?

Here is how: 1. Go to Amazon.com and search for the title of this book – "Becoming Israel". 2. Click on the title, click on the "ratings" link (right under the author's name) and click "Write a customer review" button. 3. Rate the book and leave a few words.

This will really help me a lot, especially if you genuinely love this book! After writing a review please drop me a personal note and let me know - dr.eli.israel@gmail.com. I would appreciate your help with this.

Dr. Eli Lizorkin-Eyzenberg

CHAPTER THREE: THE LIFE OF ABRAHAM

Abraham is one of the Bible's favorite characters. He is considered to be "the father" of Judaism, Christianity and Islam, since Abraham plays a central and in many ways founding role in the narrative of each religious tradition. In spite of his character flaws, he was able to exercise faith and trust towards his covenant God, especially at the critical moments in his life.

The Consistency of God's Mercy

The story of the Tower of Babel (Gen. 11:1-9) precedes the story of Abraham and his origins. It is an important bridge that establishes the consistency of God in His merciful dealings with a frail and sinful humanity. Just as God, in His mercy, exiled Adam and Eve from the Garden where their corrupt status could have been sealed forever (by eating from the Tree of Life), here, too, God displayed mercy towards the children of Adam and Eve as they attempted to build a tower that would make their name great by reaching into the very abode of God (Gen. 11:4). Human beings erected the highest building they could, but even to see it, the LORD must "descend" from His heavenly dwelling place. Just as the ground was cursed/limited/restricted in the case of Adam, so too the ability of the children of Adam to communicate was now cursed/limited/restricted. This tower forever became known as the "Tower of Babel" מִגְדַּל בָּבֶל *(migdal bavel),* or literally "the tower of confused speech."

Abraham as a Descendent of Shem

God's merciful dealings with the line of Shem continue, and in Genesis 11:10-25 we are told about the generations that God blessed with posterity, leading to the birth of Terah, Abraham's father. We are told of three children of his, of whom Abram was the oldest (Abram, Nahor and Haran). The youngest brother, Haran, had a son named Lot – Abram's nephew. In ancient Hebrew vocabulary, the Abram-Lot relationship could be described as "brotherhood" (Gen. 14:14). Terah outlived his son Haran, who died while Abram was still living in Ur of the Chaldeans (Gen. 11:28). Both Abram and his second brother Nahor were married. Sarai became the wife of Abram, while Milcah, the daughter of their deceased brother Haran, married Nahor. Before the storyteller continues with his narrative about Abram and his life, we are told that young Sarai was barren. (Gen. 11:30).

We are not told why the patriarch of this household (Terah) took his son Abram and his wife Sarai, and also his grandson Lot, and began making his way toward the Land of Canaan, leaving behind what we now know to be one of the most advanced ancient civilizations known to man – the city of the Chaldeans called Ur. Terah died in Haran, where the clan settled on the way to the Land of Canaan. According to the following chapter, Abram received a call to continue on to the Promised Land, seemingly while in Haran. The accounts certainly lack detail and are presented in a truncated fashion; this sometimes gives them the impression of self-contradiction. That realization has led a great many modern Torah scholars to conclude that many of the texts in the Torah were not simply edited or updated from time to time, but were once separate texts that were pieced together at a later time by an authorized community of editor/editors. Others retain the belief that the entire Torah can be explained without assuming any major editing.

The Call of Abram

The universalism that marked Genesis chapters 1-11 had now failed. The LORD begins anew, singling out one Mesopotamian, Abram, and promising to make of him a great nation, not numbered among the seventy nations of Genesis 10. We read in Genesis 12:1-3 that the Lord said to Abram:

וַיֹּאמֶר יְהוָה אֶל־אַבְרָם לֶךְ־לְךָ מֵאַרְצְךָ וּמִמּוֹלַדְתְּךָ וּמִבֵּית אָבִיךָ אֶל־הָאָרֶץ אֲשֶׁר אַרְאֶךָּ:

The Lord said to Abram, "Go forth from your native land and from your father's house to the land that I will show you. (Gen. 12:1)

וְאֶעֶשְׂךָ לְגוֹי גָּדוֹל וַאֲבָרֶכְךָ וַאֲגַדְּלָה שְׁמֶךָ וֶהְיֵה בְּרָכָה:

I will make of you a great nation, and I will bless you; I will make your name great, and you shall be a blessing. (Gen. 12:2)

וַאֲבָרְכָה מְבָרְכֶיךָ וּמְקַלֶּלְךָ אָאֹר וְנִבְרְכוּ בְךָ כֹּל מִשְׁפְּחֹת הָאֲדָמָה:

I will bless those who bless you and curse him that curses you; And all the families of the earth shall bless themselves by you." (Gen. 12:3)

God promised to make Abram into a great nation. This Hebrew phrase is significant: גּוֹי גָּדוֹל *(goy gadol)*, literally "big or great nation." As you may know, Hebrew places adjectives after nouns, not before, as in many other languages. So, while in English we say "big nation," in Hebrew it is גּוֹי גָּדוֹל *(goy gadol)* – "nation big." The plural of the Hebrew word for "nation" is גּוֹיִם *(goyim)*, often translated as "Gentiles" ("the [other] nations"). In Hebrew the verb "to bless" is בָּרַךְ *(barakh)*, which is related to the word for "knee" בֶּרֶךְ *(berekh)*. The meaning might therefore be connected to "bending the knee," possibly implying rendering service to someone. If so, one possible interpretation of this verse (12:3) could be: "I will serve those who serve you!" To "serve" implies doing good to someone, which will in turn result in a benefit for the recipient.

God also promises Abraham that "whoever curses him" מְקַלֶּלְךָ *(mekallekha)* will in turn "be cursed" אָאֹר *(aor)*. The strength of this promise, however, is lost in translation. The first word for "cursing" מְקַלֶּלְךָ *(mekallekha)* comes from a root that relates to "lightness." Hence, the background meaning might be "to make light of something heavy." The second word for "cursing" אָאֹר *(aor)* actually comes from a completely different root that has connotations of "damaging/destroying utterly." Taking into consideration these insights from Hebrew, an alternative translation could be presented as follows: "I will serve those who will serve you; and the one who makes light of you, I will utterly destroy."

Here begins the life of trust – the character quality for which Abram/Abraham will become most known. Abram must leave his home and begin making his way to a place that God promised to show him at a later time. In response to the trust demanded, God promises three things: 1) to make Abram into a great nation; 2) to bless Abram; and 3) to make Abram's name great. As a result of the Abram-God cooperation, the nations of the world will also receive God's blessings. God's promise to

Abram is sure, and his safety, in spite of perilous surroundings, is guaranteed. God's blessing of Abram is not the culmination, but merely the beginning. Ultimately, all nations of the earth will be blessed through him.

Abram's Obedience

Like Noah, the father of Shem, before him, Abraham too obeys God's call. Together with his wife Sarai and his nephew Lot, and along with the wealth, animals and slaves they had acquired in Haran, they set out for Canaan together. Abram's clan reached Shechem – the oak of Moreh (which in Hebrew means "teacher"). We are told by a later editor of the text that this took place when the Canaanites were living in the land (Gen. 12:6).

The Promise of the Land

Apart from choosing a particular family, God also assigned a section of His created order, a particular piece of land, to Abram and his offspring. This connection of Abram to the land was meant to invoke the history and failure of Adam in a particular land we now call the Garden of Eden. In so doing, the author may have intended to connect the promised redemptive future of Abram's children to the hope of Noah himself. After all, Noah had recently been portrayed as the second Adam from the righteous line of Seth. Abraham continues this same trajectory. Regardless of whether or not we should consider Abraham as a third Adam, the connection between Adam, Noah and Abram is clear. Like Noah (Gen. 8:20-21), Abram too set up an altar to the Lord (Gen. 12:7). It is intriguing to note that Abram settles to the east of Bethel (house of God), just as Adam was apparently situated east of the Garden of Eden (where God walked). It is there that the cherubim were placed to guard the entrance to the Garden (Gen. 3:24). God's redemptive plan continues in spite of the consistent failings of the frail children of Adam and Eve. From this point on the relationship of God to the children of Abram will dominate the remainder of the Bible, in spite of the fact that the Bible also makes it clear that the ultimate purpose of this relationship is the restoration of the entire world (Is. 65:17).

Abraham in Egypt

Because of a famine, Abram's family migrates to nearby Egypt. Being fearful for his life and the consequences of an undesirable outcome for his entire family, he asks Sarai not to reveal that she is his wife, but to inform the Egyptians that she is his sister. As expected, Sarai's beauty did not go unnoticed and she was quickly taken to join the imperial harem. Pharaoh and his household were immediately afflicted with widespread plagues (a precursor of the future event involving the children of Israel, for whom this book was originally written). It was quickly discerned that the plagues were connected to the new woman joining his harem – Sarai. Pharaoh confronted Abram about the matter and commanded him to take his wife and all that he had and leave Egypt (Gen. 12:10-20). We read in Genesis 13:3-4:

וַיֵּלֶךְ לְמַסָּעָיו מִנֶּגֶב וְעַד־בֵּית־אֵל עַד־הַמָּקוֹם אֲשֶׁר־הָיָה שָׁם אָהֳלֹה בַּתְּחִלָּה בֵּין בֵּית־אֵל וּבֵין הָעָי:

And he proceeded by stages from the Negev as far as Bethel, to the place where his tent had formerly been, between Bethel and Ai… (Gen. 13:3)

אֶל־מְקוֹם הַמִּזְבֵּחַ אֲשֶׁר־עָשָׂה שָׁם בָּרִאשֹׁנָה וַיִּקְרָא שָׁם אַבְרָם בְּשֵׁם יהוה:

… the site of the altar that he had built there at first; and there Abram invoked the LORD by name (Gen. 13:4).

We will discuss the meaning of the word יהוה (or as is it depicted in English transliteration – *YHWH*) later, when we discuss God's revelation to Moses. In this section of Genesis, suffice to say, sometimes the name of God is specified as יהוה *(yod-hey-vav-hey),* usually translated as "LORD" (in capitals), while at other times God is referred to as אֲדֹנָי *(Adonai),* also translated as "Lord." Abram's family left Egypt with much wealth because the gifts that were given to Abram for Sarai were apparently not taken back. From the wilderness of the Negev (direct connection point with Egypt) Abram returned to the place east of Bethel where he first set up an altar to the Lord (Gen. 13:1-4). Just like Noah and Enosh, son of Seth (Gen. 4:26) Abram called upon the Lord by His name. The righteous line that the Lord had established is preserved, as history continues to unfold.

Parting Ways with Lot

Not only did Abram's family grow in wealth, but Lot also benefited tremendously from his association with his uncle, becoming very wealthy in his own right (Gen. 13:5-7). After ongoing quarrelling between Lot's herdsmen and Abram's herdsmen over pasture land for the sheep, Abram proposed a wise solution to his beloved nephew (Gen. 13:8-9): So there would be no more quarrelling, for they are "brothers," they will separate and Abram gives Lot first choice of the land. Abram is full of trust and confidence in his God, whom he does not see; Lot trusts only in what he does see. This was a deal Lot could not refuse. Judging only by appearance, Lot chose for himself a piece of land that reminded him of both the prosperity of Egypt and the fabled Garden of the Lord where his forefather Adam once dwelt (Gen. 13:10-11). Thus Abram remained in Canaan, but Lot settled near Sodom. According to the text, the prosperity of Sodom was equal only to the level of its wickedness. Nevertheless, that was the place Lot chose to settle with his family (Gen. 13:12-13).

The Promise of the Land Expanded

The Lord reaffirmed the promise of the land to Abram and his offspring, asking Abram to raise his eyes and look in each direction. We read this in Genesis 13:14-17, along with the promise of innumerable offspring:

וַיהוה אָמַר אֶל־אַבְרָם אַחֲרֵי הִפָּרֶד־לוֹט מֵעִמּוֹ שָׂא נָא עֵינֶיךָ וּרְאֵה מִן־הַמָּקוֹם אֲשֶׁר־אַתָּה שָׁם צָפֹנָה וָנֶגְבָּה וָקֵדְמָה וָיָמָּה:

And the LORD said to Abram, after Lot had parted from him, "Raise your eyes and look out from where you are, to the north and south, to the east and west. (Gen. 13:14)

כִּי אֶת־כָּל־הָאָרֶץ אֲשֶׁר־אַתָּה רֹאֶה לְךָ אֶתְּנֶנָּה וּלְזַרְעֲךָ, עַד־עוֹלָם:

For I give all the land that you see to you and your offspring forever. (Gen. 13:15)

וְשַׂמְתִּי אֶת־זַרְעֲךָ כַּעֲפַר הָאָרֶץ אֲשֶׁר אִם־יוּכַל אִישׁ לִמְנוֹת אֶת־עֲפַר הָאָרֶץ גַּם־זַרְעֲךָ יִמָּנֶה:

I will make your offspring as the dust of the earth, so that if one can count the dust of the earth, then your offspring too can be counted. (Gen. 13:16)

The Hebrew words used of the four directions where Abram was asked to direct his gaze were: "North" צָפֹנָה *(tsafonah),* "South" נֶגְבָּה *(negbah),* "East" קֵדְמָה *(kedmah)* and "West" יָמָּה *(yamah).* In English, these words signify exclusive and very specific directions, but given Hebrew's intense physicality as a language we are able to see the origin of these words. Grammatically, the ending ה- *(hey)* when attached to a word signifying location shows the directional movement, similar to English "to the...." The Hebrew phrase נֶגְבָּה *(negbah),* translated as "to the South" literally means "to the Negev" (the wilderness of Negev). The phrase יָמָּה *(yamah)* translated as "to the West" literally means "to the sea." Similarly, קֵדְמָה *(kedmah),* translated as "to the east," evokes an image of "going back to something from an earlier time." Its root is connected to the idea of "antiquity" or the distant past.

From a Biblical perspective, this suggests the Garden of Eden that God planted "in the east" at the beginning of history (Gen. 2:8), as well as the direction of the rising sun. The Hebrew phrase translated as "to the North" צָפֹנָה *(tsafonah)* is connected to is connected to Mt. Tsafon or Zaphon (see Isa. 14:13), now known as Jebel Aqra on the border of Syria and Turkey. This mountain lay to Abram's north when God told him to look in all directions. Whilst we moderns consider north to be our main orientation point, ancient Israelites oriented themselves towards the east. It was a very different world from ours, where the physical landmarks took on real meaning, giving reference points to the language people used. For us to understand the world of the Bible, it is important to try to grasp how people thought in their original context.

Abram Builds an Altar to YHWH

When the Lord told Abram to walk through the length and breadth of the land, like Noah, he obeyed God's command, and he came to the vicinity of the famed oaks of Mamre in Hebron, where again he built an altar to the Lord. We read about this in the last verse of Genesis 13:

וַיֶּאֱהַל אַבְרָם וַיָּבֹא וַיֵּשֶׁב בְּאֵלֹנֵי מַמְרֵא אֲשֶׁר בְּחֶבְרוֹן וַיִּבֶן־שָׁם מִזְבֵּחַ לַיהוָה׃

And Abram moved his tent, and came to dwell at the terebinths of Mamre, which are in Hebron; and he built an altar there to the LORD. (Gen. 13:18)

The Hebrew word used for altar is מִזְבֵּחַ *(mizbeach)*. It is connected with the verb "to slaughter" and "to sacrifice." Hebrew often forms nouns from verb stems prefixed by -מ *(mem)*. For example, the verb "to fight" is לָחַם *(lacham)*, but when מ *(mem)* is added it becomes the noun מִלְחָמָה *(milchamah)* "battle, war." Abram was no longer to think of this land as a place where he dwelled among welcoming people. Instead it was promised to him and, like Adam and Noah before him, he was now given both the privilege and the responsibility associated with God's gift and grace.

The Daring Mission to Rescue Lot

The story of the capture of Lot (who now headed a separate "clan") is told in considerable detail in Genesis 14:1-12. When a rebellion between local vassal servant kings and a regional imperial power broke out, Lot and his family were captured, together with everyone else who stood in the way of the winning party. It appears that Abram had excellent people and life skills. He developed a true friendship and military alliance with Eshkol and Aner, who were his neighbors. His man came from the field of battle and reported to Abram at the oaks of Mamre (Mamre was apparently the name of the person who owned the land, as inferred from Gen. 14:24) that Lot had been captured. This was the perfect opportunity for Abram to mimic Cain's response – "Am I my brother's keeper?!"

Unlike Cain, and at great personal risk to himself and his entire household (from whom Lot had separated) Abram responded decisively and set out on a daring rescue mission. His young men were fully trained solders. He knew, given the dangers of living in the Middle East at that time (and nothing has really changed), that sooner or later their training would pay off. So he summoned over three hundred of his men, born in his household, along with the men of his military allies Aner, Eshkol and Mamre, and set out towards the very north of what would one day become Israel – the future territory of the tribe of Dan. This essentially continues to fulfill God's command to explore the entire land he was given as inheritance (Gen. 14:13-14).

Let us read carefully how Moses and the editors formulate the result of Abram's daring short-term military operation. We read in Genesis 14:16:

וַיָּשֶׁב אֵת כָּל־הָרְכֻשׁ וְגַם אֶת־לוֹט אָחִיו וּרְכֻשׁוֹ הֵשִׁיב וְגַם אֶת־הַנָּשִׁים וְאֶת־הָעָם:

He brought back all the possessions; he also brought back his kinsman Lot and his possessions, and the women and the rest of the people (Gen. 14:16)

The word אֵת *(et)* is the most frequent word in Hebrew. That is, it is a structural word that tells us something about the grammar of the sentence. The preposition אֵת *(et)* comes just before a direct object and has no equivalent in English. There are also other uses of the word אֵת *(et)*. It can also mean "with." In Modern Hebrew it rarely appears by itself with that meaning, but that meaning is still very common in combined forms, such as the word אִתּוֹ *(ito)* "with him" or אִתָּהּ *(itah)* "with her." However, in the Torah אֵת *(et)* can stand alone with this meaning. There is also another word in Hebrew that means "with" – עִם *(im)*. How we interpret these words can have a significant influence on our reading of the text.

Abram put Lot's captors to flight and drove them out of the land which God had now promised would belong to him (Gen. 13:14-17, 14:15). What is interesting is that we see here, with the rescue of Lot's clan, the direct benefit of being connected to Abram even if not part of his immediate family. We might remember that Lot's children will one day become part of the nations of the world living around Israel. In seeking to understand the Torah's positive assessment of the life of Abram, we are also forced to face his imperfections. Nevertheless, he is characterized by Moses, and later editors of the Torah, by his trust in God, despite his imperfect behavior. Abram showed himself to be a reliable friend, a loyal relative, and a committed worshiper of the LORD at almost every critical point in his life.

Meeting with Melchizedek

It is after Abram showed himself to be a loyal relative, a quality still highly valued in the Middle East, he was welcomed back home by both the King of Sodom and the King of Salem, whom the Torah later depicts as a priest of the Most High God (Most High God meaning the God of gods). The King's name was Melchizedek, and he offered Abram two very significant welcome gifts – bread and wine (Gen. 14:17-18) – the symbols of joy and sustenance. Melchizedek also spoke to Abram, as follows:

וַיְבָרְכֵהוּ וַיֹּאמַר בָּרוּךְ אַבְרָם לְאֵל עֶלְיוֹן קֹנֵה שָׁמַיִם וָאָרֶץ:

"Blessed be Abram of God Most High, Creator of heaven and earth. (Gen. 14:19)

וּבָרוּךְ אֵל עֶלְיוֹן אֲשֶׁר־מִגֵּן צָרֶיךָ בְּיָדֶךָ וַיִּתֶּן־לוֹ מַעֲשֵׂר מִכֹּל:

And blessed be God Most High, Who has delivered your foes into your hand." And [Abram] gave him a tenth of everything. (Gen.14:20)

The English word "Melchizedek" is a transliteration of the Hebrew phrase מַלְכִּי־צֶדֶק (*malki-tsedek*) which can be translated as "my king is righteousness." In Hebrew, in order to assign possessive quality to the word, a special suffix is often added to the word. In this case the ־י (*yod*) attached to "king" becomes מַלְכִּי (*malki*) and makes it mean "my king." If a different suffix were added נו־ (*-nu*), for example, then the result מַלְכֵּנוּ (*malkenu*) would mean "our king." Sometimes, however, the ־י (*yod*) is simply a connector, so that a different translation of the name could be "king of righteousness." Notice in verse 20 it is not exactly clear if it was Abram who gave Melchizedek the tenth of everything. The Hebrew simply says "and he gave him" וַיִּתֶּן־לוֹ *(va-yiten lo)*. Grammatically speaking, it could be possible that the pronoun "he" refers to Melchizedek who gave a tenth of everything he owned to Abram, and not the other way around (but see also Heb. 7:4).

The blessing on Abram by Melchizedek, king of Salem (probably the same as Jerusalem, as in Psalm 76.2), abruptly interrupts the approach of the king of Sodom, which resumes later. In the Book of Genesis, it is not unusual to find a foreigner revering the God of Israel, although that is less common in the remainder of the Hebrew Bible. It is likely that the account of Abram's interaction with the priest-king of Salem may have served to establish the antiquity of Israel's holiest site and the priestly and royal dynasties associated with it. (Jerusalem is never again mentioned by name in the Torah/Pentateuch.) Note that, technically, it is not Abram himself who is blessed by Melchizedek, but Abram's God. In the ancient world the master-servant identity was so strong that to bless the God of Abram amounted to blessing Abram himself, in our modern terms.

The Generosity of Abram

Refusing the offer of the king of Sodom to split the booty 50/50 (which would have been fair), Abram displays his generosity, graciousness, and also his understanding that he has a greater purpose than to provide an exceptional lifestyle for his clan. In Genesis 14:22, he employs almost the same depiction of God as Melchizedek did before him (Gen. 14:19). Like Melchizedek, he clearly equates the LORD with the Most High God already known and worshiped in this area of the world. This text underscores Abram's true faith in God and also his faithfulness to his neighbor. Abram was persuaded that, while he himself acted wisely and bravely, the ultimate hero of this victorious campaign was not himself, but "the LORD God Most High, Creator of heaven and earth."

A Great Promise to Abraham

Chapter 15 begins with a vision of God in which the Word of the LORD came to Abram, assuring him that he has nothing to fear because God will protect him and reward him greatly. We read in Genesis 15:1:

אַחַר הַדְּבָרִים הָאֵלֶּה הָיָה דְבַר־יהוה אֶל־אַבְרָם בַּמַּחֲזֶה לֵאמֹר אַל־תִּירָא אַבְרָם אָנֹכִי מָגֵן לָךְ שְׂכָרְךָ הַרְבֵּה מְאֹד:

Sometime later, the word of the LORD came to Abram in a vision. He said, "Fear not, Abram, I am a shield to you; Your reward shall be very great." (Gen. 15:1)

There are different ways to say "I" in Biblical Hebrew. One way is still in use in Modern Hebrew: אֲנִי (*ani*). Another more archaic term with the same meaning is used in the text above: אָנֹכִי (*anokhi*). The Hebrew literally reads "I [am a] shield to you; your pay, very much." Abram responded to God by verbalizing his ultimate pain, and challenging the real value of the promised blessing in the face of his ultimate limitation – childlessness. Abram then added that he has accepted his lot in life and is willing to leave all that he now owns, not to his child, but to his steward-servant – Eliezer of Damascus. In response, God assures him that this will not be so, then, to give him a real visual impression we read in Genesis 15:5-6:

וַיּוֹצֵא אֹתוֹ הַחוּצָה וַיֹּאמֶר הַבֶּט־נָא הַשָּׁמַיְמָה וּסְפֹר הַכּוֹכָבִים אִם־תּוּכַל לִסְפֹּר אֹתָם וַיֹּאמֶר לוֹ כֹּה יִהְיֶה זַרְעֶךָ:

He took him outside and said, "Look toward heaven and count the stars, if you are able to count them." And He added, "So shall your offspring be." (Gen. 15:5)

When God took Abram outside he said, "look towards heaven and count the stars." It is interesting that the phrase "look towards heaven" הַבֶּט־נָא הַשָּׁמַיְמָה *(hebet na ha-shamaymah)* includes a very interesting word – נָא *(na)* – which is hard to translate. There is a semantic and pragmatic distinction between an utterance in which נָא is used, and an utterance in which it is not used. The word נָא *(na)* is typically used to emphasize the action of the verb, indicating the importance the speaker attaches to it. It can express an emotional request. Here God uses this language to stress the importance of Abram looking up.

וְהֶאֱמִן בַּיהוה וַיַּחְשְׁבֶהָ לּוֹ צְדָקָה:

And because he put his trust in the LORD, He reckoned it to his merit. (Gen. 15:6)

The Hebrew word צְדָקָה *(tsedakah)* can be variously translated as "justice, righteousness, vindication, equity." In Modern Hebrew, *tsedakah* has come to mean "charitable giving" (since true charity is a righteous deed). Today a person who is referred to as a "righteous/just person" is called a צַדִּיק *(tsadik)*, while someone who is simply in the right in a disagreement is צוֹדֵק *(tsodek)*. The Hebrew word וַיַּחְשְׁבֶהָ *(vayachsheveah)* is actually a phrase that can also be translated as "and he counted it/her" (in this case, the righteousness). It could also be translated "and he accounted it" or "and he reckoned it." For example, in Modern Hebrew a word from the same root is חֶשְׁבּוֹן *(cheshbon)* "bill" or "account" (as with a bank).

Abram's Assurance

God reminded Abram that He had already promised him the gift of the land. At this point Abram asked a very simple question: How can I know this will indeed be so? (Since the Land was promised not only to him, but to his seed.) God then told him to do something that people in the Ancient Near East were very familiar with – to prepare everything for making a formal agreement – a covenant between Abram and God himself. The idea was simple: the representative of the animal life was to be cut into half and left on the floor; literally cut, torn apart. As both parties passed between of the pieces of flesh, they would make an oath to each other that would bind them by a sacred vow. The symbolism here is unavoidable – if one of the parties was unfaithful to the covenant promise, an awful curse would fall upon him – he would be torn apart – just like the animal that was laid on the floor.

In Genesis 15:13-16 God told Abram about the Egyptian slavery that was to come upon the children of Israel and last for four hundred years. Upon leaving the land of oppression, Israel would receive great wealth as reparation for their slavery. Abram was assured that he would not see this suffering in his lifetime, but that he would live a long and rewarding life. Possession of the land was still far into the future and would only happen in the fourth generation of the sons of Abraham. God could not simply remove the people already living in the Promised Land, for their iniquity had not yet reached its full measure before Him. Abram was put into a deep asleep, and a smoking pot and fiery torch appeared and walked in-between the two sides of the torn apart animals.

The implication of the words in Genesis 15:18-19 makes it clear that it was God alone who passed between the pieces. The covenant was therefore unilateral, because Abram did not take part in the ceremony. Before the Torah goes on to tell us about the drama that will develop between Hagar and Sarai over childbearing (Genesis 16), Abram was clearly assigned his territorial domain – it was a land that was large; indeed, it covered all the territory between a river in the center of Egypt (Nile) and the river Euphrates (touching the area of Haran from where the second leg of Abram's journey to the Promised Land originated). Nothing in the promises given to Abram to date specified the matriarch of the great promised Nation.
Convinced of her inability to give Abraham a son, Sarai takes matters into her own hands and, in accordance with documented ancient Near Eastern practice, offers her slave woman to Abram as a surrogate mother. Abram accepts. Given the high esteem for motherhood in biblical culture, the status of Sarai and Hagar is now in a sense reversed. According to the book of Proverbs, among the four things at which "the earth shudders," is: "a slave-girl who supplants her mistress" (Prov. 30:23). Understandably, Sarai demands justice from Abram, but instead of offering her the justice she asked for, he gives her a *carte blanche*, essentially causing injustice to Hagar.

This time the oppressor is Israelite, the slave is Egyptian (in opposition to other stories). This is reminiscent of Adam hearing bad advice from Eve and thrusting humanity into consequent havoc. Abraham is both the son of Adam and the son of Noah. He resembles both their significant failures and their great strengths.

The Sign of the Covenant

At the age of 99 God appears to Abram as *El Shaddai*, and exhorts him to live up to the high standard of the covenant that was made with him. We read in Genesis 17:1-8:

וַיְהִי אַבְרָם בֶּן־תִּשְׁעִים שָׁנָה וְתֵשַׁע שָׁנִים וַיֵּרָא יהוה אֶל־אַבְרָם וַיֹּאמֶר אֵלָיו אֲנִי־אֵל שַׁדַּי הִתְהַלֵּךְ לְפָנַי וֶהְיֵה תָמִים:

When Abram was ninety-nine years old, the LORD appeared to Abram and said to him, "I am El Shaddai. Walk in My ways and be blameless. (Gen. 17:1)

The words אֵל שַׁדַּי *(El Shaddai),* usually translated as "God Almighty" are of uncertain origin. It is possible that the root of *Shaddai* is the same as of שַׁד *(shad)* "breast." If so, the origin of this name of God might have to do with provision and sustenance. The female breast does symbolize sustenance and life-provision, fertility and offspring. So we can see how *El Shaddai* can also be translated as "God my provider."

וְאֶתְּנָה בְרִיתִי בֵּינִי וּבֵינֶךָ וְאַרְבֶּה אוֹתְךָ בִּמְאֹד מְאֹד:

I will establish My covenant between Me and you, and I will make you exceedingly numerous." (Gen. 17:2)

וַיִּפֹּל אַבְרָם עַל־פָּנָיו וַיְדַבֵּר אִתּוֹ אֱלֹהִים לֵאמֹר:

Abram threw himself on his face; and God spoke to him further, (Gen. 17:3)

אֲנִי הִנֵּה בְרִיתִי אִתָּךְ וְהָיִיתָ לְאַב הֲמוֹן גּוֹיִם:

"As for Me, this is My covenant with you: You shall be the father of a multitude of nations. (Gen. 17:4)

וְלֹא־יִקָּרֵא עוֹד אֶת־שִׁמְךָ אַבְרָם וְהָיָה שִׁמְךָ אַבְרָהָם כִּי אַב־הֲמוֹן גּוֹיִם נְתַתִּיךָ:

And you shall no longer be called Abram, but your name shall be Abraham, for I make you the father of a multitude of nations. (Gen. 17:5)

וְהִפְרֵתִי אֹתְךָ בִּמְאֹד מְאֹד וּנְתַתִּיךָ לְגוֹיִם וּמְלָכִים מִמְּךָ יֵצֵאוּ:

I will make you exceedingly fertile, and make nations of you; and kings shall come forth from you. (Gen. 17:6)

וַהֲקִמֹתִי אֶת־בְּרִיתִי בֵּינִי וּבֵינֶךָ וּבֵין זַרְעֲךָ אַחֲרֶיךָ לְדֹרֹתָם לִבְרִית עוֹלָם לִהְיוֹת לְךָ לֵאלֹהִים וּלְזַרְעֲךָ אַחֲרֶיךָ:

I will maintain My covenant between Me and you, and your offspring to come, as an everlasting covenant throughout the ages, to be God to you and to your offspring to come. (Gen. 17:7)

וְנָתַתִּי לְךָ וּלְזַרְעֲךָ אַחֲרֶיךָ אֵת אֶרֶץ מְגֻרֶיךָ אֵת כָּל־אֶרֶץ כְּנַעַן לַאֲחֻזַּת עוֹלָם וְהָיִיתִי לָהֶם לֵאלֹהִים:

I assign the land you sojourn in to you and your offspring to come, all the land of Canaan, as an everlasting holding. I will be their God." (Gen. 17:8)

The name "Abram" אַבְרָם *(Avram)* is composed of two words, *Av* and *Ram*, and means something like "father is lofty." "Abraham" אַבְרָהָם *(Avraham)*, on the other hand, contains the words אַב *(av)* and הֲמוֹן *(hamon)* within it. This refers to the phrase כִּי אַב־הֲמוֹן גּוֹיִם נְתַתִּיךָ *(ki av hamon goyim netatikha)* "because I have made you a father of a many nations" (Gen. 17:5). The change is very minor; only one letter – ה *(hey)*. But this letter inserted into the middle of the word רָם *(ram)*, essentially turns "lofty" into "multitude" or "many." The change is minor but the impact is major. The emphasis is no longer on the individual distinction of one leader, but on the collective greatness of the entire multitude of his descendants.

This theme will continue throughout the entire Hebrew Bible. God continues to address Abraham, and in Genesis 17:9-14 we are told that, as with Noah, there will be a covenantal sign present in all Abraham's children. This sign will be circumcision. When Abraham is circumcised, his future is marked as belonging to the Lord. Abraham's children would no longer belong to him, but to the God who brought him into the covenant relationship with Himself.

The Promise of Isaac

It is clear that when Abram heard God's promise of fertility, he did not understand what was to come – a son through the womb of Sarah, who was now well past child-bearing age. The Torah goes on to speak of the nature of this very interesting communication between God and Abraham (Gen. 17:15-22). God now tells Abraham that he is not the only one in the family to change names. Sarai, his wife, would now be known as Sarah. God further promised that she would also bear Abraham a son; indeed a multiplicity of people groups and nations will descend from her. When Abraham laughed at God's promise, he made his own proposal to God: "Oh that Ishmael might live before you!" God responded in the negative, saying that it would be through the son of his wife Sarah that the covenant blessing would flow.

His name will be called "Isaac" יִצְחָק *(Yitschak),* which in Hebrew means "he laughs" or "he will laugh" (Gen. 17:19, 21-22). God's choice of Isaac did not discount his love and care for "Ishmael" יִשְׁמָעֵאל *(Yishmael),* whose name means "God will hear" or "God hears." God stated that because of Abraham's request the blessings on Ishmael would also come into effect. He too will become a great nation and father twelve princes. (Gen. 17:20). That very day, in radical Noah-like obedience, Abraham circumcised Ishmael and every male in his household (Gen. 17:23-27).

Three Heavenly Beings Meet Abraham

In Genesis 18 we are invited to consider a crucial encounter between Abraham and Sarah, and three "men" who come to Abraham's tent and are welcomed by him as honored guests. This happened at the above-mentioned oaks of Mamre. At their sudden appearance Abraham quickly approached them and begged them to allow him to show them hospitality. The three men agree (Gen. 18:1-5).

Abraham hurried to request Sarah to bake cakes to feed their guests, then ran to the herd, chose a calf, and delegated a servant to prepare it. He then placed the prepared food before his guests while acting as a waiter, catering to their every need (Gen. 18:6-8). They asked him where Sarah was. When Abraham answered that she was in the tent, the LORD, one of the three, told Abraham that when He returned about the same time next year, Sarah will have a son. Sarah was eavesdropping and when she heard this, she laughed, just as Abraham had done previously, since her menstrual cycle had long since ceased (Gen. 18:9-12).

We continue reading in Genesis 18:13-15:

וַיֹּאמֶר יהוה אֶל־אַבְרָהָם לָמָּה זֶּה צָחֲקָה שָׂרָה לֵאמֹר הַאַף אֻמְנָם אֵלֵד וַאֲנִי זָקַנְתִּי:

Then the LORD said to Abraham, "Why did Sarah laugh, saying, 'Shall I in truth bear a child, old as I am?' (Gen. 18:13)

הֲיִפָּלֵא מֵיהוה דָּבָר לַמּוֹעֵד אָשׁוּב אֵלֶיךָ כָּעֵת חַיָּה וּלְשָׂרָה בֵן:

Is anything too wondrous for the LORD? I will return to you at the same season next year, and Sarah shall have a son." (Gen. 18:14)

וַתְּכַחֵשׁ שָׂרָה לֵאמֹר לֹא צָחַקְתִּי כִּי יָרֵאָה וַיֹּאמֶר לֹא כִּי צָחָקְתְּ:

Sarah lied, saying, "I did not laugh," for she was frightened. But He replied, "You did laugh." (Gen. 18:15)

Abraham and God's Secrets

Abraham's hospitality is once again highlighted as he walks with them to escort them on their way (Gen. 18:16). In Genesis 18:17-19 we read about God questioning Himself as to whether He should keep secrets from Abraham, given his glorious future:

וַיהוה אָמָר הַמְכַסֶּה אֲנִי מֵאַבְרָהָם אֲשֶׁר אֲנִי עֹשֶׂה:

Now the LORD had said, "Shall I hide from Abraham what I am about to do (Gen. 18:17)

וְאַבְרָהָם הָיוֹ יִהְיֶה לְגוֹי גָּדוֹל וְעָצוּם וְנִבְרְכוּ בוֹ כֹּל גּוֹיֵי הָאָרֶץ:

Since Abraham is to become a great and populous nation and all the nations of the earth are to bless themselves by him? (Gen. 18:18)

כִּי יְדַעְתִּיו לְמַעַן אֲשֶׁר יְצַוֶּה אֶת־בָּנָיו וְאֶת־בֵּיתוֹ אַחֲרָיו וְשָׁמְרוּ דֶּרֶךְ יהוה לַעֲשׂוֹת צְדָקָה וּמִשְׁפָּט לְמַעַן הָבִיא יהוה עַל־אַבְרָהָם אֵת אֲשֶׁר־דִּבֶּר עָלָיו:

For I have singled him out, that he may instruct his children and his posterity to keep the way of the LORD by doing what is just and right, in order that the LORD may bring about for Abraham what He has promised him." (Gen. 18:19)

God's conclusion is positive, and he proceeds to explain to Abraham the true nature of His mission – to inspect the alleged evil-doing of the residents of Sodom and Gomorrah (Gen. 18:21-22).

Abraham the Intercessor

As the three "men" depart (he now seems to understand that they are heavenly visitors), Abraham appeals to the righteousness and justice of God's own nature, pleading that surely He would not destroy the righteous together with the wicked. This leads to a fascinating dialogue, which became one of the key texts for Rabbinic Judaism's development of the idea of *minyan* – the quorum of ten men needed for certain communal prayers (Gen. 18:23-33). We read in Genesis 18:25-26:

חָלִלָה לְּךָ מֵעֲשֹׂת כַּדָּבָר הַזֶּה לְהָמִית צַדִּיק עִם־רָשָׁע וְהָיָה כַצַּדִּיק כָּרָשָׁע חָלִלָה לָּךְ הֲשֹׁפֵט כָּל־הָאָרֶץ לֹא יַעֲשֶׂה מִשְׁפָּט:

Far be it from You to do such a thing, to bring death upon the innocent as well as the guilty, so that innocent and guilty fare alike. Far be it from You! Shall not the Judge of all the earth deal justly?" (Gen. 18:25)

The phrase translated as "far it be from you" is the Hebrew חָלִלָה לְּךָ *(chalilah lekha)*. The meaning is something like "may it never be," "God forbid" or "far it be from you!" The simple meaning of this is that the one who pronounces these words believes that something is really not a good idea to do. In this context, the meaning connotes the idea of Abram saying something like this: "Don't do it! It is so out of character for You!"

וַיֹּאמֶר יהוה אִם־אֶמְצָא בִסְדֹם חֲמִשִּׁים צַדִּיקִם בְּתוֹךְ הָעִיר וְנָשָׂאתִי לְכָל־הַמָּקוֹם בַּעֲבוּרָם:

And the LORD answered, "If I find within the city of Sodom fifty innocent ones, I will forgive the whole place for their sake." (Gen. 18:26)

וַיַּעַן אַבְרָהָם וַיֹּאמַר הִנֵּה־נָא הוֹאַלְתִּי לְדַבֵּר אֶל־אֲדֹנָי וְאָנֹכִי עָפָר וָאֵפֶר:

Abraham spoke up, saying, "Here I venture to speak to my Lord, I who am but dust and ashes: (Gen. 18:27)

אוּלַי יַחְסְרוּן חֲמִשִּׁים הַצַּדִּיקִם חֲמִשָּׁה הֲתַשְׁחִית בַּחֲמִשָּׁה אֶת־כָּל־הָעִיר וַיֹּאמֶר לֹא אַשְׁחִית אִם־אֶמְצָא שָׁם אַרְבָּעִים וַחֲמִשָּׁה:

What if the fifty innocent should lack five? Will You destroy the whole city for want of the five?" And He answered, "I will not destroy if I find forty-five there." (Gen. 18:28)

As Abraham realizes the gravity of the situation (after all he is arguing with the supreme judge of the whole earth), he acknowledges his essential connection to the first Adam. The phrase אָנֹכִי עָפָר וָאֵפֶר *(anokhi afar ve-efer)* is more or less accurately translated as "dust and ashes." Clearly a connection is being made to Adam's origins in Genesis 2:7. There the sentence וַיִּיצֶר יהוה אֱלֹהִים אֶת־הָאָדָם עָפָר מִן־הָאֲדָמָה *(va-yitser YHWH Elohim et ha-adam afar min ha-adamah)* is translated as: "And the LORD God formed man from the עָפָר *(afar)* dust of the earth." Abraham, like Noah before him, continues to be connected in a typological sense to the figure of Adam (among others). Notice also that Abraham's demand is not that the guilty be destroyed and the innocent spared, but rather that the LORD spares the entire city for the sake of the righteous who live in it. This point is made more explicit in verse 26. The underlying theology here asserts that a righteous minority can effect deliverance for the entire community.

Abraham is Remembered, Lot is Saved

Genesis 19 deals largely with the judgment of Sodom and Gomorrah brought about by the three visitors who had previously been hospitably received at the tent of Abraham. As in the account of the judgment against wicked humanity in the story of Noah, here too God remembered his conversation with Abraham, and spared his nephew Lot and his family from the fire that rained down on Sodom and Gomorrah. We read about it in Genesis 19:27-29:

וַיַּשְׁכֵּם אַבְרָהָם בַּבֹּקֶר אֶל־הַמָּקוֹם אֲשֶׁר־עָמַד שָׁם אֶת־פְּנֵי יהוה:

Next morning, Abraham hurried to the place where he had stood before the LORD. (Gen. 19:27)

וַיַּשְׁקֵף עַל־פְּנֵי סְדֹם וַעֲמֹרָה וְעַל־כָּל־פְּנֵי אֶרֶץ הַכִּכָּר וַיַּרְא וְהִנֵּה עָלָה קִיטֹר הָאָרֶץ כְּקִיטֹר הַכִּבְשָׁן:

And, looking down toward Sodom and Gomorrah and all the land of the Plain, he saw the smoke of the land rising like the smoke of a kiln. (Gen. 19:28)

The phrase translated: "before the LORD" אֶת־פְּנֵי יהוה (*et pene YHWH*) in Genesis 19:27 might serve to make a connection with two other uses of the word פָּנִים (*panim*), which literally means "face": עַל־פְּנֵי סְדֹם וַעֲמֹרָה (*al pene Sedom ve-Amorah*) "upon Sodom and Gomorrah"; and וְעַל־כָּל־פְּנֵי אֶרֶץ (*ve-al kol pene erets*) "and upon all the land of the Plain."

וַיְהִי בְּשַׁחֵת אֱלֹהִים אֶת־עָרֵי הַכִּכָּר וַיִּזְכֹּר אֱלֹהִים אֶת־אַבְרָהָם וַיְשַׁלַּח אֶת־לוֹט מִתּוֹךְ הַהֲפֵכָה בַּהֲפֹךְ אֶת־הֶעָרִים אֲשֶׁר־יָשַׁב בָּהֵן לוֹט:

Thus it was, that when God destroyed the cities of the Plain and annihilated the cities where Lot dwelt, He was mindful of Abraham and removed Lot from the midst of the upheaval (Gen. 19:29).

Abraham and Abimelech

The previous time that Abram said his wife Sarah was his sister, he was in Egypt fleeing the famine in the Promised Land. At some point after the destruction of Sodom and Gomorrah, Abraham made his way towards the region of the Negev (which includes the modern city of Beer Sheva) and stayed some time in Gerar, again asserting that Sarah was his sister (a half-truth). Abimelech, the King of Gerar, sent for Sarah and took her to his residence. After God's gracious intervention, Sarah is returned to her family. We read about the ironic description relating to the fear of God in the court of Abimelech and the explanation Abraham gives for his actions in Genesis 20:8-13:

וַיַּשְׁכֵּם אֲבִימֶלֶךְ בַּבֹּקֶר וַיִּקְרָא לְכָל־עֲבָדָיו וַיְדַבֵּר אֶת־כָּל־הַדְּבָרִים הָאֵלֶּה בְּאָזְנֵיהֶם וַיִּירְאוּ הָאֲנָשִׁים מְאֹד:

Early next morning, Abimelech called his servants and told them all that had happened; and the men were greatly frightened. (Gen. 20:8)

וַיִּקְרָא אֲבִימֶלֶךְ לְאַבְרָהָם וַיֹּאמֶר לוֹ מֶה־עָשִׂיתָ לָּנוּ וּמֶה־חָטָאתִי לָךְ כִּי־הֵבֵאתָ עָלַי וְעַל־מַמְלַכְתִּי חֲטָאָה גְדֹלָה מַעֲשִׂים אֲשֶׁר לֹא־יֵעָשׂוּ עָשִׂיתָ עִמָּדִי:

Then Abimelech summoned Abraham and said to him, "What have you done to us? (Gen. 20:10)

וַיֹּאמֶר אַבְרָהָם כִּי אָמַרְתִּי רַק אֵין־יִרְאַת אֱלֹהִים בַּמָּקוֹם הַזֶּה וַהֲרָגוּנִי עַל־דְּבַר אִשְׁתִּי:

"I thought," said Abraham, "surely there is no fear of God in this place, and they will kill me because of my wife. (Gen. 20:11)

The irony of this story is that Abimelech and his men were truly terrified of the wrath of Abraham's God, whilst Abraham was persuaded that there was no fear of God among them. Like Noah, Abraham is shown as a fully righteous, but nevertheless imperfect, man. Like Noah, he certainly does not live up to the perfection of pre-fall humanity and yet, in spite of his shortcomings, it is clear that Abraham does display the real trust and faithfulness important in any close relationship. When Abimelech returns Sarah, he blesses both her and Abraham with many gifts, thus vindicating himself and clearing Sarah of any wrong-doing by her, or to her (Gen. 20:14-22). While we may concentrate on whether or not Abraham did what is right, the text shows no concern with our moral dilemma. Rather, it highlights the priestly, intercessory power of Abraham the prophet (Gen. 20:7, 17).

Sarah Conceives Isaac

As the tension between Sarah and Hagar developed over time, Abraham found himself in a very difficult position. His wife Sarah has developed a real animosity towards Ishmael and has requested that Abraham remove Ishmael from the borders of their family settlement. Abraham was devastated because he loved Ishmael (Gen. 21:1-11). God told Abraham, however, to go ahead and to do what Sarah asked him to do. This command also specified that while the covenantal promise will be carried through the line of Isaac, Ishmael too will be greatly blessed because he, too, is Abraham's son. Despite the intense emotional agony Abraham felt, in obedience he hurriedly prepared for their departure. What he did not yet know was that more emotional agony was awaiting him regarding his son Isaac. He too, like Ishmael, will be offered up to the Lord, albeit in a very different and far more significant way.

Abraham Swears to Abimelech

Because of his early experience with Abraham, Abimelech is certain that Abraham is truly blessed by God. He has seen that Abraham is successful in all he does, so God must surely be on his side. He therefore asks Abraham to promise him that the goodwill and loyalty that Abimelech showed to Abraham will not be betrayed by him. He seeks assurance that, if and when the time comes for Abraham to show his loyalty to Abimelech, he will do so. Without hesitation Abraham swore an oath, that indeed he would always deal honestly and kindly with Abimelech and his descendants (Gen. 21:22-24). Sometime later, Abraham tells Abimelech that a well he had dug had been confiscated by Abimelech's servants. When Abimelech pleaded ignorance, Abraham offered him animals from his herd, after which a pact was made between the two. Abraham, however, did not stop there.

He took another seven fully grown sheep and asked Abimelech, probably in a public ceremony, to accept them as proof that he did indeed dig the well and therefore it belonged to him. Abimelech agreed, and from this point on the place where Abraham dwelled among Philistines for a very long time, was called Beer Sheva. It is there, as with Noah before him, that Abraham invoked the name of the Lord, the Everlasting God (Gen. 21:25-34). The modern city of Beer Sheva is built in the general vicinity of this very place where the ceremony involving the seven fully grown sheep to secure Abraham's claim on the ownership of the well, took place. The names of both the ancient and modern cities makes the connection clear to the careful reader of this Torah narrative in Hebrew – בְּאֵר *(beer)* means "well," and שֶׁבַע *(sheva)* means "swearing" (i.e., an oath) or "seven."

Abraham's Ultimate Test

Abraham was no stranger to challenges, but everything he had gone through up to this point only prepared him for the ultimate challenge that his God would ask of him – offering to God his son, Isaac. As we have seen, Abraham is no stranger to challenging tests of faith to carry out his God's instructions, even to the point of anguish and failure to grasp the reasoning in God's mind. Yet it is here, in Genesis 22, that the ultimate test of Abraham's trust is spelled out: When God called Abraham's name, he responded – "Here I am." (Gen. 22:1).

Like Noah, Abraham was willing and ready to answer God's call immediately. He was his servant, ever-ready to do his God's bidding. This story would come to epitomize the determination of every true Israelite to serve his God, no matter what the circumstances. Indeed, this faithful service to God is the ultimate reason for Israel's existence. The difficulty of this tenth and final test lay not only in Abraham's love for his son Isaac, but also in the promises that God had given Abraham in connection with him. If Isaac was to die, those promises could never be fulfilled. What is Abraham to make of the words of his God?

The Demand

We read in Genesis 22:2-4:

וַיֹּאמֶר קַח־נָא אֶת־בִּנְךָ אֶת־יְחִידְךָ אֲשֶׁר־אָהַבְתָּ אֶת־יִצְחָק וְלֶךְ־לְךָ אֶל־אֶרֶץ הַמֹּרִיָּה וְהַעֲלֵהוּ שָׁם לְעֹלָה עַל אַחַד הֶהָרִים אֲשֶׁר אֹמַר אֵלֶיךָ׃

And He said, "Take your son, your favored one, Isaac, whom you love, and go to the land of Moriah, and offer him there as a burnt offering on one of the heights that I will point out to you." (Gen. 22:2)

The order of the Hebrew is "your son, your favored one, the one whom you love, Isaac," indicating increasing tension. The expression "go" or "get going" לְךָ־לְךָ (*lekh lekha*), which previously occurred only in Genesis 12:1, the initial divine command to Abraham, connects this story to the very beginning of Abraham's dealings with his God. Note also the parallel between "on one of the heights that I will point out to you" in this verse with "to the land that I will show you" in Genesis 12:1. All these stories form one coherent narrative of the faith and trust relationship between Israel and her God. Of course, Isaac was not the only son of Abraham. Ishmael was both his son, and was acknowledged by God as such, but here Abraham is told to take his son, the only son, whom he loves – Isaac. While Ishmael was also blessed by God due to being Abraham's son, it was Isaac who was the sign of God's ultimate commitment to him.

The giving of Isaac to Abraham in the most improbable of circumstances possibly produced in Abraham (along with prophetic statements about Isaac) an exceptional love and hope for this son born to Sarah. Will the child of "laughter" now turn into the child of "sadness"? Were Abraham and his family simply part of some crude, heavenly experiment? Abraham did not know. But he trusted God. So early the next morning, Abraham saddled his ass and took with him his two servants and his son Isaac. He split the wood for the burnt offering, and set out for the place that God had told him about (Gen. 22:3). It is clear that Isaac is singled out as Abraham's most "treasured possession." Now he faced his greatest test – to give up the son he loved; the one he had hoped and waited for, for so long. Yet, it was not just the giving up that was difficult for Abraham – he had passed similar tests before. This time the righteousness, faithfulness and goodness of Abraham's God – his reputation – was at stake.

The Chosen Mountain

בַּיּוֹם הַשְּׁלִישִׁי וַיִּשָּׂא אַבְרָהָם אֶת־עֵינָיו וַיַּרְא אֶת־הַמָּקוֹם מֵרָחֹק:

On the third day Abraham looked up and saw the place from afar. (Gen. 22:4)

The journey to the mountain of God's choosing, "Moriah" מֹרִיָּה (*Moriah*), took three days. The third day must have been the most difficult. Abraham actually saw the very place where he needed to kill his Isaac, just as he would an animal sacrifice, and offer him to God. About a thousand years later, at this very location, King David bought the threshing floor of

Araunah the Jebusite and built an altar to the Lord so that a "plague may be held back from the people" (2 Sam. 24:18-21). After David's death, his son King Solomon built a glorious temple on the same site. We read in 2 Chronicles 3:1: "Then Solomon began to build the house of the LORD at Jerusalem on Mount Moriah…" The story of the significance of this place will not stop here, but we must return and continue with the story of Abraham and Isaac as they continued their journey to Mount Moriah.

The Challenge of Faith

When they arrived at the foot of the mountain Abraham told his servants to stay while he and the young man continued together. So he put the wood for fire on the back of Isaac (adding enormous tension to the story), while he took the stones he used to set fire and the knife for the killing of Isaac (Gen. 22:5-6). We continue reading in Genesis 22:7-8:

וַיֹּאמֶר יִצְחָק אֶל־אַבְרָהָם אָבִיו וַיֹּאמֶר אָבִי וַיֹּאמֶר הִנֶּנִּי בְנִי וַיֹּאמֶר הִנֵּה הָאֵשׁ וְהָעֵצִים וְאַיֵּה הַשֶּׂה לְעֹלָה:

Then Isaac said to his father Abraham, "Father!" And he answered, "Yes, my son." And he said, "Here are the firestone and the wood; but where is the sheep for the burnt offering?" (Gen. 22:7)

The text emphasizes the pain Abraham must have experienced when the word "Father!" (אָבִי) were uttered by Isaac. Since the ancient text did not have punctuation marks, we must practice reading original Hebrew very slowly and with holy imagination, in order to feel together with Abraham, the redemptive pain of Isaac's address, recalling perhaps all the faithfulness and goodness of Abraham's God. This pain and sensitivity from an old warrior is epitomized in his immediate and tender response: "Here am I, my son" הִנֶּנִּי בְנִי *(hineni beni)*. The ancient Hebrew divides up the dialogue with repetitions of the simple: "and he said" וַיֹּאמֶר *(va-yomer)*, whereas today we might use different words.

וַיֹּאמֶר אַבְרָהָם אֱלֹהִים יִרְאֶה־לּוֹ הַשֶּׂה לְעֹלָה בְּנִי וַיֵּלְכוּ שְׁנֵיהֶם יַחְדָּו:

And Abraham said, "God will see to the sheep for His burnt offering, my son." And the two of them walked on together. (Gen. 22:8)

Abraham's response continues with firm, consistent and modern mind-boggling faith that earned him his fame. Literally the text says, reflecting the Hebraic structure of the language, "God will see for him the lamb" or "God will see for himself the lamb" אֱלֹהִים יִרְאֶה־לּוֹ הַשֶּׂה *(Elohim yireh lo ha-seh)*. This binding of the father and the son under the enormous challenge of God is evoked in the phrase "and the two of them walked on together" וַיֵּלְכוּ שְׁנֵיהֶם יַחְדָּו *(va-yelkhu sheneyhem yakhdav)*. While nothing in the text indicates the age of Isaac, it seems he could have been anywhere from a teenager to a grown adult. Either way, he appears to be a willing participant, together with Abraham, in the sacrifice that his God has demanded (to whatever extent he understands the proceedings).

Isaac on the Altar

As we have already seen, wherever the great men of God of Genesis went they built altars consecrating new places to the worship of their God. This is no exception. What is different here is the intensity and difficulty of God's demand.

וַיָּבֹאוּ אֶל־הַמָּקוֹם אֲשֶׁר אָמַר־לוֹ הָאֱלֹהִים וַיִּבֶן שָׁם אַבְרָהָם אֶת־הַמִּזְבֵּחַ וַיַּעֲרֹךְ אֶת־הָעֵצִים וַיַּעֲקֹד אֶת־יִצְחָק בְּנוֹ וַיָּשֶׂם אֹתוֹ עַל־הַמִּזְבֵּחַ מִמַּעַל לָעֵצִים׃

They arrived at the place of which God had told him. Abraham built an altar there; he laid out the wood; he bound his son Isaac; he laid him on the altar, on top of the wood. (Gen. 22:9)

וַיִּשְׁלַח אַבְרָהָם אֶת־יָדוֹ וַיִּקַּח אֶת־הַמַּאֲכֶלֶת לִשְׁחֹט אֶת־בְּנוֹ׃

And Abraham picked up the knife to slay his son. (Gen. 22:10)

It is interesting to see how beautifully the author speeds up and slows down the narrative presentation. The relatively slow development of the story as they travelled to Mount Moriah took eight verses to cover (Gen. 22:1-8). The action picks up in verse 9, with the building of the altar and binding of Isaac upon wood, being described quite quickly. Then, in verse 10, the narrative motion slows considerably as it describes Abraham lifting up the knife. This is masked in some English translations (as in NJPS that we are using here), where the first part of the sentence is missing in translation altogether: וַיִּשְׁלַח אַבְרָהָם אֶת־יָדוֹ *(va-yishlach Avraham et yado)*, literally something like "and Abraham sent out his hand." Only after this does the text continue וַיִּקַּח אֶת־הַמַּאֲכֶלֶת לִשְׁחֹט אֶת־בְּנוֹ (*va-yikach et ha-maachelet lishchot et beno*), which means "and he picked up the knife to slay his son."

So, whilst those translations do not really lose any of the basic meaning by omitting the first part, the literary skill and intention of the author who intended the text to have a slower, fast, and extra-slow tempo, goes unnoticed. The specific word used for the knife Abraham lifted up – מַאֲכֶלֶת (*maakhelet*) – probably meant "slaughtering knife" and is connected by root to אֹכֶל (*okhel*) "food." Yet that kind of knife does not simply prepare food for consumption, but is actually meant to end the life of an animal. Hebrew is a root language, so we can see how words that are unconnected in other languages, like "slaughtering knife" and "food," can be etymologically connected in Hebrew. In the language of worship, a sacrifice is just that – "food" offered to God for His "consumption." So Abraham prepared the instrument of food for action as he stretched out his hand with a knife in it.

The Angel of the LORD (YHWH)

וַיִּקְרָא אֵלָיו מַלְאַךְ יהוה מִן־הַשָּׁמַיִם וַיֹּאמֶר אַבְרָהָם אַבְרָהָם וַיֹּאמֶר הִנֵּנִי:

Then an angel of the LORD called to him from heaven: "Abraham! Abraham!" And he answered, "Here I am!" (Gen. 22:11)

וַיֹּאמֶר אַל־תִּשְׁלַח יָדְךָ אֶל־הַנַּעַר וְאַל־תַּעַשׂ לוֹ מְאוּמָה כִּי עַתָּה יָדַעְתִּי כִּי־יְרֵא אֱלֹהִים אַתָּה וְלֹא חָשַׂכְתָּ אֶת־בִּנְךָ אֶת־יְחִידְךָ מִמֶּנִּי:

And he said, "Do not raise your hand against the boy, or do anything to him. For now I know that you fear God, since you have not withheld your son, your favored one, from Me." (Gen. 22:12)

There are many instances in the Bible where the figure of a very special messenger of God's presence appears. He is referred to in verse 11 as מַלְאַךְ יהוה (*malakh YHWH*) "the angel/messenger of the LORD," when he calls on Abraham to cease the intended sacrifice of Isaac. Most Bibles translate this phrase as "the angel of the LORD," though some translations, such as the NJPS translation, using the indefinite article ("a") rather than the definite article ("the"). However, the Hebrew for "angel" and "messenger" are one and the same word – מַלְאָךְ (*malakh*). So, while the translation "a/the messenger of the LORD" is probably the most accurate, the designation "angel of the Lord" is less helpful, because in our minds the word "angel" immediately conjures up a particular extra-biblical and culture-specific image.

"The angel of the LORD" speaks from the first person, as if he is God (as we will see below in vs. 12). In other biblical usage of this term, "the angel of the LORD" executes judgment on behalf of God Himself, slaying 185,000 Assyrian soldiers in their camp, saving Jerusalem (2 Kings 19:35). "The angel of the LORD" is the commander of the Lord's army who commissions Joshua to undertake the Lord's battles for Canaan (Josh. 5:1-15), just as Moses had been commissioned to confront Pharaoh.

"The angel of the LORD" also carries out priestly duties of reconciliation. He asks how long God will withhold mercy from Jerusalem and Judah (Zech. 1:12). After Manoah meets "the angel of the LORD," he declares that he has seen *Elohim* – i.e., God or angels. The messenger/angel accepts blood-sacrifice worship from Manoah (Judges 13:9-22). "The angel of the LORD" apparently even has authority to forgive sins (Ex. 23:20-21). Historic Christian tradition has largely understood this "angel of the LORD" to be the pre-incarnate Lord Jesus, while Rabbinic Judaism has branded him with a Judeo-Greek word מֶטַטְרוֹן (*Metatron*), which in Hebraized Greek means something like "the one next to the throne," being made up of two Greek words μετά (*meta*) "between, beside" and θρόνος (*thronos*) "throne."

The Replacement Sacrifice

וַיִּשָּׂא אַבְרָהָם אֶת־עֵינָיו וַיַּרְא וְהִנֵּה־אַיִל אַחַר נֶאֱחַז בַּסְּבַךְ בְּקַרְנָיו וַיֵּלֶךְ אַבְרָהָם וַיִּקַּח אֶת־הָאַיִל וַיַּעֲלֵהוּ לְעֹלָה תַּחַת בְּנוֹ:

When Abraham looked up, his eye fell upon a ram, caught in the thicket by its horns. So Abraham went and took the ram and offered it up as a burnt offering in place of his son. (Gen. 22:13)

וַיִּקְרָא אַבְרָהָם שֵׁם־הַמָּקוֹם הַהוּא יהוה יִרְאֶה אֲשֶׁר יֵאָמֵר הַיּוֹם בְּהַר יהוה יֵרָאֶה:

And Abraham named that site Adonai-Yireh, hence the present saying, "On the mount of the LORD there is vision." (Gen. 22:14)

The substitution of a male sheep for the firstborn son has parallels in the ancient Near East and foreshadows the story of the paschal lamb (Ex. 12.1-42) in both its temporary and ultimate fulfillments. The story is not about the superiority of animal to human sacrifice; nor is it a polemic against human sacrifice. Note that God commands the sacrifice of Isaac at the beginning of the story (Gen. 22:2) and commends and rewards Abraham for being willing to carry it through at the end (Gen. 22:12-18).

וַיִּקְרָא מַלְאַךְ יהוה אֶל־אַבְרָהָם שֵׁנִית מִן־הַשָּׁמָיִם:

The angel of the LORD called to Abraham a second time from heaven (Gen. 22:15).

One of the names of God in the Bible is יהוה יִרְאֶה (*YHWH yireh*). It appears in Genesis 22:14, and most Bibles translate it as "the LORD will provide." The four-letter name of God comes first, but the יִרְאֶה (*yireh*) part comes from the Hebrew verb רָאָה (*raah*), which means "to see, to perceive, to look." This same root is used to describe someone who has an ability to see things others cannot, a רֹאֶה (*roeh*) "seer" or "prophet." So the phrase can be translated more literally to say "the LORD will (fore)see" instead of the usual "The Lord will provide." The comparison of "providing" vs. "seeing," although not identical, is actually not dissimilar. In Genesis 22, this verb is used several times where God is being described as "one who will see to it" or "one who will look out for his interest." When God sees His people in need, He acts to provide for them all that is needed. There may also be a play on words here, as the Messenger of the Lord in a sense *saw* that Abraham feared God יְרֵא אֱלֹהִים (*yere Elohim*). The word יְרֵא (*yere*) means "feared," but the similar-sounding word יִרְאֶה (*yireh*) used in יהוה יִרְאֶה (*YHWH Yireh*) means "sees."

The Confirmation of Blessing

וַיֹּאמֶר בִּי נִשְׁבַּעְתִּי נְאֻם־יהוה כִּי יַעַן אֲשֶׁר עָשִׂיתָ אֶת־הַדָּבָר הַזֶּה וְלֹא חָשַׂכְתָּ אֶת־בִּנְךָ אֶת־יְחִידֶךָ:

And said, "By Myself I swear, the LORD declares: Because you have done this and have not withheld your son, your favored one (Gen. 22:16)

כִּי־בָרֵךְ אֲבָרֶכְךָ וְהַרְבָּה אַרְבֶּה אֶת־זַרְעֲךָ כְּכוֹכְבֵי הַשָּׁמַיִם וְכַחוֹל אֲשֶׁר עַל־שְׂפַת הַיָּם וְיִרַשׁ זַרְעֲךָ אֵת שַׁעַר אֹיְבָיו׃

I will bestow My blessing upon you and make your descendants as numerous as the stars of heaven and the sands on the seashore; and your descendants shall seize the gates of their foes. (Gen. 22:17)

וְהִתְבָּרֲכוּ בְזַרְעֲךָ כֹּל גּוֹיֵי הָאָרֶץ עֵקֶב אֲשֶׁר שָׁמַעְתָּ בְּקֹלִי׃

All the nations of the earth shall bless themselves by your descendants, because you have obeyed My command." (Gen. 22:18)

The second angelic address conveys the LORD's final blessing on Abraham, using language similar to previous blessings (Gen. 12:3; 13:16; 15:5). However, this time the earlier promises are restated as a consequence of Abraham's obedience to the voice of God. A further promise is also added: "Your offspring shall possess the gate of their enemies." This definitive response from God establishes absolute and final approval of Abraham in this covenantal relationship, secured by the surety of the vow sworn by God to Himself.

Abraham has passed the ultimate test – he has given all to the One who will Himself one day give all to the children of Abraham. Because Abraham did not spare his one and only son, God confirms His promise to multiply Abraham's seed into a great nation, too numerous to count. The promise of blessing upon the nations of the earth through Abram is now confirmed to Abraham.

וַיָּשָׁב אַבְרָהָם אֶל־נְעָרָיו וַיָּקֻמוּ וַיֵּלְכוּ יַחְדָּו אֶל־בְּאֵר שָׁבַע וַיֵּשֶׁב אַבְרָהָם בִּבְאֵר שָׁבַע׃

Abraham returned to his servants, and they departed together for Beer-sheva; and Abraham stayed in Beer-Sheva. (Gen. 22:19)

This verse closes the *inclusio* that began in verse 1. The story of faith will now turn to Isaac and Jacob, the direct descendants of Abraham's covenantal relationship with his God.

MY REQUEST

Dear reader, may I ask you for a favor? Would you take three minutes of your time and provide an encouraging feedback to other people shopping on Amazon.com about this book (assuming you like it of course!)?

Here is how: 1. Go to Amazon.com and search for the title of this book – "Becoming Israel". 2. Click on the title, click on the "ratings" link (right under the author's name) and click "Write a customer review" button. 3. Rate the book and leave a few words.

This will really help me a lot, especially if you genuinely love this book! After writing a review please drop me a personal note and let me know - dr.eli.israel@gmail.com. I would appreciate your help with this.

Dr. Eli Lizorkin-Eyzenberg

CHAPTER FOUR: THE LIFE OF ISAAC

Like an excellent book or a great movie, the Torah moves back and forth in time shedding light on the fascinating events in the life of the person we call Isaac. Although the story of Isaac formally begins in Genesis 25:19, where we read the words: "This is the story of Isaac, Son of Abraham," we have already been introduced to Isaac's miraculous conception by post-menopausal Sarah (Gen. 21), and even him becoming the focal point of God's testing of Abraham (Gen. 22). The Hebrew word יִצְחָק *(Yitshak)* translated as "Isaac" literally means "he laughed" (or "he will laugh," "he laughs). It is an unmistakable reference to three laughs that were heard surrounding the events connected with the birth of Isaac. First, the laugh of Abraham, when God first broke the news to him (Gen. 17:17); second, the laugh of Sarah when she heard of it from the heavenly delegation that was entertained by Abraham in his tent (Gen. 18:11-13); and third (we may presume) was of course the good-natured laugh of God Himself when Sarah did become pregnant and gave birth nine months later.

Rebekah Arrives in the Promised Land

As the story begins to switch gears away from Abraham and Sarah, it first moves, not to Isaac, but to Rebekah the daughter of Bethuel and sister of Laban (Gen. 23-25). The narrative now develops around her willingness to leave her father's house and join Isaac, whom Abraham does not want to let leave the Promised Land. Yet at the same time, Abraham made his senior servant swear not to allow Isaac to take a wife from the local daughters of the Canaanites (24:2-4). We read of Abraham's response to the reluctant agreement by Eliezer, Abraham's trusted servant, in Genesis 24:6-7:

וַיֹּאמֶר אֵלָיו אַבְרָהָם הִשָּׁמֶר לְךָ פֶּן־תָּשִׁיב אֶת־בְּנִי שָׁמָּה:

Abraham answered him, "On no account must you take my son back there!" (Gen. 24:6)

יהוה אֱלֹהֵי הַשָּׁמַיִם אֲשֶׁר לְקָחַנִי מִבֵּית אָבִי וּמֵאֶרֶץ מוֹלַדְתִּי וַאֲשֶׁר דִּבֶּר-לִי וַאֲשֶׁר נִשְׁבַּע-לִי לֵאמֹר לְזַרְעֲךָ אֶתֵּן אֶת-הָאָרֶץ הַזֹּאת הוּא יִשְׁלַח מַלְאָכוֹ לְפָנֶיךָ וְלָקַחְתָּ אִשָּׁה לִבְנִי מִשָּׁם:

The LORD, the God of heaven, who took me from my father's house and from my native land, who promised me on oath, saying, "I will assign this land to your offspring" – He will send His angel before you, and you will get a wife for my son from there. (Gen. 24:7)

Abraham was emphatic, הִשָּׁמֶר לְךָ פֶּן-תָּשִׁיב (*hishamer lekha pen tashiv*), literally "guard yourself, least you return (him)." It was extremely important to Abraham that Isaac secure the promise already made. He must stay in the land God has promised to him and his children. Based on Abraham's previous experience in Genesis 22, when the promise of God (a nation through Isaac), which seemed to run against God's commandment (to offer up Isaac), was resolved by the appearance of the Lord's heavenly messenger (the Angel of the Lord), now Abraham trusts that Eliezer's mission to bring a wife to the Promised Land will be successful because God's angel is sure to prepare the way before him. As we read above in verse 7, Abraham said הוּא יִשְׁלַח מַלְאָכוֹ (*hu yishlach malakho*) "He will send his angel/messenger." After the providentially guided meeting of Rebekah by Abraham's servant, we read of the blessing upon Rebekah's departure, along with her maids, to meet her husband Isaac, of whose miraculous birth and God's sure blessing she has already heard so much (24:35-41). We read in Genesis 24:60:

וַיְבָרְכוּ אֶת-רִבְקָה וַיֹּאמְרוּ לָהּ אֲחֹתֵנוּ אַתְּ הֲיִי לְאַלְפֵי רְבָבָה וְיִירַשׁ זַרְעֵךְ אֵת שַׁעַר שֹׂנְאָיו:

And they blessed Rebekah and said to her, "O sister! May you grow into thousands of myriads; may your offspring seize the gates of their foes." (Gen. 24:60)

The meaning of the name רִבְקָה (*Rivkah*) "Rebekah" is unclear. It's possible that the meaning may be derived from a word for "tying up," "securing" or "capturing" something or someone. It may be connected with the noun מַרְבֵּק (*marbek*) which means a "stall" or "place for securing animals" in Amos 6:4. Notice that in the blessing she is called אֲחֹתֵנוּ (*achotenu*), which means "our sister." She was no longer just a daughter, but a daughter of their people, probably highlighting her coming of age, being old enough to marry and to start her own family unit.

What is interesting is that Abraham did not cut all ties with his family and the place of his origin. After all, it is from there that Abraham commends the wife for Isaac to be selected. We read in Genesis 24:15 about Eliezer's first meeting with Rebekah:

וַיְהִי־הוּא טֶרֶם כִּלָּה לְדַבֵּר וְהִנֵּה רִבְקָה יֹצֵאת אֲשֶׁר יֻלְּדָה לִבְתוּאֵל בֶּן־מִלְכָּה אֵשֶׁת נָחוֹר אֲחִי אַבְרָהָם וְכַדָּהּ עַל־שִׁכְמָהּ:

He had scarcely finished speaking, when Rebekah, who was born to Bethuel, the son of Milcah the wife of Abraham's brother Nahor, came out with her jar on her shoulder. (Gen. 24:15)

This can be seen in stark contrast with Abraham's unwillingness for his son to be united with the indigenous people of Canaan (Gen. 24:2-4). The phrase used in Rebekah's blessing, וְיִירַשׁ זַרְעֵךְ אֵת שַׁעַר שֹׂנְאָיו (*ve-yirash zarekh et shaar sonav*), literally means something like "and your seed will conquer the gate of their haters." The gate of a city was considered to be the seat of power, so to burn the gates of the city meant to destroy the city itself. It is possible that this blessing was given in the hope that Rebekah's blessing would be similar to the kind of blessing with which Abraham himself was blessed by God at his call: "And I will bless them that bless thee, and him that curseth thee will I curse; and in thee shall all the families of the earth be blessed." (Gen. 12:3).

The Initial Meeting

Isaac had been in Beer-lahai-roi (בְּאֵר לַחַי רֹאִי) and was coming from there when the caravan carrying Rebekah approached. We read in Genesis 24:63-67:

וַיֵּצֵא יִצְחָק לָשׂוּחַ בַּשָּׂדֶה לִפְנוֹת עָרֶב וַיִּשָּׂא עֵינָיו וַיַּרְא וְהִנֵּה גְמַלִּים בָּאִים:

And Isaac went out walking in the field toward evening and, looking up, he saw camels approaching. (Gen. 24:63)

וַתִּשָּׂא רִבְקָה אֶת־עֵינֶיהָ וַתֵּרֶא אֶת־יִצְחָק וַתִּפֹּל מֵעַל הַגָּמָל:

Raising her eyes, Rebekah saw Isaac. She alighted from the camel (Gen. 24:64)

וַתֹּאמֶר אֶל־הָעֶבֶד מִי־הָאִישׁ הַלָּזֶה הַהֹלֵךְ בַּשָּׂדֶה לִקְרָאתֵנוּ וַיֹּאמֶר הָעֶבֶד הוּא אֲדֹנִי וַתִּקַּח הַצָּעִיף וַתִּתְכָּס:

...and said to the servant, "Who is that man walking in the field toward us?" And the servant said, "That is my master." So she took her veil and covered herself. (Gen. 24:65)

וַיְסַפֵּר הָעֶבֶד לְיִצְחָק אֵת כָּל־הַדְּבָרִים אֲשֶׁר עָשָׂה:

The servant told Isaac all the things that he had done. (Gen. 24:66)

וַיְבִאֶהָ יִצְחָק הָאֹהֱלָה שָׂרָה אִמּוֹ וַיִּקַּח אֶת־רִבְקָה וַתְּהִי־לוֹ לְאִשָּׁה וַיֶּאֱהָבֶהָ וַיִּנָּחֵם יִצְחָק אַחֲרֵי אִמּוֹ:

Isaac then brought her into the tent of his mother Sarah, and he took Rebekah as his wife. Isaac loved her, and thus found comfort after his mother's death. (Gen. 24:67)

Rebekah's Troubled Pregnancy

In Genesis 25:19 we are told that it is here in this section that the formal telling of Isaac's story commences. Isaac was 40 years old when he took Rebekah to be his wife but, like Sarah, Rebekah was barren. Again God gave a promise, but the reality on the ground was different. This mention of Rebekah's barrenness is certainly reminiscent of Abraham and Sarah's struggle with not being able to bring posterity into the world. We are told in Genesis 25:21:

וַיֶּעְתַּר יִצְחָק לַיהוה לְנֹכַח אִשְׁתּוֹ כִּי עֲקָרָה הִוא וַיֵּעָתֶר לוֹ יהוה וַתַּהַר רִבְקָה אִשְׁתּוֹ:

Isaac pleaded with the LORD on behalf of his wife, because she was barren; and the LORD responded to his plea, and his wife Rebekah conceived. (Gen. 25:21)

The Hebrew word for "and he pleaded/entreated/petitioned" וַיֶּעְתַּר *(va-ye'etar)* carries the sense of a passionate plea and commitment to continue until the desired result is achieved. Notice that וַיֶּעְתַּר יִצְחָק לַיהוה *(va-ye'etar Yitschak la-YHWH)* "and Isaac pleaded with the LORD" and וַיֵּעָתֶר לוֹ יהוה *(va-ye'ater lo Adonai)* "the LORD responded to his plea" actually use different forms of the same Hebrew verb. The literal meaning would be that when Isaac pleaded to the LORD, the LORD accepted the plea or "allowed himself to be entreated" and replied with an affirmative answer. The word עֲקָרָה *(akarah)* means "barren." Interestingly this word carries not only a meaning as "unfruitful", but also relates to "displaced," "destroyed" and "uprooted."

The ancient linguistic logic goes as follows: If a woman has no children, she has no roots, and therefore embodies a type of displacement. On the other hand, the word for "womb" is רֶחֶם *(rechem)* and beautifully connects with another Hebrew word רַחֲמִים *(rachamim)*, which means "mercy/mercies." The connection seems to indicate that a woman who becomes pregnant has received mercy from above. Another connection may be understood from the "compassion" typically felt by a mother for her own offspring, the "fruit of her womb" (Isaiah 49:15).

Rebekah conceived and after some months began to feel unusually strong and harsh movements within her womb. It felt like there was a war going on in her womb. To her and to other woman that she most likely consulted concerning this turmoil, it may have seemed like something that could result in miscarriage. Remember that she had been barren. Rebekah was truly discouraged, so she inquired of the LORD (Gen. 25:22).

וַיִּתְרֹצֲצוּ הַבָּנִים בְּקִרְבָּהּ וַתֹּאמֶר אִם־כֵּן לָמָּה זֶּה אָנֹכִי וַתֵּלֶךְ לִדְרֹשׁ אֶת־יְהוָה׃
But the children struggled in her womb, and she said, "If so, why do I exist?" She went to inquire of the LORD. (Gen. 25:22).

The word וַיִּתְרֹצֲצוּ *(va-yitrotsetsu)*, usually translated "and they struggled" does not really convey the full meaning. The root רָצַץ *(ratsats)* communicates the idea of "breaking," "crushing" and "oppressing." Alternatively, the root might be רוּץ *(ruts)* "running." In either case, what she felt inside her was no small struggle; it was a great contest or even war. The story then quickly moves to introducing the future "struggle" between Esau and Jacob – the two sons of Rebekah who warred with each other prophetically within her womb. We will return to this story and the Lord's answer later when we look at the person of Jacob, but for now, let us stay with the life of Isaac.

Like Father, Like Son

Like his father Abraham before him, Isaac experienced a famine in the land and decided to go to Abimelech, the king of the Philistines in Gerar (not far from the modern city of Beer Sheva). This was exactly the same place where Abraham stayed for a short time when he sought to pass Sarah off as his sister. It is possible that it was the very same king that now ruled Gerar, but it is likely that the Abimelech mentioned here is actually the son of Abimelech in Abraham's story. Although this is not mentioned, the Lord's warning and commandment not to travel to Egypt presupposes the fact that Isaac wanted to move to Egypt, just as Abram once did under very similar circumstances.

We read in Genesis 26:2-5 of the renewed promise of God to Isaac, which caused him to reconsider his plans and stay in the place chosen by God for His clan – Gerar of the Philistines:

וַיֵּרָא אֵלָיו יהוה וַיֹּאמֶר אַל־תֵּרֵד מִצְרָיְמָה שְׁכֹן בָּאָרֶץ אֲשֶׁר אֹמַר אֵלֶיךָ׃

The LORD had appeared to him and said, "Do not go down to Egypt; stay in the land." (Gen. 26:2)

גּוּר בָּאָרֶץ הַזֹּאת וְאֶהְיֶה עִמְּךָ וַאֲבָרְכֶךָּ כִּי־לְךָ וּלְזַרְעֲךָ אֶתֵּן אֶת־כָּל־הָאֲרָצֹת הָאֵל וַהֲקִמֹתִי אֶת־הַשְּׁבֻעָה אֲשֶׁר נִשְׁבַּעְתִּי לְאַבְרָהָם אָבִיךָ׃

Reside in this land, and I will be with you and bless you; I will assign all these lands to you and to your heirs, fulfilling the oath that I swore to your father Abraham. (Gen. 26:3)

וְהִרְבֵּיתִי אֶת־זַרְעֲךָ כְּכוֹכְבֵי הַשָּׁמַיִם וְנָתַתִּי לְזַרְעֲךָ אֵת כָּל־הָאֲרָצֹת הָאֵל וְהִתְבָּרֲכוּ בְזַרְעֲךָ כֹּל גּוֹיֵי הָאָרֶץ׃

I will make your heirs as numerous as the stars of heaven, and assign to your heirs all these lands, so that all the nations of the earth shall bless themselves by your heirs (Gen. 26:4)

עֵקֶב אֲשֶׁר־שָׁמַע אַבְרָהָם בְּקֹלִי וַיִּשְׁמֹר מִשְׁמַרְתִּי מִצְוֹתַי חֻקּוֹתַי וְתוֹרֹתָי:

Inasmuch as Abraham obeyed Me and kept My charge: My commandments, My laws, and My teachings." (Gen. 26:5)

Like his father before him, Isaac too was assured of God's presence with him and of the much-needed help to sustain his family and survive the famine. While it was because of Abraham's faithfulness and his merits that the covenant is now being transferred to Isaac, Isaac himself also needed to be tested and tried through his own trials, albeit not as dramatic as those of his father. The close correlation between the events in the lives of Isaac and Abraham are not coincidental. The Book of Genesis goes out of its way to highlight how similar some of these stories are. The reason for this is that the original audience had in many ways encountered the same challenges as their forefathers. They needed to be shown that God remained faithful to His promises and carried the forefathers of Israel through every imaginable difficulty. Since this was so, the presumption was that He would do the same for their covenant children – the Children of Israel who left Egypt and were the original recipients of the Book of Genesis.

These parallels are even more numerous between the lives of Abraham and Jacob, and their families as well as other key figures (and people groups) of the biblical narrative. This may mean that there is a broader purpose across the Torah of narrative typology and its purpose is far beyond simple similarity of challenges for each generation. For example, the descent to Egypt and return by Abraham is a harbinger of Israel's descent and return to the same place. The Torah narratives, therefore, are connected to form one narrative of God's engagement with both Israel in particular and humanity in general. In Genesis 26:6 we read that in obedience to God's instruction, Isaac stayed in Gerar during the time of the famine: וַיֵּשֶׁב יִצְחָק בִּגְרָר *(va-yeshev Yitschak bi-Gerar)* "And Isaac dwelt in Gerar."

The word יָשַׁב *(yashav)* is usually translated as "to dwell." Its root relates to words for "seating," "being located," "populating," "residing," "colonizing," and "exercising dominion." For example, even in Modern Hebrew when someone asks where a particular office staff is located, we answer (literally) they are "sitting" in such and such a place. While readers should not get the erroneous idea that Modern Hebrew usage serves as a legitimate lens through which biblical meanings can be understood, we are, nevertheless, justified in considering the modern use that may have some connection to the ancient one as something that may shed further light on the issues at hand.

The name of the place גְּרָר (*Gerar*) "Gerar" is of unknown origin. It may mean simply "a place of living." Interestingly, however, the Hebrew verb גָּרַר (*garar*) can mean "to drag (away)." People are "dragged away" like fish in nets (Hab. 1:15), strong winds "sweep through" (Jer. 30:23), and violent people are "dragged off" by their own violence (Prov. 21:7). It is certainly intriguing to think that both Abraham and Isaac were afraid that their wives, Sarah and Rebekah, would be "dragged away" from them when they dwelt amongst the Philistines; maybe the name of the place in the story helped to evoke such associations among early hearers.

We are also told that Isaac, too, just like Abraham, decided to tell everyone that Rebekah was his sister, failing to mention that she was also his wife. He feared that his wife could have been taken from him and he be murdered to clear the way for her remarriage or concubine status to someone locally important and powerful. But, as the story has it, Abimelech king of Philistines noticed the romantic relationship between Isaac and Rebekah and realized that she was more to Isaac than he had admitted.

Abimelech confronted Isaac about his lie. Isaac gave his justification. It was exactly the same justification as the one given by Abraham to Abimelech's father. The king reacted in anger and disbelief. Sleeping with another man's wife (as long as the man was still alive) was rightly considered a grave sin in that time and place. Therefore, Abimelech's accusation was justified:

מַה־זֹּאת עָשִׂיתָ לָּנוּ כִּמְעַט שָׁכַב אַחַד הָעָם אֶת־אִשְׁתֶּךָ וְהֵבֵאתָ עָלֵינוּ אָשָׁם׃

"What have you done to us! One of the people might have lain with your wife, and you would have brought guilt upon us." (Gen. 26:10)

Ancient Hebrew, both original paleo-Hebrew and later Hebrew, did not use punctuation, so there was no way to identify that something was a question other than by looking at the text and its contexts. An example is מַה־זֹּאת עָשִׂיתָ לָּנוּ (*mah zot asita lanu*), which translated means "What (is) this you did to us?" When we read our Bibles in the English language, we must not blindly trust the translation committee's placement of commas and periods in the text, nor especially trust the parsing of literary units into chapter and paragraph sections, since the meaning of the text may in some cases be changed dramatically by these insertions. The translation decisions are justified most of the time, although sometimes they are purely arbitrary. Translation is essentially a work of interpretation as well.

In Genesis 26:11 we read:

וַיְצַו אֲבִימֶלֶךְ אֶת־כָּל־הָעָם לֵאמֹר הַנֹּגֵעַ בָּאִישׁ הַזֶּה וּבְאִשְׁתּוֹ מוֹת יוּמָת׃

And Abimelech charged all the people, saying: 'He that touches this man or his wife shall surely be put to death.' (Gen. 26:11)

Notice how differently people in ancient times thought of communal vs. individual responsibility. There was absolutely no doubt in Abimelech's mind that if one of his men violated Rebekah, everyone in Gerar would have experienced the curses of the carefully watching God/gods. Therefore, Abimelech issued a very stern warning to any individual who will be found guilty of it, exposing everyone to real danger. We have trouble thinking of it in this corporate way. We believe in the individual responsibility of each person, unless that person is an official representative of a greater number of people. But this was not so in the ancient world. Another line of reasoning may have been coming from Abimelech's father who had dealings with Abram many years before if he had warned his son ahead of time to be very careful with any member of Abram's household. Surely Isaac as Abram's direct descendent would have been included in that fatherly warning. Having relations with a married woman was forbidden in the ancient society not because of great respect for the woman, but because the woman literally belonged to a man. She was his possession. She was his and his alone. Ancient societies by and large respected and held this idea in high regard.

Isaac Becomes Great

Just like Abram before him, Isaac, too, is shown to be truly blessed by God. In every way he became exceedingly wealthy, as his father before him, as to invoke the envy of those around. The blessings upon Isaac are summarized in Genesis 26:12-14, where we read:

וַיִּזְרַע יִצְחָק בָּאָרֶץ הַהִוא וַיִּמְצָא בַּשָּׁנָה הַהִוא מֵאָה שְׁעָרִים וַיְבָרֲכֵהוּ יהוה:

And Isaac sowed in that land, and found in the same year a hundredfold; and the LORD blessed him. (Gen. 26:12)

וַיִּגְדַּל הָאִישׁ וַיֵּלֶךְ הָלוֹךְ וְגָדֵל עַד כִּי־גָדַל מְאֹד:

And the man grew, and going he went, and he grew until he became very great. (Gen. 26:13)

וַיְהִי־לוֹ מִקְנֵה־צֹאן וּמִקְנֵה בָקָר וַעֲבֻדָּה רַבָּה וַיְקַנְאוּ אֹתוֹ פְּלִשְׁתִּים:

And he had possessions of flocks, and possessions of herds, and a great household; and the Philistines envied him. (Gen. 26:14)

The פְּלִשְׁתִּים (Pelishtim) "Philistines" were an ancient people group whose name was eventually adapted by the Romans to refer to much of the Land of Israel (as "Palestine"). Modern Palestinians are not the same people as the ancient Philistines, but their name derives from the Biblical term. The Modern Hebrew word for "Palestinians" is פְּלֶסְטִינִים (Palestinim), a transformed loan word from English (i.e., "Palestinian" with Hebrew plural ending ־ים). In the Bible the פְּלִשְׁתִּים (Pelishtim) "Philistines" never ruled the whole Land of Israel, and their name referred to a smaller area. The southwestern coastal area of the territory that would become Israel was called Philistia, while the central highlands constituted Canaan. Both the Canaanites and the Philistines disappeared as distinct peoples by the time of the Babylonian Captivity of Judea (586 B.C.E.), most likely assimilating with other people groups in the region.

Before 135 C.E., the Romans used the terms Judea, Samaria and Galilee to refer to the Land of Israel as a whole. When Titus destroyed Jerusalem in 70 C.E., the Roman government produced coins with the phrase *Judea*

Capta ("Judea Captive"). The term "Palestine" was not used at this time. It was only when the Romans brutally crushed the second Jewish revolt against Rome in 135 C.E. (the Bar Kochba uprising) that Emperor Hadrian applied the term "Palestine" to the entire Land of Israel. He took the name of the ancient enemies of Israel, the Philistines, Latinized it, and applied it to the Land of Israel. He hoped to erase the name of Israel from all memory.

Philistia for Philistines

The Philistines were afraid and took measures to cut the water supplies of Isaac's clan, filling up with earth the wells used by Isaac's people. It was clear Isaac's time in Gerar was up. Abimelech told Isaac, "Go away from us, for you have become far too big for us." The Book of Genesis was not written during the life of Abraham and Isaac, but (according to my view) much later when the Israelites had just left Egypt. It gives direction and inspiration to the Israelites in the wilderness, showing them how in many ways the struggles and wonderings of the Israelites resembled those of Abraham and Isaac. The children of Israel were not disconnected from the origins and their history. While the history moved forward, it clearly repeated itself many times over. What happened to Abraham and Isaac, will happen to them, too. They should be prepared and not taken by surprise by the suffering and unpredictability of life ahead of them. Instead, they must remember that God will be faithful to them just as He was faithful to their forefathers – Abraham and Isaac.

New Beginning

Isaac moved away from the city of Gerar and pitched his tents in the wadi of Gerar. There he dug again the very wells that his father Abraham had dug, before the Philistines of his time filled them up with earth seeking to destroy Abraham's source of drinking water. Isaac restored the wells symbolically giving them the same names that were once given to them by his father (Gen. 26:17-18). Isaac was a man who sought uncontested peace with his neighbors. When his newly-dug wells (and digging a well was a very expensive construction project) were unfairly challenged by the men from Gerar as belonging to them, he did not fight them but moved away from two wells that he dug.

We must understand that digging of wells was a very serious financial and time investment. This non-confrontational attitude by Isaac came to him at a high cost. The third well was uncontested so he named it *Rechovot* (today it is the name of a modern Israeli city), saying, "Now at last the Lord has granted us ample space to increase in the land" (Gen. 26:22). We read about it as follows:

וַיַּעְתֵּק מִשָּׁם וַיַּחְפֹּר בְּאֵר אַחֶרֶת וְלֹא רָבוּ עָלֶיהָ וַיִּקְרָא שְׁמָהּ רְחֹבוֹת וַיֹּאמֶר כִּי־עַתָּה הִרְחִיב יהוה לָנוּ וּפָרִינוּ בָאָרֶץ:

And he removed from thence, and dug another well; and for that they strove not. And he called the name of it Rehoboth; and he said: 'For now the LORD hath made room for us, and we shall be fruitful in the land.' (Gen. 26:22)

There are thousands of names of people and places in the Bible that are connected to some kind of event (like this one) or an idea. When the men of Gerar "did not argue about the third well" that he dug וְלֹא רָבוּ עָלֶיהָ *(ve-lo ravu aleah)*, Isaac called the place רְחֹבוֹת *(Rechovot)*, כִּי־עַתָּה הִרְחִיב יהוה לָנוּ *(ki ata hirchiv YHWH lanu)*, which literally means "because now the LORD has widened (it) for us/on our behalf." In Modern Hebrew רְחוֹב *(rechov)* means "street" (literally a widened place), translated correctly as a city square in Nehemiah 8:1.

When Isaac moved from there to Beer Sheva the Lord appeared to him, confirming to him that He was the God of his father Abraham and that he must not fear because He would be present with him every step of the way. God also reminded him of the promise to bless and increase in number his offspring, because of the proven faithfulness of his father. (Gen. 26:23-25). Just like Abraham and other holy men before him, Isaac built an altar there and evoked the name of the Lord (Gen. 26:25).

Making Peace with Abimelech

Immediately after the Lord appeared to him and promised to be with him, Isaac and his men pitched their tents and began the work to acquire drinking water in Beer Sheva. Abimelech, with his chief consular and the chief commander arrived to meet with Isaac. Isaac, expressing bewilderment at their arrival, asked them why they would come to him now, given their hostile actions towards him in the not so distant past. We read in Genesis 26:28-30:

וַיֹּאמְרוּ רָאוֹ רָאִינוּ כִּי־הָיָה יהוה עִמָּךְ וַנֹּאמֶר תְּהִי נָא אָלָה בֵּינוֹתֵינוּ בֵּינֵינוּ וּבֵינֶךָ וְנִכְרְתָה בְרִית עִמָּךְ:

And they said: 'We saw plainly that the LORD was with thee; and we said: Let there now be an oath between us, even between us and thee, and let us make a covenant with thee. (Gen. 26:28)

אִם־תַּעֲשֵׂה עִמָּנוּ רָעָה כַּאֲשֶׁר לֹא נְגַעֲנוּךָ וְכַאֲשֶׁר עָשִׂינוּ עִמְּךָ רַק־טוֹב וַנְּשַׁלֵּחֲךָ בְּשָׁלוֹם אַתָּה עַתָּה בְּרוּךְ יהוה:

That thou wilt do us no hurt, as we have not touched thee, and as we have done unto thee nothing but good, and have sent thee away in peace; thou art now the blessed of the LORD.' (Gen. 26:29)

וַיַּעַשׂ לָהֶם מִשְׁתֶּה וַיֹּאכְלוּ וַיִּשְׁתּוּ:

And he made them a feast, and they did eat and drink. (Gen. 26:30)

On the following morning, both parties held a covenant-making ceremony. Then the delegation departed back to Gerar. On that same day Isaac's men brought him a piece of excellent news. They had found water! He named the new well שִׁבְעָה *(shivah)* (Gen. 26:31-33). This event parallels a previous covenant between Abraham and Abimelech (presumably the father of Isaac's Abimelech), when Abraham told that king that a well he had dug had been confiscated by the ruler's servants.

At that time Abraham took שֶׁבַע *(sheva)* "seven" fully grown sheep and asked Abimelech, probably in a public ceremony, to accept them as proof of the king's acknowledgement that Abraham had indeed dug that well – and thus it belonged to him. Abimelech agreed, and from this point on the place where Abraham dwelled for some time among the Philistines was called בְּאֵר שֶׁבַע *(Beer Sheva)* "the well of an oath [or: of seven]" (Gen. 21:25-34).

Hebrew שבועה *(shevuah)* "oath, curse" seems to share a root with the word שבע *(sheva)* "seven" and may have originated from the practice of using sets of seven in maledictions (cf. Lev. 26:18, 21, 24). Thus, the sense of swearing an oath may originally have been "to lay curses in sevens on someone" or "to be willing to accept seven curses upon oneself" should the oath be broken. In this way an oath could become a curse.

Isaac's Family Problems

In Genesis 26:34 we are told that Esau's marriage to Judith, the Hittite, was a source of bitterness for Isaac and Rebekah. While we are not told the exact reason behind this was, we can clearly see that Isaac's life was certainly not a life of bliss and ease, but rather blessing and victory. Chapter 27 of Genesis tells the story of Jacob – one of Isaac's children – deceiving his father and receiving the blessing that Isaac meant for Esau. While we will study this in-depth when we get to the story of Jacob's life, it is important to point out that the deceptive events in the life of Isaac (in particular his dealings with Abimelech concerning Rebekah) come back to haunt him. It is now someone else that through deception gets his way. (This applies to both Jacob and to Isaac's wife Rebekah herself, who no doubt learned the acceptability of deception from her husband Isaac in critical cases). The anguish of Isaac after painful realization that he has blessed "the wrong" son is explicitly described in the story. He is, however, able to accept the inevitability of God's will (the blessing already granted) and bless Jacob, now knowingly and instruct him about his future life choices (Gen. 28:1-5). When Isaac was at Mamre (now Hebron) at hundred and eighty years old, he passed away. He was buried by his sons Esau and Jacob (Gen. 35:27-29).

CHAPTER FIVE: THE LIFE OF JACOB

Jacob is one of the most fascinating characters in the entire Hebrew Bible. He is considered the patriarch of the Israelites. After all, not all the children of Abraham and Isaac can claim to be the father of the nation of Israel. The covenant originally made with Abram continues only through his son Isaac, and then specifically through Isaac's son – Jacob.

The Struggle in the Womb

The story of Jacob begins with his mother Rebekah's initial inability to conceive, which we discussed briefly when we dealt with Isaac. Rebekah's barrenness confirms upon her a line of succession to her late mother-in-law – Sarah (Gen. 24.67). Although the story of Rebekah is much more compressed and less complex than the corresponding story of Sarah (Gen. 16) the parallel is obvious and intentional. As her pregnancy advanced, Rebekah felt vigorous movements of what turned out to be two children in her womb (Esau and Jacob). She inquired of the LORD about this intense struggle that she felt going on inside her. The babies' movements in her womb were but a sign, foretelling the relationship they would have as siblings, which indicates their separate, but related purposes in God's plan. We have already seen that the Hebrew word for "struggle" used in the text speaks of a struggle that is very intense, harsh, even a crushing battle. We continue here where we left off. When Rebekah petitioned the Lord about her situation, He answered her:

וַיֹּאמֶר יהוה לָהּ שְׁנֵי גיִים בְּבִטְנֵךְ וּשְׁנֵי לְאֻמִּים מִמֵּעַיִךְ יִפָּרֵדוּ וּלְאֹם מִלְאֹם יֶאֱמָץ וְרַב יַעֲבֹד צָעִיר:

"Two nations are in your womb, two separate peoples shall issue from your body; One people shall be mightier than the other, and the older shall serve the younger." (Gen. 25:23)

We can appreciate how the translators saw what we also see, i.e. the literal and ambiguous meaning, but struggled with how to best translate the intricacies of Hebrew for the greatest benefit of their readers. They sought to keep two very important factors in balance: the accuracy of the text translated, and its readability. To find an equivalent to Hebrew in another language is not always easy and sometimes not possible. Therefore the translators used the *dynamic equivalence method* – that is, instead of translating *word-for-word*, they translate *thought-for-thought*. Some English language translations adopt this method even when it is possible to translate word-for-word, preferring the increased readability (with essential meaning preserved) to a more literal translation (with original wording preserved).

Often it is very helpful to see a literal translation in order to appreciate that the vast majority of Bible translations, such as the one above (NJPS), use *dynamic equivalence* rather than a strictly *literal* method of translation. It is important to keep in mind that a more literal translation is not necessarily more faithful. The meaning can be diluted and easily lost by preserving obscure grammatical structures of another language. Nevertheless, reading a text translated from Hebrew literally can enrich our understanding of the text (especially if we know some Hebrew). This practice always safeguards us from thinking that translations are free from interpretive errors and can be trusted uncritically.

When translated literally we see this idea: "Two peoples are in your stomach" שְׁנֵי גוֹיִם בְּבִטְנֵךְ *(shene goyim be-vitnekh)*. "And two peoples from your body will be separated [from each other]" וּשְׁנֵי לְאֻמִּים מִמֵּעַיִךְ יִפָּרֵדוּ *(u-shene leumim mi-meayikh yiparedu)*. "One people from another people will exercise effort/strength" וּלְאֹם מִלְאֹם יֶאֱמָץ *(u-leom mi-leom yeemats)*. It is the last portion of this verse that introduces a considerable ambiguity וְרַב יַעֲבֹד צָעִיר *(ve-rav yaavod tsair)*. Traditional translations render it as "the older will serve the younger." However, there is a potential problem with such translation. The Hebrew phrase is indefinite; it does not say "the older" or "the younger" but literally just "great" and "young." If the words were definite, it would include the particle את *(et)* to indicate the direct object. Without that marker, the text is not entirely clear as to whether the younger will serve the older or the other way around, since Hebrew syntax can sometimes be flexible.

The second feature alerting us to an ambiguity is that we expect the opposite of "young" צָעִיר *(tsair)* to be "old," not רַב *(rav)* "great/big" as is written here in Hebrew. Yet English translations set the sentence up as if the two opposites are in view (younger vs. older). Can you imagine having to make a translation decision when the text in Hebrew clearly has a built-in ambiguity? The text of Genesis then goes on to tell the reader that when Rebekah did give birth, it became clear that she was not imagining things – the twins, still struggling with each other, were finally born (Gen. 25:24-26). We read the detailed description of this birth as follows:

וַיֵּצֵא הָרִאשׁוֹן אַדְמוֹנִי כֻּלּוֹ כְּאַדֶּרֶת שֵׂעָר וַיִּקְרְאוּ שְׁמוֹ עֵשָׂו:

The first one emerged red, like a hairy mantle all over; so they named him Esau. (Gen. 25:25)

When Esau, the first of the twins, emerged, his appearance determined both his name and the name of the nations that will proceed from him. The word אַדְמוֹנִי *(admoni)* is related to the word for "Adam" אָדָם *(adam)* and other words, such as אָדֹם *(adom)* "red" and אֲדָמָה *(adamah)* "earth." We should also not forget the sound similarity with דָּם *(dam)* "blood." This is why the people group descended from Esau was called Edom or the Edomites. Esau became the father of the Edomites, and Jacob the father of the Israelites, with the two nations continuing their struggle throughout most of their history. But this baby also needed a name that was somehow connected to him. Those who were present at his birth saw that he was "fully covered with hair" כֻּלּוֹ כְּאַדֶּרֶת שֵׂעָר *(kulo ke-aderet sear)*. Although the etymology of the name "Esau" is unknown, it seems to have something to do with his hairy body. The Hebrew word for "hair" is שֵׂעָר *(sear)* and for "Esau" עֵשָׂו *(Esav)*.

The connection between these words is unclear. Nonetheless, there are cases in which words do have root connections in Biblical Hebrew even if this is not obvious at first glance. Possibly there was once a root word that meant "hair" which fell out of use in Hebrew (עָשָׂה). The Biblical Hebrew root word from those letters עָשָׂה *(asah)* means "to make" or "to do." This Semitic root does also survive, interestingly enough, in the Arabic language, a language related to Hebrew, and it means "hair" or "hairy." Given that there does not seem to be any obvious connection between Esau's birth and "to do/make," it stands to reason that the suggestion related to the ancient Hebrew root that is now lost, is a plausible one. However, this is only one interpretive option. A second one, at least, should be thought of in terms of connection with the above-mentioned

Hebrew root עָשָׂה *(asah)*, which carries the meaning of "making and doing." In this scenario the name of Esau has a meaning close to the English expression "fully made" and communicates the idea of being perfect and ready.

On the surface this connection does not seem to work, since we are accustomed to thinking of Esau as a negative character in the story (being very hairy is a negative connotation in the Western world). But this does not mean that "hairy" means unattractive or anything negative in the world of the Bible. If we consider the beginning of the story (Jacob's and Esau's birth) in light of the end of this very story, we see that Esau exhibited a strong, generous, forgiving character. This can be clearly seen in the scene of his reconciliation with Jacob (Gen. 33). None of the stolen blessings came true in the life of Jacob (especially those having to do with power and domination, but more about this later). In the end it was Jacob who called Esau "his lord" to his face and prostrated before him seven times, thereby acknowledging his fault in stealing his brother's blessing. Contrary to expectations, Esau is blessed with a good and successful life, free of his brother's unconditional superiority and domination (Gen. 27:39-40).

Jacob actually lives out the blessing that was indeed intended by Isaac for him from the beginning. It is this second blessing that Isaac gave him that actually comes true in his lifetime. God promised to bless Jacob with the blessing of Abraham and grant him the perpetual inheritance of the Promised Land and children (Gen. 28:3-4). While Jacob stole the blessing of wealth and domination, it was the blessing of the land and posterity that God had in mind for him. If we allow ourselves to see Esau in a positive (at least not exclusively negative) light, then we can see how his name could be related to perfection being "fully made or complete."

The Jewish sages in their commentaries accurately observed that no one honored his father more than Esau in the Bible. The covenant blessing of land and children, however, had to go through Jacob, not because he earned it, but because God decided that it would be so, for reasons known to God alone.

וְאַחֲרֵי־כֵן יָצָא אָחִיו וְיָדוֹ אֹחֶזֶת בַּעֲקֵב

Then his brother emerged, holding on to the heel of Esau; so they named him Jacob... (Gen. 25:26)

When Esau first emerged, they observed something amazing. His twin brother was holding on to his heel, as if not willing to let him go and be born first. Jacob's name in Hebrew יַעֲקֹב *(Yaakov)* relates to the word for "heel" עָקֵב *(akev)*. For this reason his parents called him a "heel-grabber." In modern Hebrew, instead of saying that we are "following someone", we literally say "we are going after their heel" לַעֲקֹב אַחֲרֵי מִשֶׁהוּ *(laakov acharei mishehu)*. So it's amusing to think that to "follow someone" could be interpreted as "to Jacob someone."

Trouble in the Making

The Book of Genesis (or at the very least its basic narrative structure) was authored to encourage the Israelites who left Egypt and were struggling with their troubles and identity. It was not written "in real time." In other words, the author of Genesis did not claim that it described events as they were happening at that time. Genesis describes how historical events that took place long time ago relate to, determine and inform the current situation on the ground. The stories are told to speak deeply and convincingly to Israelites (the children of Jacob) who at the moment seek to survive as a people, and eventually, as the covenant promise states, come into the Promised Land and establish themselves as a nation.

The stories of families portrayed in the Bible are brutally honest and oftentimes shock the readers with "naked truth," the kind of narratives that most families would try very hard to keep private. Take parental favoritism, for example. Today it is considered the gravest of parental sins, but in reality such things often happen. Just as the biblical reality of sibling rivalry happens far more often than we like to acknowledge. Parents often do connect better with some children than with others, for a variety of reasons. While it can be said that all parents love all their children in same way, it can also be established that they often favor one over another. In fact, the idea of "disliking, hating or favoring someone less" works quite differently in Biblical Hebrew.

This is especially true when it is expressed in contrast of "loving someone." The phraseology expresses the idea of intensity of feeling in comparison. In other words, "Jacob I loved... Esau I hated" (Mal. 1:2-3) is rendered quite literally in our modern terms. Translated from ancient Hebrew and interpreted into our modern way of speaking it could arguably mean something like "Esau I loved, but Jacob I favored with my great covenantal love." The same is the case with Jesus' statement that one must love Him and hate his parents (Luke 14:26). This is an idiomatic Hebraism that makes a comparison and does not actually instruct one to express hatred towards one's parents. That would be absurd, given God's explicit commandment to honor them.

What is clear is that the Book of Genesis is Torah for all of Israel; it is not a manual on parenting and should not be read as such. The loving and favoring of one child over another is stated as a matter of fact and is not in any way criticized or judged. What is evident from this story, as we will shortly see, is that one of the parents makes a right choice and the other makes a wrong choice in which child they chose to favor. If we realize that Genesis was written for Israelites who struggled with Edomites (among others), we will clearly and quickly see why the narrative of Esau and Jacob's births and the choices of their parents were very important to know and to internalize for the original readers/hearers of Genesis. Only when we understand how the texts apply to the original audience for which they were intended, can we ever hope to be able to apply them accurately to our modern times and our very different lives.

We read about the continued post-womb struggle of Esau and Jacob in Genesis 25:27-28:

וַיִּגְדְּלוּ הַנְּעָרִים וַיְהִי עֵשָׂו אִישׁ יֹדֵעַ צַיִד אִישׁ שָׂדֶה וְיַעֲקֹב אִישׁ תָּם יֹשֵׁב אֹהָלִים:

When the boys grew up, Esau became a skillful hunter, a man of the outdoors; but Jacob was a mild man who stayed in camp. (Gen. 25:27)

וַיֶּאֱהַב יִצְחָק אֶת־עֵשָׂו כִּי־צַיִד בְּפִיו וְרִבְקָה אֹהֶבֶת אֶת־יַעֲקֹב:

Isaac loved Esau because he had a taste for game, but Rebekah loved Jacob (Gen. 25:28).

Isaac seems blind (for the time being) to the higher purpose that his God has for his son Jacob. These purposes would become clear to the readers of the Genesis account only later. Isaac is blinded by his own personal preferences and connects with Esau better than with Jacob. God's own preference for the younger son over the older has already become a familiar pattern from the story of Cain and Abel (Gen. 4.4-5). The same idea is seen in the narrative of Ishmael and Isaac (Gen. 21:12). This same principle will also become a prominent feature in the story of Joseph and his relationship with his older brothers (Gen. 37:3). While the reason for Rebekah's choice is not given, Isaac's wrong choice is clearly explained. We read in the above-cited Genesis 25:28 וַיֶּאֱהַב יִצְחָק אֶת־עֵשָׂו כִּי־צַיִד בְּפִיו *(va-yeehav Yitschak et Esav ki tsayid be-fiv)* which, if translated literally, would say: "And Isaac loved Esau because hunting was in his (Isaac's) mouth." This expression specifies exactly why Isaac loved Esau more than Jacob – his taste for hunted game.

This may be a point of another connection between Isaac and Abraham. When Abraham agreed to take Hagar and endeavor to father a son through her, he too was blinded to God's will because of his natural desire for an heir. Esau's descendants eventually dominated the southern lands and made their living by agriculture and trade. One of the ancient trade routes, the King's Highway (Num. 20:17), passed through Edom, and when the Israelites requested permission to use this route on their exodus from Egypt, they were forcefully forbidden to pass. The Book of Deuteronomy, however, clearly states that Edomites should not be hated by Israelites because there are brothers (Deut. 23:7). Moreover, the warning is issued to Israelites by God not to provoke Edomites because God Himself guarantees Esau's inheritance (Deut. 2:4-5). It is interesting that the prophet Amos connects Edom with all the nations of the world that are called by the name of the LORD (Amos 9:12).

Not-So-Brotherly Love

In the previous section we finished by referring to the verse that spoke of Isaac's favor towards Esau because he had a taste for hunted game; but Jacob was a mild young man who was described as staying in the camp (Gen. 25:28), and he was favored by Rebekah. God's favoring of a younger son is already familiar from the story of Cain and Abel (Gen. 4:4-5) and, in a different way, with Ishmael and Isaac (Gen. 21:12), and will soon be the prominent feature of the story of Joseph (37:3) as the book of Genesis unfolds.

The line of thought about God favoring the younger brother in the Esau and Jacob story continues with the account of the "sold" and "bought" birthright. Jacob was "stewing a stew" וַיָּזֶד יַעֲקֹב נָזִיד *(va-yazed Yaakoov nazid)* when Esau came in, וְהוּא עָיֵף *(ve-hu ayef)* "and he was famished/exhausted" from his hunting. Esau had spent an entire day seeking wild meat, not bred and grown in Isaac's family flocks. We read in Genesis 25:30-31:

וַיֹּאמֶר עֵשָׂו אֶל־יַעֲקֹב הַלְעִיטֵנִי נָא מִן־הָאָדֹם הָאָדֹם הַזֶּה כִּי עָיֵף אָנֹכִי עַל־כֵּן קָרָא־שְׁמוֹ אֱדוֹם:

And Esau said to Jacob, "Give me some of that red stuff to gulp down, for I am famished" – which is why he was named Edom. (Gen. 25:30)

The Hebrew word Esau used to tell Jacob to "feed him" is הַלְעִיטֵנִי *(haliteni)* which communicates the idea of "devouring greedily/gulping down," or translated even more literally "cause/enable me to devour greedily." The Hebrew phrase that Esau used to describe the "stew" נָזִיד *(nazid)* mentioned earlier is מִן־הָאָדֹם הָאָדֹם *(min ha-adom ha-adom)* or literally "from this red-red (thing)." This event with stew is very significant for the greater story. So much so that the later connection of Esau with his posterity, the Edomites, is rooted in this explanation: "which is why he was named Edom" עַל־כֵּן קָרָא־שְׁמוֹ אֱדוֹם *(al ken kara shemo Edom)*. We have to understand that "red" and "Edom" are closely related words in Hebrew.

It is intriguing that the word translated as "stew" in the text (vs.29) is נָזִיד *(nazid),* which means something like "the thing boiled," but the verb related to this noun, in addition to the meaning "to boil," sometimes can mean "to presume" or even "to act proudly/arrogantly." If this connection is meant to be seen in the story, then perhaps the author seeks to align the reader's sympathies not with Jacob, but with Esau. He is the hardworking family man; the son that his father can be proud of in a good sense. Is Jacob going about his milder affairs with pride or a heart full of presumption? We don't know; but the story will seek at times to evoke sympathy for the one who will not be chosen to continue the covenantal line of blessing. Though not chosen, Esau will be greatly loved and personally protected by Israel's God.

וַיֹּאמֶר יַעֲקֹב מִכְרָה כַיּוֹם אֶת־בְּכֹרָתְךָ לִי:

Jacob said, "First sell me your birthright." (Gen. 25:31)

Now Jacob, seeing his older brother's weakness, demands that Esau should מִכְרָה כַיּוֹם אֶת־בְּכֹרָתְךָ לִי *(mikhra kha-yom et bekhoratkha li)* "sell me your firstborn rights this very day." As the story continues we will see that Jacob's actions (when he fools Isaac into thinking that he is Esau) will not be honored by Abraham's God. There will be a series of severe setbacks to Jacob's life (Laban's dealings with him) which will look remarkably similar and as dishonest as Jacob's dealings with Esau. Jacob will ultimately be blessed, but certainly not with the blessings he believed he could steal from his brother. Isaac and God had a much greater blessing in store for him – one that was prepared, and did not need to be stolen. But Jacob did not know that at the moment.

Despising Birthright

The Hebrew root word connected to the idea of the "birthright" and "being firstborn" is בָּכַר *(bakhar)*. It basically refers to the idea of "being first." While Esau is portrayed as a hard-working man, he is also clearly shown as someone who did not distinguish the spiritual significance of being "firstborn" בְּכֹרָה *(bekhorah)*, from the right of being blessed with a mighty "blessing" בְּרָכָה *(berakhah)* that would come later. To the seemingly unreasonable request of his younger brother, "First sell me your birthright," Esau responds: אָנֹכִי הוֹלֵךְ לָמוּת וְלָמָּה־זֶּה לִי בְּכֹרָה *(anokhi holekh lamut ve-lama zeh li bekhorah)* "I am at the point of death, so of what use is my birthright to me?"

True, Esau was tired and hungry. Still, one who has a high esteem for his status as the firstborn will not give up this high status for simple food. The story is clear: when Jacob finally served Esau לֶחֶם וּנְזִיד עֲדָשִׁים *(lechem u-nezid adashim)* "bread and lentil stew" Esau simply ate and went away. In so doing, the text of Genesis 25:34b says, וַיִּבֶז עֵשָׂו אֶת־הַבְּכֹרָה *(va-yivez Esav et ha-bekhorah)* "so Esau spurned the birthright." The verb בָּזָה *(bazah)* has a connotation of "being careless" or "having contempt" – despising something as useless.

Esau's Marriages

As the story in Genesis 26:6-33 continues, it describes a severe famine in Isaac's time, just as in the time of Abraham. That comes to an end and the text makes a brief but poignant remark that when Esau was forty years old, which signifies the age of full maturity, he took Judith, daughter of Beeri the Hittite, and Basemath, daughter of Elon the Hittite, to be his wives. Both of these women were to become a source of real emotional distress for both Isaac and Rebekah. The Hebrew phrase used to describe this distress in the original text is מֹרַת רוּחַ *(morat ruach)*. It literally means "bitterness of spirit."

The letter ת *(tav)* replaces ה *(hey)* at the end of the word מָרָה *(morah)*, which means "bitterness." The reason is that this term comes before the word for "spirit" רוּחַ *(ruach)*, which causes a state of *smikhut* here. *Smikhut* is a Hebrew grammatical situation that arises from a combination of nouns and can articulate possession. It is similar to the possessive function of the word "of" in the English language. Hence, "bitterness of spirit." So Esau's marriages were not a blessing to his family. While the Edomites would be blessed and protected by Israel's God because of His concern and promised blessing to Esau, they can still cause a lot of pain. This statement speaks loudly to later Israelite readers of Genesis. They should not be surprised that Edomites were then, and still are in their time, a cause of "bitter stress." Their matriarchs brought "bitterness" to Isaac and Rebekah, a situation that persists.

The Stolen Blessing

Sibling rivalry is a central motif of the Book of Genesis: Cain and Abel, Isaac and Ishmael, Jacob and Esau, Rachel and Leah, and Joseph and his brothers. Sibling rivalry also plays a central role in human conflict, and it begins with a very simple desire – the desire to have what your brother has, or even to be what your brother is. Such coveting and craving will one day be forbidden by the Ten Words/Commandments, which will still later come to underlie the morality of the Western world. Chapter 27 presents one of the most difficult stories of Genesis. It is certainly one of the masterpieces of biblical narrative artistry.

We all know it as the story of the stolen blessing. The "white elephant in the room" is that, while the tricking of Isaac was ethically wrong, God's covenant still continued through Jacob, who was in the end truly blessed. We will take time to walk through this story in order to understand exactly what happened and how we should understand this foundational story of Genesis. The deceit of Isaac, the aged and blind son of Abraham by promise, lays at the root of the very birth of God's covenant people Israel. These stories are full of ironies and unexpected twists, so we should be ready to be surprised. Walter Brueggemann writes:

> The narrator seems unaware of the incongruity that may appear to us: a blessing gotten by deception! While that may be a problem for us, we do better to stay inside the story itself, to perceive that the narrative is simply that way (as is life itself). Settlement of property and inheritance is seldom achieved without coveting and calculation. That is how it is in this family. The story is powerful enough to speak for itself.[1]

The story begins by stating that Isaac was old, and his eyes were dim, so that he could not see. When Isaac began to ponder his death (vs. 2),[2] he determined, without further delay, to give his blessing, as was traditionally done, to his firstborn and favorite son – Esau. Most of this narrative makes very little sense to many modern people, as we ascribe virtually no value to the paternal blessing of the firstborn son. However, this story, and naturally the characters in the story, treat the blessing very seriously. It can be stolen, just as anything of value can be taken away. This concept should challenge us to rethink our idea of blessing, and move away from seeing it as something spiritual or theoretical to something real and, in fact, very tangible.

"Isaac called his oldest son Esau" וַיִּקְרָא אֶת־עֵשָׂו בְּנוֹ הַגָּדֹל *(va-yikrah et Esav beno ha-gadol)*. Esau answered him with the typical הִנֵּנִי *(hineni)* "Here I am" refrain. It is likely that the text here recalls a similar triple refrain in the binding of Isaac (Gen. 22.1, 7, 11), where Isaac's own father Abraham had answered with the same word. This textual similarity is arguably an indication that the narrator seeks to align the ancient readers' and hearers'

---

[1] Walter Brueggemann, *Genesis: Interpretation: A Bible Commentary for Teaching and Preaching* (Louisville: Westminster John Knox Press, 2010), 229.
[2] Isaac was wrong about the nearness of his death. Jacob and Esau did not bury their father until decades later at the age of 180. (Gen. 35:29)

sympathy with Esau, rather than with Jacob (although the expression is a common one).

Isaac told him that he was now old and had been considering his own passing, not knowing when he would die. We read in Genesis 27:3-4:

וְעַתָּה שָׂא־נָא כֵלֶיךָ תֶּלְיְךָ וְקַשְׁתֶּךָ וְצֵא הַשָּׂדֶה וְצוּדָה לִּי צֵידָה

Take your gear, your quiver and bow, and go out into the open and hunt me some game. (Gen. 27:3)

וַעֲשֵׂה־לִי מַטְעַמִּים כַּאֲשֶׁר אָהַבְתִּי וְהָבִיאָה לִּי וְאֹכֵלָה בַּעֲבוּר תְּבָרֶכְךָ נַפְשִׁי בְּטֶרֶם אָמוּת

Then prepare a dish for me such as I like, and bring it to me to eat, so that I may give you my innermost blessing before I die." (Gen. 27:4)

Isaac chooses the timing of bestowing the firstborn blessing very carefully. This is not a spur-of-the-moment decision. As we have already seen, Isaac had a special fondness for Esau כִּי־צַיִד בְּפִיו *(ki tsayid be-fiv)* "because he had a taste for wild game" or, more literally, "for hunting was in his mouth" (Gen. 25:28). So here Isaac sends Esau out to hunt and to bring back the food he desires Esau to prepare for him. There is something precious that Isaac and Esau are anticipating here: the son is feeding the father; the father is blessing the son. Isaac states that he wants the blessing to be full, heartfelt, and thorough – the concepts that are most likely behind the Hebrew phrase תְּבָרֶכְךָ נַפְשִׁי *(tevarekh'kha nafshi)* which literally means something like "my soul/being will bless you."

It is here, in verse 5, that the plan of Isaac and Esau came undone. Rebekah, who favored her younger son, Jacob, was eavesdropping on their conversation and was persuaded that she needed to act quickly. It is striking that Rebekah did not refer to the motivation for her actions, or at least we don't have that recorded. Most likely they were rooted in God's words to her when she was pregnant:

שְׁנֵי גיים בְּבִטְנֵךְ וּשְׁנֵי לְאֻמִּים מִמֵּעַיִךְ יִפָּרֵדוּ וּלְאֹם מִלְאֹם יֶאֱמָץ וְרַב יַעֲבֹד צָעִיר:

"Two nations are in your womb, two separate peoples shall issue from your body; one people shall be mightier than the other, and the older shall serve the younger." (Gen. 25:23)

Since the texts in chapters 25 and 27 were meant to be read together, not separately, it may be safe to assume that this earlier statement (Gen. 25:23) is not repeated here explicitly because it was presumed to be understood as related to Rebekah's decision. We previously discussed the ambiguity of the phrase וְרַב יַעֲבֹד צָעִיר *(ve-rav yaavod tsair)* "the greater will serve the younger." The consequences are by no means clear. There are essentially two schools of thought as to whether Rebekah did something good by acting with holy zeal, thus forcing history to go "God's way," or whether what she (and Jacob) did was actually evil, which subsequently caused much pain and suffering to all involved. After all, Jacob was never mentioned as seeing his mother alive again. Astonishingly, she literally invoked upon herself any curse that may rightly have befallen the guilty party in such a questionable transaction (Gen. 27:13).

If Rebekah was right in what she did, then her actions could be compared to Zipporah's, in saving the life of Moses in a later story, when she circumcised their child, thereby saving Moses from God's severe judgment (Ex. 4:25). If the view is taken that Rebekah was not right, then her actions could be compared to those of Sarah, when she encouraged Abraham to have relations with Hagar, her servant, in order to ensure that God's promise would not become void. But again in such interpretations, we are not being led by the story itself, which does not seem very concerned to explain the wrong or right here. Rather, the story is about the manifestation of God's mighty promises (and yes, there are more blessings than one) in the context of an intense and true-to-life family drama.

When Esau went out to the field to hunt, his mother quickly sprang into action by telling Jacob about the timing of Isaac's intention to bless Esau, its content, and then imploring Jacob to do exactly as she directed. She instructed Jacob to go to the flock and to bring to her two choice young lambs, promising that she will then prepare and cook them exactly as his father likes. "Once that is accomplished, you will take it to your father and he will bless you before he dies," said Rebekah to Jacob (Gen. 27:5-10). Jacob expressed some serious doubts about his mother's plan. We read in Genesis 27:11-13:

וַיֹּאמֶר יַעֲקֹב אֶל־רִבְקָה אִמּוֹ הֵן עֵשָׂו אָחִי אִישׁ שָׂעִר וְאָנֹכִי אִישׁ חָלָק

Jacob answered his mother Rebekah, "But my brother Esau is a hairy man and I am smooth-skinned. (Gen. 27:11)

The biggest problem to overcome, as far as Jacob was concerned, was that he and Esau were not identical twins – Esau was hairy and Jacob was smooth-skinned. Hebrew phrases such as אִישׁ שָׂעִר *(ish sair)* and אִישׁ חָלָק *(ish chalak)* are forms of expression specifying the kind of אִישׁ *(ish)* "man" or "person" being spoken of. The first literally means "man of hair" or "hairy man" and the second literally "man of (something) smooth" or "smooth man."

אוּלַי יְמֻשֵּׁנִי אָבִי וְהָיִיתִי בְעֵינָיו כִּמְתַעְתֵּעַ וְהֵבֵאתִי עָלַי קְלָלָה וְלֹא בְרָכָה

If my father touches me, I shall appear to him as a trickster and bring upon myself a curse, not a blessing." (Gen. 27:12)

Jacob feared that Isaac may lovingly caress him, believing him to be Esau. The verb מָשַׁשׁ *(mashash)* indicates "touch." The use of this word may have been meant to highlight the intimate father-son relationship that Isaac and Esau shared. Jacob is afraid that, if he were to follow his mother's instructions, he may be thought by his father as a "mocker" or "deceiver" מְתַעְתֵּעַ *(metatea)* and be in danger of being cursed by him. The risk is indeed high – either he will receive his father's blessing, which will forever change his life for the better, or it may be the other way around – his father's curse will follow him all the days of his life. Jacob was at loss as to what to do.

The Hebrew word קְלָלָה *(kelalah)* means a "curse," but it has a very interesting meaning which can be better understood if we compare the word to an opposing concept, the Hebrew word כָּבוֹד *(kavod)* meaning "honor" or "glory." This word is connected with the general idea of being כָּבֵד *(kaved)* "being heavy." The opposite of "being heavy" or "honored" is the idea of being "made light of" or "dishonored" and is expressed by the Hebrew word קָלוֹן *(kalon)*. The word we are looking at in this text, קְלָלָה *(kelalah)* is usually translated as "curse," which is related and therefore might have originally means something like "being made light of." The idea is simple – a heavy object is steady, a light object is not. Something heavy is difficult to move from its place, something light can be moved with no real effort. Therefore, the issue here is true-to-life stability and security on every level.

וַתֹּאמֶר לוֹ אִמּוֹ עָלַי קִלְלָתְךָ בְּנִי אַךְ שְׁמַע בְּקֹלִי וְלֵךְ קַח־לִי

But his mother said to him, "Your curse, my son, be upon me! Just do as I say and go fetch them for me." (Gen. 27:13)

Rebekah told Jacob not to be concerned about receiving a curse. She was prepared to bear any curse herself, if such were in fact rendered instead of a blessing. Jacob was still young and was expected not to argue with his mother, but to do just what she asked of him. Remember that it seems the story is not being told with the question of ethics in mind. (Did he do right? Did she do wrong?) So we, too, must follow the logic of the story, seeking to grasp the meaning in its original text free from our modern ideas and concerns. Jacob listened to his mother and their plan was set in motion. The time for Esau to receive his birthright-related blessing was quickly running out. Rebekah then brought to Jacob his brother's festive clothes to wear as he went to Isaac to impersonate Esau. She then covered the bare areas of skin (neck and hands) with the skins of the kids she had used to prepare the food, in order to disguise Jacob to feel like Esau.

Once again Jacob found himself holding a dish of food. This time he will offer it not to Esau, but to his father Isaac. Although the text is, as it is typical for the Book of Genesis, silent about some of the private conversations that must have gone on in the family, it very well may be that Rebekah and Isaac did previously discuss the oracle given by God to Rebekah and the strange events where Esau actually sold his birthright to Jacob for a bowl of soup. If so, it may have been a matter of disagreement between them. Rebekah believed that Isaac should now bless Jacob with the blessing generally belonging to the firstborn, whereas Isaac sought to bless the older son first, as he planned before the birthright sale.

This narrative about Jacob portrays Israel, the patriarch of an entire people in his earthiest and most scandalous appearance in Genesis. It is not edifying in any conventional religious or moral sense. Indeed, if one comes to the narrative with such an agenda, one would find it offensive. But for that very reason, the Jacob narrative is most real, believable and life-like. The Jacob narrative permits candor about the offensiveness of Israel and the resilience of God despite his scandalous actions. As we continue to read the developing story, Jacob approaches his blind father (vs. 18). Jacob greets Isaac with the word "Father." Isaac then asked the most important question: "Which one of my two sons are you?" Isaac answered: "I am Esau, your first-born; I have done as you told me. Please, sit and eat what I hunted, so that you can give me your innermost blessing." Isaac expressed surprise that Esau was able to complete the task so quickly, to which Jacob answered: "Because the Lord your God granted me good fortune" (Gen. 27:18-20).

Even though Isaac sensed that it was Jacob's voice he heard, not Esau's, he chose to ignore this and rely, instead, on his sense of touch. In so doing, he was fooled by Rebekah and Jacob's crafty camouflage, and blessed Jacob in this well-staged identity. In verse 24 the story returns to the time before Isaac rendered the blessing and more conversation between Isaac and Jacob is revealed. At some point Jacob (perhaps remembering his disagreement with Rebekah) asks: "Are you really my son Esau?" Jacob then answers: "I am." Isaac then tells him to serve him the food so that, once consumed, Isaac can proceed with the ceremony of bestowing the blessing. Jacob duly served the food to his father. Isaac beckons Jacob to draw near and kiss him. Upon smelling the clothing of Esau, Isaac was mistakenly convinced that before him there stood his favorite son – Esau (Gen. 27:24-27), so he said:

וַיֹּאמֶר רְאֵה רֵיחַ בְּנִי כְּרֵיחַ שָׂדֶה אֲשֶׁר בֵּרֲכוֹ יהוה

"Ah, the smell of my son is like the smell of the fields that the LORD has blessed. (Gen. 27:24)

As we continue to trace Jacob's troublesome life, we will soon encounter his travels to Padan Aram, where Laban, Rebekah's brother, lived. There Jacob will fall in love, serve Laban for seven years, only to find that Laban used the same trick on him as he did on his father Isaac. Leah, the oldest daughter, was given to be his wife, instead of Rachel, whom Jacob loved with all his heart. Jacob will experience at the hands of his uncle Laban the same level of deceit with which he deceived his father, Isaac. The similarities will be stunning, but more about that later.

As we continue in our journey through the life of Jacob, it is imperative that we look carefully at the content of the actual blessing given to Jacob by mistake. We should consider how and why this blessing is different from the second blessing that Isaac gave to Jacob knowingly. This time there will be no case of mistaken identity and every word of blessing to Jacob will be intended for him. We read the exact text of the blessing stolen by Jacob in Genesis 27:28-29:

וְיִתֶּן־לְךָ הָאֱלֹהִים מִטַּל הַשָּׁמַיִם וּמִשְׁמַנֵּי הָאָרֶץ וְרֹב דָּגָן וְתִירֹשׁ

"May God give you of the dew of heaven and the fat of the earth, abundance of new grain and wine. (Gen. 27:28)

The basic idea here is that Jacob will not have to work hard in his livelihood, or at least not to an inordinate extent. The earth and the heavens will work for him instead, giving him the fruit of the earth as is symbolized in this text by grain and wine. He will be rich. This part of the blessing did not come to fruition for Jacob at first. Ironically, perhaps, the opposite was true at the start. Jacob had to work fourteen hard years for Laban just to marry Rachel. Later he did become wealthy because God blessed the hard work that he did with care and success. But the wealth and success did not come easy.

יַעַבְדוּךָ עַמִּים וְיִשְׁתַּחֲווּ לְךָ לְאֻמִּים הֱוֵה גְבִיר לְאַחֶיךָ וְיִשְׁתַּחֲווּ לְךָ בְּנֵי אִמֶּךָ

Let peoples serve you, and nations bow to you; Be master over your brothers, and let your mother's sons bow to you. (Gen. 27:29)

Another part of the blessing is stated here explicitly. Jacob will be blessed with enormous power and authority. The nations around Jacob will become his slaves, they will pay homage to his great rule. This part of the stolen blessing also did not seem to come true in his lifetime. As we will see Jacob struggled with the peoples around him all his life. He was far from the position of power that this blessing described. Addressing the Pharaoh whom Joseph served, Jacob said, "Few and hard have been the years of my life..." (Gen.47:9).

So perhaps Jacob did not get the blessing he had stolen. In fact, it was Jacob as he sought to make peace with his older brother Esau, who called himself his servant or slave and not the other way around (Gen.32:28-20). This is especially clear in what words Jacob's servants were instructed to say to Esau about the animals he encountered, "Your servant Jacob's; they are a gift sent to my lord Esau." Then upon the actual meeting of brothers, Jacob "himself went on ahead and bowed low to the ground seven times until he was near his brother" (Gen.33:3). Another part of this stolen blessing said:

אֹרְרֶיךָ אָרוּר וּמְבָרֲכֶיךָ בָּרוּךְ

Cursed be they who curse you, blessed they who bless you." (Gen. 27:29)

It is hardly a surprise that this part of the blessing will not have an immediate fulfillment in the life of Jacob either.

The Real Blessing

Later the same day when Rebekah found out what Esau said about his decision to eventually put Jacob to death, Isaac and Rebekah sent their younger son Jacob to Haran to Rebekah's brother Laban. Abraham and his father Terah settled in Haran after leaving Ur of the Chaldees while en route to the Promised Land (Gen. 11:31). It was located in Paddan Aram (the field of Aram in Aramaic). Returning there perhaps constituted a "setback" as far the promises of the covenant are concerned. It did not look like things were going well for the heir of Abraham's covenant. After all, Jacob had to go back to where Abraham his grandfather had come from. There was no visible progress, only visible regress. But, as is often the case, what in our eyes may look as "going back" is simply a part of God's plan. In reality, true spiritual progress takes place in times of adversity and struggle.

It is at this precise point, when Jacob is characterized by ultimate weakness (hiding out from the revenge of his furious duped brother) that Isaac blesses Jacob with a different blessing – the blessing that was meant for him. We read the exact text of that second blessing given by Isaac to Jacob in Genesis 28:3-4. All of these words came to full fruition. They promised Jacob that God the Provider will grant him a large number of offspring and that they will have their own Land.

וְאֵל שַׁדַּי יְבָרֵךְ אֹתְךָ וְיַפְרְךָ וְיַרְבֶּךָ וְהָיִיתָ לִקְהַל עַמִּים

May El Shaddai bless you, make you fertile and numerous, so that you become an assembly of peoples. (Gen. 28:3)

This particular blessing invokes the name of God as אֵל שַׁדַּי (*El Shaddai*). As mentioned above, the Hebrew etymology of this special name is not certain. Several theories have been put forward about its meaning. One explains that *El Shaddai* is "God Almighty," a name connected with the Hebrew verb שָׁדַד, meaning "to destroy, despoil." Another theory speaks of "God of the Mountains" – a name connected with the Acadian word *shadau*. It is also quite possible that *El Shaddai*, instead, should be translated as "God the Provider," "God who is Sufficient" or "God the Sufficient One." There are two basic reasons for such interpretations. The word שַׁדַּי (*shaddai*) may be connected with the Hebrew root word for "breast" שַׁד (*shad*). The female breast is one of the clear symbols of provision for the beginning and the very substance of human life and nourishment. Alternatively, the letter שׁ (*shin*) may be understood as a prefix that means "then." In this scenario, דַי (*dai*) may be taken to mean "sufficiency" which in Hebrew literally means "enough."

The blessing promises וְיַפְרְךָ וְיַרְבֶּךָ (*ve-yafrekha ve-yarbekha*), that God will "make (Jacob) fertile and numerous." Simply put, it promises him a large number of descendants with the purpose of becoming an "assembly of the peoples" לִקְהַל עַמִּים (*li-kehal amim*). The verbs are the same ones that were used in Genesis 1:28 when God told Adam and Eve to be "fruitful and multiply" פְּרוּ וּרְבוּ (*peru u-revu*). Just as we saw in the lives of Noah, Abraham and Isaac a clear connection to the first human being – Adam – so now we see the same link with Jacob.

וְיִתֶּן־לְךָ אֶת־בִּרְכַּת אַבְרָהָם לְךָ וּלְזַרְעֲךָ אִתָּךְ לְרִשְׁתְּךָ אֶת־אֶרֶץ מְגֻרֶיךָ אֲשֶׁר־נָתַן אֱלֹהִים לְאַבְרָהָם

"May He grant the blessing of Abraham to you and your offspring that you may possess the land where you are sojourning, which God assigned to Abraham." (Gen. 28:4)

This is truly a very different blessing from the other one. It does not focus on wealth and power, but instead covenantal continuity is stressed. What is promised to Jacob is only the descendants and the land. This blessing is clearly identified with the blessing of Jacob's grandfather, Abraham himself. Rabbi Jonathan Sacks explained it this way: "Time and again God blesses the patriarchs – but always and only in terms of children and a land. He never promises them 'the richness of the earth,' or that they will 'Rule over their brothers.' Wealth and power have nothing to do with the covenant. They are not part of Israel's destiny."[3]

One can wonder what would have happened if Sarah never suggested to Abraham to ensure the fulfillment of God's promise through Hagar and Ishmael? And also, how would the world look if Jacob never stole the blessing that belonged to Esau? The Hebrew Bible, however, does not encourage us to think in this direction. Instead the Scriptures seek to make sense of our reality, the situation on the ground. The ancient texts give visionary directions for lives of individuals (Genesis) and nations (Exodus) in an imperfect and broken world.

Later, when Jacob grows old, he will bless his son Judah with a special blessing. He will bless a son who comes from the womb of the wife that he ironically loved less, Leah. Judah's blessing is closely connected to the blessing that that was stolen from Esau. It will not pertain to the days of the patriarchs, but to the days of the kings, and even to the "latter days" (Gen. 49:1). This would not be simply the blessing of the patriarchs Abraham, Isaac and Jacob (posterity and land). Instead, this blessing is for the King of Israel. Judah's dynasty was divinely chosen to rule over Israel and the world-at-large (prosperity, strength, rule and assured protection). In Genesis 49:1, 8-10 we read:

> And Jacob called his sons and said, "Come together that I may tell you what is to befall you in the latter days בְּאַחֲרִית הַיָּמִים *(be-acharit ha-yamim)*. You, O Judah יְהוּדָה אַתָּה *(Yehudah atah)*, your brothers shall praise יוֹדוּךָ אַחֶיךָ *(yodukha achekha)*; Your hand shall be on the nape of your foes יָדְךָ בְּעֹרֶף אֹיְבֶיךָ *(yadkha be-oref oyvekha)*; Your father's sons shall bow low to you יִשְׁתַּחֲווּ לְךָ בְּנֵי אָבִיךָ *(yishtachavu lekha bene avikha)*. Judah is a young lion גּוּר אַרְיֵה יְהוּדָה *(gur aryah Yehudah)*… The scepter shall not depart from Judah לֹא־יָסוּר שֵׁבֶט מִיהוּדָה *(lo yasur shevet mi-Yhudah)*, nor the ruler's staff from between his feet וּמְחֹקֵק מִבֵּין רַגְלָיו *(u-mechokek mi-ben raglav)*; Until that tribute shall come to him and the homage of peoples be his עַד כִּי־יָבֹא שִׁילֹה וְלוֹ יִקְּהַת עַמִּים *(ad ki yavo shiloh ve-lo yikhat amim)*."

---

[3] Jonathan Sacks, *Not in God's Name: Confronting Religious Violence* (New York: Schocken Books, 2015), 135.

In the book of Numbers we read about Balaam who is forced by God to pronounce a blessing upon Israel, which resounds Jacob's words. It becomes clear that Israel's king is destined for victorious rule over the nations in fulfillment of Jacob's blessing to Judah (Num. 24:2-9). It is through this ultimate King of Israel that mankind's return to "the garden of Eden," which was lost, will be accomplished. This King, unlike Adam, will rule and exercise His God-given responsibility, but without sin (Num. 24:19; Gen. 1:26).

Jacob's Dream

One of the most famous human encounters with God in the Bible is the dream of "Jacob's Ladder." This immensely significant event took place when Jacob was on the way from Beer Sheva to Haran. Jacob had been on the run from Esau for some time when he came to "a certain place" which, at that time, was unknown. It was, however, destined to become one of the most important religious sites in the world. We are of course talking about Bethel – the House of God. While the precise location of Bethel today is disputed, its significance is not. Significant holy places in the Ancient Near East were not considered chosen by humans, but quite the opposite. In the minds of the people, it was the gods who chose places on earth because of their inherent holiness and uniqueness. Then they revealed their will to the holy men.

We see something similar here at Bethel, and yet, also something very different. Upon reaching this "place," the sun had set and the weary Jacob stopped there to rest for the night. He took a stone and placed it under his head as a pillow and laid down to sleep. During the night something happened that neither he nor his descendants could ever forget. While Jacob slept he had a dream. We read the details in Genesis 28:12-15:

וְהִנֵּה סֻלָּם מֻצָּב אַרְצָה וְרֹאשׁוֹ מַגִּיעַ הַשָּׁמָיְמָה וְהִנֵּה מַלְאֲכֵי אֱלֹהִים עֹלִים וְיֹרְדִים בּוֹ

"… *a stairway was set on the ground and its top reached to the sky, and angels of God were going up and down on it." (Gen. 28:12)*

Brueggemann says: "The framework of the journey (vv. 10–11) is not very important except that the event happens "between places," where nothing unusual was expected. Jacob's encounter with God happened between safe, identifiable places, but here, everything is uncertain. Suffice to say at this point, that this "non-place" is transformed by a visitation from God into a crucially important place. The transformation takes place during sleep, when Jacob has lost control of his destiny… in the process, this "non-person" (i.e., exiled, threatened) is transformed by the coming of God to a person crucial for the promise."[4]

The fivefold repetition of the term מָקוֹם *(makom)* "place" between vs. 11 and 17 demands our attention. This leads us to ask what was the significance of this *place*? The "non-place" becomes *"the place,"* and the "non-person" becomes *"the person."* The marvel is the grace of God which makes this miraculous encounter a reality.

Since we don't really know what "Jacob's ladder" looked like, we should entertain at least a few possibilities when trying to visualize it. One can visualize a traditional portable wooden ladder we use today for climbing hard to reach places. Hypothetically, something like that could have appeared in Jacob's vision. But what is more likely is that he saw a stone staircase. Perhaps something that looked more like an ancient Ziggurat. This was a common sacred structure in the ancient Near East, a hill with long stairs leading up to the deity situated on the top of those ascending series of stones.

The word סֻלָּם *(sulam)* is difficult to translate accurately because this is the only passage in Hebrew Bible where it is used. Thus "ramp" and "stairway" have been justifiably suggested in addition to "ladder" as possible translations. What is important is that this "ladder" was set up on earth and its top reached heaven. The most important revelation that Jacob must grasp in this dream is that the God of heaven is truly involved with what is happening on earth. Jacob's eyes were opened to see the traffic moving between heaven and earth, which could not be seen with the natural, naked eye. Angels of God (His obedient servants/ messengers) were ascending and descending to fulfill God's will on Earth. In Psalm 91:10-11 this heaven/earth connection is stated clearly: "There will no evil befall you,

---

[4] Brueggemann, *Genesis: Interpretation*, 242.

neither will any plague come near to your tent. For He will give His angels charge over you, to keep you in all thy ways."

It is interesting that when Jacob returns to Canaan, the Promised Land, the LORD appears to him once again at Bethel (Gen. 35:1), where an altar is built and the covenant is reiterated along the lines of the covenant with Isaac and Abraham (35:12). The angels of God meet him when leaving the land (Gen. 28:12) and when he returns (Gen. 32:2), forming a literary *inclusio* (everything that happens with him in exile happens between these two angel-related visions/dreams). While Jacob was not expecting a spiritual encounter at this point, but concerned only for his own survival, the God of Abraham and Isaac appeared to this deceitful fugitive. In His grace and covenant mercy God made Himself known to Jacob. The first step was to enable Jacob to comprehend something that he had not previously known.

The Resource of Heaven

The God of his forefathers speaks to Jacob in his dream and His words are incredible:

וְהִנֵּה יהוה נִצָּב עָלָיו וַיֹּאמַר אֲנִי יהוה אֱלֹהֵי אַבְרָהָם אָבִיךָ וֵאלֹהֵי יִצְחָק הָאָרֶץ אֲשֶׁר אַתָּה שֹׁכֵב עָלֶיהָ לְךָ אֶתְּנֶנָּה וּלְזַרְעֶךָ

And the LORD was standing beside him and He said, "I am the LORD, the God of your father Abraham and the God of Isaac: the ground on which you are lying I will assign to you and to your offspring. (Gen. 28:13)

In Brueggemann's words: "The element in the narrative that surprises Jacob and seems incredible to us is not the religious phenomenon of appearance. It is the wonder, mystery, and shock that this God should be present in such a decisive way to this exiled one. The miracle is the way this sovereign God binds himself to this treacherous fugitive. The event is told as an inexplicable experience. It cannot be assessed by any comparisons or norms outside itself."[5]

---

[5] Brueggemann, *Genesis: Interpretation*, 242.

From time to time deities were known to appear to holy men of the Ancient Near East, but this God was unusual, He made self-binding promises. The LORD confirmed that the second blessing that Isaac gave to Jacob could be fully relied upon (unlike the first one that was stolen). The same God who spoke to Jacob's grandfather Abraham, and his own father Isaac, is now addressing him directly. God's message was unequivocal: Jacob and his descendants would be given the very land upon which he was now sleeping. God's goodness and promises to him and his forefathers must not be doubted.

The time will come when Jacob and his descendants *will* possess this land. The fact that this happened in a dream when Jacob was, by definition, fully passive is very significant. What God said and did had absolutely nothing to do with any manipulation on the part of Jacob. This encounter was instigated by God alone and it was He who was fully in charge of all the events that took place. Curiously, God provided Eve for Adam by causing him to sleep deeply. This part of the story should also remind the readers that Abraham, as well, fell asleep when God made the covenant with him. Now the pattern repeats. The Earth is not left to its own resources, and heaven is not a remote self-contained realm for the gods. Heaven is intrinsically tied up with earth, and earth finally may count on the resources of heaven. The LORD God is connected with Israel and even with the very place where Jacob slept.

וְהָיָה זַרְעֲךָ כַּעֲפַר הָאָרֶץ וּפָרַצְתָּ יָמָּה וָקֵדְמָה וְצָפֹנָה וָנֶגְבָּה וְנִבְרְכוּ בְךָ כָּל־מִשְׁפְּחֹת הָאֲדָמָה וּבְזַרְעֶךָ

"Your descendants shall be as the dust of the earth; you shall spread out to the west and to the east, to the north and to the south. All the families of the earth shall bless themselves by you and your descendants." (Gen. 28:14)

According to the promise of God, Jacob will not simply be blessed with children as his forefathers were. It is important to see that he will be blessed with an immeasurable number of children. Not only that, but Jacob and his offspring will become a blessing to all "peoples/families of the earth" מִשְׁפְּחֹת הָאֲדָמָה *(mishpechot ha-adamah)*. Here the word for "earth" אֲדָמָה *(adamah)* is etymologically connected with "Adam" אָדָם *(adam)*. It is not simply a promise of well-being for Israel, but a promise of well-being for the nations through Israel.

God's Guarantee

God continued to speak to Jacob:

וְהִנֵּה אָנֹכִי עִמָּךְ וּשְׁמַרְתִּיךָ בְּכֹל אֲשֶׁר־תֵּלֵךְ וַהֲשִׁבֹתִיךָ אֶל־הָאֲדָמָה הַזֹּאת כִּי לֹא אֶעֱזָבְךָ עַד אֲשֶׁר אִם־עָשִׂיתִי אֵת אֲשֶׁר־דִּבַּרְתִּי לָךְ

"Remember, I am with you: I will protect you wherever you go and will bring you back to this land. I will not leave you until I have done what I have promised you." (Gen. 28:15)

As the story of Israel builds, the parallels between Jacob and Joseph (although chronologically still in the future) should not be overlooked. Both Jacob and Joseph are younger brothers whose future is predicted by dreams. Both are exiled because of conflicts with their brothers. These conflicts are such that there was a clear intent to kill both in Jacob's and in Joseph's stories. In the end both reconcile with their brothers. They both die in Egypt and are buried in the Promised Land.

Just as the promise of Abraham (also given in a dream), Jacob's promise receives full clarification in a dream revelation to Jacob. We see three distinct promises: 1) God's own continual presence, 2) God's own protection everywhere, and 3) Jacob's eventual return to the Promised Land.

First – God's Presence: This is one of the most important themes throughout the Holy Scriptures – the idea that the God of Heaven will be "with us, with His people" and in this case with this fugitive on the run – Jacob. What can be counted as a better assurance of avoiding life's danger than the constant presence of the most powerful being anywhere – the God of Abraham, Isaac and now Jacob?! It is amazing that God, who spoke to Jacob from the top of the ramp, promised that his own personal presence would remain with him. God was not going to merely send His representatives (angels) to be with this heir of the Abrahamic covenant. So important was Jacob to God, that He stated these astounding words: אָנֹכִי עִמָּךְ *(anokhi imakh)* "I am with you."

Second – God's Protection: God promised to protect Jacob in all his travels. Of course this protection will far outlast Jacob's personal wonderings. Whether Jacob remains in the Promised Land or departs from it would not matter – he will be protected wherever he goes because God's personal presence will guard him. What an astounding promise! In the ancient world the gods were connected to particular lands/territories. Probably in most people's minds no single God ruled supreme all over the world. People could leave the domain of one god and enter the domain of another. This ancient worldview of gods and lands was something similar to our understanding of criminally-run cities of today where all neighborhoods are clearly delineated and covered by a particular gang. If you are under the protection of a powerful gang in one place, such protection is not guaranteed in another area. Here God tells Jacob that it makes no difference where his travels take him. God will protect him absolutely anywhere, even in the pagan Padan-Aram from which his grandfather left to settle in Canaan.

Third – Jacob's Return: Not only did God promise Jacob that he could count on His personal presence to protect him anywhere, but also that Jacob's exile was temporary. God will bring him home. "The search for a bride" in Padan-Aram was clearly presented as an excuse for what is actually a flight for Jacob's life, an excuse engineered by Rebekah with her melodramatic complaint about paganism in Canaan (27:46)[6] – even if that also has parallels in the earlier stories of the family. One day Jacob's exile will come to an end and he will be able to return home to the Land of Promise. God, Himself, guaranteed that, and now Jacob was assured of it. The Lord of the Covenant will not rest until all the words of His promise become a reality. The day will come when Jacob will no longer be a fugitive from Esau's justice.

Decades later, peace, forgiveness and brotherly love will prevail, and Jacob and Esau will bury their father Isaac together in the Land of Promise (Gen. 35:29). Jacob's exile may be compared to the time the Israelites will wander in the wilderness after their exodus from Egypt. They were waiting for the Lord to come through on His words of promise as well. The message of God's story is clear. Just as God can be trusted to do what He promised to Jacob, He can also be trusted to fulfill what He promised regarding Jacob's descendants – deliverance of the children of Israel from Egypt.

---

6   Robert Alter, *Genesis: Translation and Commentary* (New York: W.W. Norton, 1998): 147.

Jacob's Vow

When Jacob awoke from his sleep he said to himself, יֵשׁ יהוה בַּמָּקוֹם הַזֶּה וְאָנֹכִי לֹא יָדָעְתִּי *(yesh YHWH ba-makom ha-zeh ve-anokhi lo yadati)*, which translated means "The LORD is in this place, and I did not know." As Jacob was awakened to the realization of the significance of the place where he unintentionally slept that night, his language reflected the awesome truth that had become profoundly real to him. "Is this not a house of God?" אֵין זֶה כִּי אִם־בֵּית אֱלֹהִים *(eyn zeh ki im bet Elohim)*; "this is the gate to heaven!" זֶה שַׁעַר הַשָּׁמָיִם *(zeh shaar ha-shamaim)*. Though prior to Jacob's encounter with God this place was known as Luz, Jacob re-named it Bethel – meaning "House of God" – setting up a stone as a memorial of the revelation he received.

The setting up of stones as memorials seems to have been a way to mark significant times and places (as continues even today). This practice will be repeated by many Israelite leaders to commemorate significant events in their lives as well. Moses, in particular in Exodus 24, will set up 12 stones, representing each of the Israelite tribes, as a sign of their full participation in the covenant with the LORD God at Mt. Sinai. Jacob responded to God with his own very significant vow, saying that if LORD keeps His three promises (to be with him and keep him safe, to sustain him with food and clothing, and to bring him home to his father's house) then he, Jacob, will honor God:

וְהָיָה יהוה לִי לֵאלֹהִים

The LORD shall be my God. (Gen. 28:21)

In the ancient times the main question was not whether or not God existed, as it is today for many people. The issue in ancient times also was not what interpretation (religion) of that God was the correct one. Instead, the ancients asked one principal question: Which god (in this god-congested universe) should/will be my god? Or which deity should I be in covenant with and serve? Jacob decides that, if יהוה *(YHWH)* "the LORD" keeps His word, then he will choose Him (presumably Him alone) to be his God, saying: וְהָיָה יהוה לִי לֵאלֹהִים *(ve-haya YHWH li l-Elohim)* "The LORD will be my God."

וְהָאֶבֶן הַזֹּאת אֲשֶׁר־שַׂמְתִּי מַצֵּבָה יִהְיֶה בֵּית אֱלֹהִים

And this stone, which I have set up as a pillar, shall be God's abode. (Gen. 28:22a)

While it is of no special significance here, it is a good place to note that the word אֶבֶן (*even*), preceded by its definite article ה- (*ha-*), is grammatically feminine (translated it means "stone"). In Hebrew, as in many other languages, the feminine gender of a word does not necessarily mean the object has some distinct feminine qualities. The feminine gender is just the grammatical form for reasons that are not always clear. The word is, therefore, being used with feminine demonstrative pronoun זֹאת (*zot*) "this" and not the masculine one זֶה (*zeh*). By the way, Hebrew has no neuter gender, so all objects (animate or inanimate) will be either masculine or feminine. It is interesting to note that Jacob does not say that the stone that he is setting up as a memorial will be "a sign" of where the House of God will be, but that the stone itself will be the house of God (perhaps an idiom used at the time to denote a site of worship).

Jacob makes another promise:

וְכֹל אֲשֶׁר תִּתֶּן־לִי עַשֵּׂר אֲעַשְּׂרֶנּוּ לָךְ:

And of all that You give me, I will set aside a tithe for You. (Gen. 28:22b)

Jacob makes his conditional commitment concrete by promising to set aside a tithe of everything that the LORD God gives him. As Walter Brueggemann says, "Jacob the trickster is now bound to this God who presides over all the trickery yet to come in the narrative," notably with Laban-related stories.[7] Genesis has described Jacob as אִישׁ תָּם (*ish tam*), sometimes translated as "a simple man" or "a peaceful man," but better understood as "whole" or "blameless" or arguably even "single-minded" (Gen. 25:27). It is interesting that the prophet Micah associates Jacob with truth – "You give truth to Jacob, kindness to Abraham" (Micah 7:20). Jacob's life embodies the fact that truth must be fought for with determination. It rarely comes without a struggle and the pain of experience.[8]

---

[7] Brueggemann, *Genesis: Interpretation*, 248.
[8] See Jonathan Sacks, *Covenant & Conversation: a Weekly Reading of the Jewish Bible*. Genesis: The Book of Beginnings (New Milford, CT: Maggid Books & The Orthodox Union, 2009): 225-227.

Truth was learned by Jacob through pain acquired through his dangerous journeys and owned by him, though imperfectly, through his vows. What is that truth? Jacob does not belong to himself or even to his family, but to the LORD God who bound Himself to Jacob by His promises. Jacob's end response is fully appropriate – from everything that God gives him, he will give a tenth portion to God. The imperfect vow that Jacob gave has successfully led him to "sustained, disciplined worship."[9] There is hope for Jacob; there is hope for Israel; there is hope for the nations of the world.

An Imperfect Family

The story of Jacob arriving in the Haran area begins in Genesis 29 and immediately places us, as hearers of the story, next to the well, not far from Laban's house and land. A large stone covered the opening of the water delivery system in such a way that it was rolled away only when the flock of all the owners living in the area were assembled. Jacob inquired about Laban from the people that were at the well. The shepherds pointed out to Jacob that Rachel, a shepherdess and Laban's daughter, was in fact approaching the well with her flock. Jacob meets Rachel and breaks into tears. Jacob moves the rock to give water to her flock. It is interesting that both his ability to move the rock and Rachel's work in the family (shepherdess) speak of strength of both character and body. In response Rachel ran to her father Laban and, together, she and Laban ran back to Jacob. Jacob leveled with Laban about his troubles with Esau (Gen. 29:13), to which Jacob interestingly responds in the words of Adam: עַצְמִי וּבְשָׂרִי אָתָּה *(atsmi u-vesari atah),* which means "You are my bone and my flesh!" (Gen. 2:23; 29:14). As the readers find out from the rest of the story, Jacob has met his match. Laban would turn out to be as manipulative and deceptive as Jacob. Behind Laban's warm Eastern-style family welcome lay the self-seeking, manipulative heart of an impossible-to-satisfy, ungrateful man.

What Goes Around...

Laban had two daughters. The older daughter's name was Leah, of whom it is said that her eyes were weak. And a younger daughter Rachel, of whom

---

[9] Brueggemann, *Genesis: Interpretation,* 248.

it was said that she was very beautiful. So when Laban told Jacob to name the price for his work in Laban's family business, Jacob did not hesitate and said that he will work for seven full years to get Rachel to become his wife. Time passed and Jacob's years of service were up so Laban agreed to have a wedding feast. Nothing alerted Jacob to an impending disappointment. After the feast, when it was already very dark, Laban led Leah instead of the promised Rachel to Jacob's tent. The two consummated their union but, when the sun rose and first rays of light began to break into the tent, Jacob realized how Laban and Leah tricked him. Next to him was a sister-like figure he had perhaps grown to love, care for and respect as a relative. But his beloved Rachel was not in sight.

When Jacob confronted Laban about this, Laban said that it was not their custom to marry off a younger daughter before the older. In one of the later rabbinic midrashim (creative interpretive rethinking of the biblical text) we read the following imagined reenactment of Jacob-Leah conversation: "Said he [Jacob] to her [Leah]: 'You are a deceiver and the daughter of a deceiver!' 'Is there a teacher without pupils?' she retorted. 'Did not your father call you Esau, and you answered him! So did you too call me and I answered you!'" (Midrash Rabbah, Bereishit 70:19) There is no doubt that in this story Jacob is being treated by Laban and Leah exactly how he and his mother Rebekah treated Esau and Isaac. What goes around, they say, comes around.

A Faithless Competition

After the wedding week was completed Laban gave Rachel to Jacob as his second wife in exchange for another seven years of work. Jacob probably cared for both women as a good husband would, but he clearly loved the younger daughter more (Gen. 29:30). Rachel knew it and so did Leah. In the Hebrew Bible "loved less" can be expressed as "unloved" or even "hated." The LORD who promised to be with Jacob at all times does something that Jacob and Rachel could not understand. The narrative that establishes the origins of Jacob's family begins with barrenness, just as was the case with Abraham and Sarah, and Isaac and Rebekah. He opened up Leah's womb, but closed the womb of Rachel. The text says very clearly that this was so because "the LORD saw that Leah was unloved" (Gen. 29:31).

Thus, the story of Jacob introduces the themes of injustice and love. This love will be a characteristic of Jacob and will one day become extremely important for the nation of Israel as well. Sacks writes:

> Nowhere in Genesis do we read that Abraham loved Sarah. Once we hear that Isaac loved Rebekah. Three times we read that Jacob loved Rachel, and three times that he loved Joseph. The Hebrew Bible is a book of love: love God with all your heart, soul and might (Deut. 6:5); love your neighbor as yourself (Lev. 19:18); love the stranger (Lev. 19:34). But love is not unproblematic. Given to one but not another, to one more than another, it creates tensions that can turn to violence. More than any other character in Genesis, Jacob loves, but the result is conflict between Leah and Rachel and between Joseph and his brothers. The message of Genesis is that love is necessary but not sufficient. You also need sensitivity to those who feel unloved.[10]

The firstborn of Jacob is Reuben and, as the narrative continues in predicable fashion, we find out that in time it would be other sons of Jacob who would outshine Reuben. Being born first does not equal automatic entitlement to true leadership in Israel. To lead one must have moral courage, a selfless attitude, and a life marked by a true ability to repent (change of actions). The time will come when both Joseph, Jacob's youngest son, and Judah, a son of the woman less loved, will demonstrate their leadership character traits. Leah gave Jacob four sons in a row: Reuben, Simeon, Levi and Judah. Each time she gave a name to a son, she did it in a way that reflected her deep desire to be loved by Jacob as much (or more) as Rachel. We will take a closer look at names later. Leah's feelings of being loved less, unloved and even hated were the defining factor in her life and it would be a mistake to think that this insecurity was not passed onto her children in the form of disdain towards the firstborn of Rachel, supremely loved by Jacob – Joseph.

Judah seemed to be Leah's last son after a period of several births (Gen. 29:35), but her misguided passion and methodology to get into the center of Jacob's love did not stop. She was competing against Rachel. She, the unloved one, desperately wanted to be loved by Jacob. Rachel's envy towards her sister reached a high point when, in the depth of her despair, she demanded of Jacob to give her children, too, (Gen. 30:1) as if he was withholding this from her. Naturally this placed even more strain on a

---

[10] Sacks, *Not In God's Name*, 145.

difficult relationship between Jacob and his first love, Rachel. Jacob lashed back at Rachel. Rachel gave Jacob a concubine who bore him Dan and Naphtali in the name of Rachel. Judging from the names she gave, envy and a sense of not-being-loved-enough by Jacob's God defined her life just as it defined Leah's. One can only imagine how Jacob struggled with both of them being part of one family.

It was now Leah's turn to hit back at her chief rival. Persuaded that Judah was her last son, she offered her servant as a concubine to Jacob as well. As a result, came Gad and Asher in the name of Leah. So the child-bearing and child-counting race continues. Leah was still in the lead, but neither the winner nor the looser felt loved. The story of manipulation on the part of Israel's matriarchs goes into the next scene. It moves from the domain of surrogate births to herbal therapy. In Genesis 30:14 we read that Leah's oldest son found a rare root plant that was believed to increase fertility in women (mandrake plant). Rachel bargained with Leah, offering her Jacob for the night in exchange for some of the plant. This is very similar to how Jacob bargained with Esau for his birthright at a time of desperate need. Rachel does not get pregnant soon after this, but Leah goes on to give Jacob two more sons – Issachar and Zebulun – and one daughter – Dinah. Mandrakes did not work. At least they did not work for Rachel, but God remembered Rachel, had compassion on her, finally opened her womb, and she gave birth to Joseph. Later, Jacob will formally count both sons of Joseph's Egyptian wife (Ephraim and Manasseh) as his own during his blessing preferring the younger (Manasseh) and giving him the largest portion of land from all the twelve tribes.

Jacob's Family

The sons of Jacob from both Leah and Rachel (whether born by them or in their name) are:

Leah	Rachel
1. Rueben	1. Dan
2. Simeon	2. Naphtali
3. Levy	3. Joseph
4. Judah	4. Benjamin
5. Gad	
6. Asher	
7. Issachar	
8. Zebulun	

רְאוּבֵן **Reuben** כִּי־רָאָה יהוה בְּעָנְיִי *"Because the LORD saw my poverty"* (Gen. 29:32)

שִׁמְעוֹן **Simeon** כִּי־שָׁמַע יהוה כִּי־שְׂנוּאָה אָנֹכִי *"Because the LORD heard that I was unloved/hated"* (Gen. 29:33)

לֵוִי **Levy** הַפַּעַם יִלָּוֶה אִישִׁי אֵלַי *"This time my man will accompany me"* (Gen. 29:34)

יְהוּדָה **Judah** הַפַּעַם אוֹדֶה אֶת־יהוה *"This time I will praise the LORD."* (Gen. 29:35)

דָּן **Dan** דָּנַנִּי אֱלֹהִים *"God vindicated me."* (Gen. 30:6)

נַפְתָּלִי **Naphtali** נִפְתַּלְתִּי עִם־אֲחֹתִי *"I wrestled with my sister."* (Gen. 30:8)

גָּד **Gad** בְּגָד *"In the luck/fortune."* (Gen. 30:11)

אָשֵׁר **Asher** בְּאָשְׁרִי כִּי אִשְּׁרוּנִי בָּנוֹת *"In happiness, because the girls (will deem me?) happy/blessed."* (Gen. 30:13)

יִשָּׂשכָר **Issachar** נָתַן אֱלֹהִים שְׂכָרִי אֲשֶׁר־נָתַתִּי שִׁפְחָתִי לְאִישִׁי *"God gave me my reward because I gave my maidservant to my man."* (Gen. 30:18)

זְבֻלוּן **Zebulun** זְבָדַנִי אֱלֹהִים אֹתִי זֵבֶד טוֹב הַפַּעַם יִזְבְּלֵנִי אִישִׁי *"God bestowed upon me a good gift; this time my man will honor me (make me his legitimate wife)."* (Gen. 30:20)

יוֹסֵף **Joseph** יֹסֵף יהוה לִי בֵּן אַחֵר *"God will/ may add me another son."* (Gen. 30:24)

בִּנְיָמִין **Benjamin** בִּנְיָמִין *"Son of my strength/ right hand"* – changed from Rachel's original name בֶּן־אוֹנִי *"Son of my sorrow"* (Gen. 35:18)

The story of the birthright bought and the blessing stolen by Jacob, as well as the stories of manipulation by Leah and Rachel, show that the origins of Israel as a family were far from perfect. Jacob's family was very much like Jacob himself, flawed. Yet the wonder of it all is that the narrator, far from hiding these facts, parades them to the readers/hearers instead. This is the point. The people in these stories are imperfect, but God who chose to do His will through them, He is perfect! They do not "deserve" the benefits of His commitment and covenantal love, but the LORD God enters into covenant relations with these imperfect sons and daughters of Adam. There is hope. All these stories are really not about these characters, but about the character of God.

Jacob's Exodus

Genesis 30:25 informs the reader that after Rachel gave birth to Joseph, Jacob asked Laban to allow him to return to his father's home and his own land. Laban sought to slow down and defraud Jacob through further trickery, but all his cunning amounts to nothing. Jacob continues to prosper (his flocks grow exponentially) under the most unpromising of circumstances, as we find out later, all because of God's revelation through a dream (Gen. 31:11-13). As Jacob prepares to return and face Esau, God prospers him. His newly found prosperity is described in Genesis 30:43 as follows:

וַיִּפְרֹץ הָאִישׁ מְאֹד מְאֹד וַיְהִי־לוֹ צֹאן רַבּוֹת וּשְׁפָחוֹת וַעֲבָדִים וּגְמַלִּים וַחֲמֹרִים׃

So the man grew exceedingly prosperous, and came to own large flocks, maidservants and menservants, camels and asses. (Gen. 30:43)

The root word פָּרַץ *(parats)* is used here to describe Jacob's growth in wealth. It carries a meaning of "breaking through," "breaking away" and "spreading wide," and is used here in connection with breaking away from the situation of being "limited," "restricted" and "bound." So when God's blessing on Jacob is described, it is depicted in terms of "breaking away" from the limitations placed upon his life, both by his own prior actions toward Esau and Laban's wicked enslavement of Jacob and his unwillingness to set him free.[11]

In Hebrew, we commonly see repetition of the same words used as a way of emphasis. Here, Jacob's prosperity is described as מְאֹד מְאֹד *(me'od me'od)*, which translated means "very-very" or "exceedingly." This repetitive

---

[11] The same verb is used in Gen. 28:14 promising that he would "expand" in all directions with his seed. In Ex. 1:12 it describes the multiplication of Israel while oppressed by Pharaoh.

phrase מְאֹד מְאֹד *(me'od me'od)* also appears in the promise to Abraham (Gen. 17:2, 6 twice!) and again in Ex. 1:7 showing that this language refers to the promise given and fulfilled with both Abraham and Jacob and yet to be fulfilled in the future in Egypt. The use of the פָּרַץ *(parats)* verb and מְאֹד מְאֹד *(me'od me'od)* repetition refers to the same promise.

Word endings in Hebrew often determine whether nouns are masculine or feminine. In Hebrew, the suffix תוֹ- *(-ot)* is a plural feminine ending, while ים- *(-im)* is plural masculine. We see these endings in words like שְׁפָחוֹת *(shefachot)* "maidservants" (feminine plural), and וַעֲבָדִים וּגְמַלִים וַחֲמֹרִים *(va-avadim u-gemalim va-chamorim)* "and servants and camels and donkeys" (plural masculine endings).

Jacob heard that Laban's sons were talking behind his back, saying that he had taken what belonged to their father and prospered from that capital. At about the same time Jacob noticed that Laban began to treat him differently. Sometime before that (even before Jacob's prosperity) the LORD God spoke to Jacob and told him to prepare to make this move (Gen. 31:1-13). Jacob told his wives about his grievance with their father and about the dream he had received from God with deliberate instructions for acquiring what would become his newfound wealth. He told them of God's command that Jacob must now return to Canaan. Both Rachel and Leah agreed with him without reservation.

Rachel and Leah speak about the "bride price" or "bridal dowry" – a gift the groom paid to his father-in-law. The text may suggest that it (the price of the gift) was meant to go to the bride herself as she entered her new husband's house. Laban, they both complained, had used the bride price (presumably Jacob's labor wages for him) without any concern for them, in effect disowning them. "His daughters thus see themselves reduced to chattel by their father, not married off but rather sold for profit, as though they were not his flesh and blood."[12] For this reason they were now favoring their husband over their father. It's been said that people should "use money and love people." Laban, we might say, consistently acted in just the opposite manner. He "loved money and used people." His daughters' justified disloyalty exemplifies the truth of another folk proverb: "The stingy man pays twice." Through the process of defrauding and

---

[12] Alter, *Genesis: Translation and Commentary*, 168.

using Jacob, Laban himself ended up losing valuable possessions. Everything was now set for Jacob's escape, this time away from Haran and back to his father's house.

Jacob's exodus from the land of servitude, which had once been a land of salvation, resonates with the story of Israel's exodus from Egypt. The children of Israel went to Egypt (in the time of Joseph) to escape a severe famine that was in the land, but in time became slaves of a new Pharaoh who was unwilling to let them go. Just as Jacob experienced God's intervention through dreams, so too did Joseph. Just as Jacob "breaks away" from a land of bondage with great wealth, Israel too, will leave Egypt with great wealth as a reparation payment for their forced slave labor. Another strong connection with the Exodus story is found in Genesis 46:3-4 where God says to Israel (Jacob): "Do not be afraid to go down to Egypt, for I will make you into a great nation there. I will go down to Egypt with you and I will surely bring you back again." This is similar to the words God spoke to Jacob at Bethel (Gen. 28:15). While there are differences between these stories, the similarities are stunning and clearly show authorial intent to draw such connections and parallels.

Jacob's exodus is back to the "land of your [i.e., his] birth" אֶל אֶרֶץ מוֹלַדְתֶּךָ *(el erets moladtekha)* in Gen. 31:13 while Abram's exodus from the same place was described as going "from the land of his birth" מֵאַרְצְךָ מוֹלַדְתֶּךָ *(me-artsekha moladtekha)*. This indicates further evidence for the deliberately and artistically paralleled lives of these two men. Both journeys originate in Haran (11:31, 27:43, 28:10, 29:4), where they marry close relatives and leave fathers (Laban, Terah) and siblings (Abram's brothers and Laban's sons). They will follow the same itinerary through the land upon arriving and separating from other close relatives (Lot and Esau) because the land could not sustain their flocks (Gen. 13:6; 36:7). Genesis 31:20 speaks of Jacob literally "stealing the heart of Laban the Aramean":

וַיִּגְנֹב יַעֲקֹב אֶת־לֵב לָבָן הָאֲרַמִּי עַל־בְּלִי הִגִּיד לוֹ כִּי בֹרֵחַ הוּא

Jacob kept Laban the Aramean in the dark, not telling him that he was fleeing. (Gen. 31:20)

The verb גָּנַב *(ganav)* "to steal" has a wide range of meanings in Hebrew (as in English). We may infer that not all actions described by this verb necessarily constitute morally negative acts. Here the phrase means to do something "quietly concealing," "without notice" or "in secret." We should note that Rachel in the previous verse 19 had also "stolen" תִּגְנֹב *(tignov)* idols from Laban, her father, so the story seems to be playing on the different meanings of the word. There may be other word plays, here, too. "Laban" לְבָן *(Lavan)*, whose name means "white," shares some sounds with the Hebrew word for "heart" לֵב *(lev)*, while the Hebrew word for "Aramean" אֲרַמִּי *(Arami)* sounds a bit like a Hebrew word for "deceiving" רָמָה *(ramah)*. What a fitting play on words, because when one thinks of Laban, one thinks of deception.[13]

Laban is called an "Aramean" in Gen 31, as if on purpose. "The stage is being set for the representation of the encounter between Laban (the Aramean) and Jacob (the Hebrew) as a negotiation between national entities."[14] Later on in the story, when Laban and Jacob make a peace and borders pact, they will both name the same heap of stones in their appropriate languages – Laban will use Aramaic and Jacob Hebrew (both meaning one and the same thing – "the heap of witness") – but for now we must not get too far ahead in the narrative.

When Jacob escaped, Laban was shearing his flock and was caught unaware. "Laban had earlier set a precedent of grazing his herds at a distance of three days' journey from Jacob's herds.... Other references to shearing of the flocks in the Bible indicate it was a very elaborate procedure involving large numbers of men, and accompanied by feasting, and so would have provided an excellent cover for Jacob's flight."[15]

Laban found out about it three days later, while his relatives were still with him. Laban pursued Jacob for seven days before catching up with him in the hill country of Gilead (Gen. 31:19-25). Some time prior to their meeting, God had appeared to Laban and warned him not to say anything to Jacob, either good or bad. In fact, both Abimelech and Laban received similar warnings regarding any mistreatment of Abram and Jacob (Gen. 20:3; 31:29). The one thing that Laban cannot understand is this: Why would Jacob (given his commitment to Abraham's God) steal his

---

[13] Adele Berlin, and Marc Zvi Brettler, *The Jewish Study Bible: Torah, Nevi'im, Kethuvim*, 2nd ed. (New York: Oxford University Press, 2014), 59.
[14] Alter, *Genesis: Translation and Commentary*, 169.
[15] *Ibid.*

household gods/idols? Neither Jacob nor Laban imagined that Rachel was responsible for this. Jacob's rash statement, that anyone found with Laban's gods would be put to death, may have been a harbinger of Rachel's premature death at the birth of Benjamin (Gen. 35:16-20). It is not at all clear why she did what she did. As the narrative continues, the reason she remains undiscovered is because she remained seated upon the camel's packsaddle where the idols were hidden, offering the excuse that she was going through her menstrual period.

This may have been a personal revenge towards her father. Taking something that was very dear to him, in return for him having taken something important from her (both Jacob during the wedding, and her bridal dowry). On the other hand, "There is no reason to assume that Rachel would have become a strict monotheist through her marriage."[16] Like many people of that time she may have come to hold a henotheistic view (only one God is supreme and should be worshiped, but other gods also exist). A more positive reading of Rachel is proposed by Rashi – one of the key Jewish medieval Bible commentators. Rashi thinks that her intention was a noble one. Namely, to keep her father from the worship of idols.

Later, we will find that some Israelites when they left Egypt did not let go of the Egyptian idols, but took them on their journey. As late as the Israelite conquest of Canaan, Joshua had to issue his call to make a final break with the idols of Egypt: "If it is disagreeable in your sight to serve the LORD, choose for yourselves today whom you will serve: whether the gods which your fathers served which were beyond the River, or the gods of the Amorites in whose land you are living; but as for me and my house, we will serve the LORD" (Josh. 24:15).

Despite its seriousness, this story also contains a lot of humor and irony, especially if we pay attention to its literary style. There are many instances. One example is how Laban's paganism is ridiculed. His gods are protected and sat on by a menstruating woman. Lev. 15:22 will later state that everything upon which a menstruating woman sits is ceremonially unclean. In their direct speech, Laban (vs. 30) and Jacob (vs. 32) both refer to these stolen figurines as his "gods." But the story's narrator (vs. 34) describes

---

[16] Alter, *Genesis: Translation and Commentary*, 169.

them as idols or graven images תְּרָפִים *(terafim)*.[17] Now Jacob speaks boldly to Laban, telling him what he always wanted to say to him face-to-face. He brings up all the unfaithfulness and trickery, and highlights his own endurance in the hardships of his service. Jacob describes his personal faithfulness to Laban over twenty long years.

Jacob also credits his current prosperity to the faithfulness of his God. We read in Genesis 31:42:

לוּלֵי אֱלֹהֵי אָבִי אֱלֹהֵי אַבְרָהָם וּפַחַד יִצְחָק הָיָה לִי כִּי עַתָּה רֵיקָם שְׁלַּחְתָּנִי אֶת־עָנְיִי וְאֶת־יְגִיעַ כַּפַּי רָאָה אֱלֹהִים וַיּוֹכַח אָמֶשׁ

Had not the God of my father, the God of Abraham and the Fear of Isaac, been with me, you would have sent me away empty-handed. But God took notice of my plight and the toil of my hands, and He gave judgment last night. (Gen. 31:42)

As we read this interaction, we cannot help but see Jacob as a man of integrity in his service of Laban; a man with a clear conscience as he boldly faces his uncle and publicly argues his case with the conviction of a righteous man. This may be the idea behind a later statement by the prophet Micah תִּתֵּן אֱמֶת לְיַעֲקֹב *(titen emet le-Yaakov)* "you (the LORD) gave truth to Jacob" (Mic. 7:20). Laban and Jacob agree to make a pact. This happens possibly because of the pressure of other relatives who listened as Laban was not able to establish any wrongdoing on the part of Jacob. Jacob agrees to treat his wives (Laban's daughters) well and commits not to take any additional wives. Laban's part was to leave Jacob alone and in peace.

The pact was made and was marked, characteristically, by the erection of a stone monument, followed by an oath exchange and communal meal to seal their agreement. Jacob's response to Laban's vows is set forth in Genesis 31:53:

אֱלֹהֵי אַבְרָהָם וֵאלֹהֵי נָחוֹר יִשְׁפְּטוּ בֵינֵינוּ אֱלֹהֵי אֲבִיהֶם וַיִּשָּׁבַע יַעֲקֹב בְּפַחַד אָבִיו יִצְחָק

---

[17] Adele Berlin, and Marc Zvi Brettler, *The Jewish Study Bible: Torah, Neviim, Kethuvim*, 2nd ed (New York: Oxford University Press, 2014), 171.

'May the God of Abraham and the god of Nahor" (their respective ancestral deities) "judge between us" and Jacob swore by the fear of his father Isaac. (Gen. 31:53)

"Although it is not stated that Nahor emigrated with his father and brother from Ur of the Chaldees, Haran is called 'the city of Nahor' (Gen. 24:10), so it may be inferred that Nahor took part in the emigration and settled at Haran. Nahor was the progenitor of twelve Aramean tribes through his twelve sons, of whom eight were born to him by his wife Milcah, and four by his concubine Reumah (Gen. 22:20-24)."[18]

Alter writes, "Jacob swore by the Terror of his father Isaac. …Jacob resists the universal Semitic term for God, *'elohim*, and the equation between the gods of Nahor and Abraham. He himself does not presume to go back as far as Abraham, but in the God of his father Isaac he senses something numinous, awesome, frightening."[19]

While in most English translations יִשְׁפְּטוּ בֵינֵינוּ *(yishfetu benenu)* is translated as "(God) judge between us," implying a single subject, the Hebrew actually uses a plural verb. The original thus clearly implies that it is not just one God, but two – the God of Abraham and the God of Nahor – who will give judgment jointly. It is easy to understand why people who live in a multi-god society would say something like this.

Jacob's confidence in fleeing Laban and his public confrontation with clear and fair charges were all based on his imperfect, yet real, confidence in the promises of God. God promised to keep Jacob safe and, in spite of all his deserved and undeserved troubles, to have him become the father of a great nation with its own land, protected and blessed by Abraham's God.

The Danger of Return

Over twenty years have passed since Jacob ran away from his brother destitute and alone. More than twenty years have passed since Esau swore his revenge for the theft of his blessing. Now the brothers are about to meet again. In the past Esau had sworn to kill Jacob. Will he do so now?

---

[18]   Emil G. Hirsch and Seligsohn, M. (1906), "Nahor." *Jewish Encyclopedia*, accessed December 19, 2015, http://www.jewishencyclopedia.com/articles/11287-nahor

[19]   Alter, *Genesis: Translation and Commentary*, 176.

Or could it be that time (and the God of Abraham, Isaac and Jacob) had softened his heart? Now, in the final stage of Jacob's struggle with his brother, he must come face-to-face with him once again. God's covenant promise is God's gift for the future. But God endowed Jacob with entrepreneurial ingenuity, a gift he used all the time. I realize that I have just stated something here that goes completely against the usual interpretation. The traditional Christian interpretation proposes that all Jacob's "survival plans" were an expression of his doubt.

There is a notion that only after meeting with God at Penuel did Jacob gain trust towards God and, because of that, was renamed Israel. I clearly don't think that this is a good reconstruction of the events. Jacob's faith does not have to be in conflict with Jacob's shrewd preparations. As we will see later, Jacob is not simply bribing his way back to peace; but something else, something far more important, is happening in the story. When Laban and his company left, Jacob continued on his way to Canaan. In Genesis 32:2 we read about an unexplained and unannounced encounter with the "angels of God" מַלְאֲכֵי אֱלֹהִים *(malakhe Elohim)*. After this brief mention we are told that Jacob declared, "This is God's camp" and named the place מַחֲנָיִם *(machanayim)*. This word translated literally means "the two camps" or "a pair of camps."

Jacob understood that he had just encountered God's angels carrying out His will (i.e. protecting him) while he was heading to Canaan, just as he saw them at Bethel on the way out of Canaan many years earlier. "There is a marked narrative symmetry between Jacob's departure from Canaan, when he had his dream of angels at Bethel, and his return, when again he encounters a company of angels. That symmetry will be unsettled when later in the chapter he finds himself in fateful conflict with a single divine being."[20]

Jacob divided everything into two camps. His plan was simple. If things don't work out as he hopes, at least one of his camps will remain alive and survive the meeting with Esau and his 400 warriors. Perhaps, Jacob reasoned that this is what God had in mind. This sounds remarkably similar to Abraham and Sarah's struggle with child-conception, and their creative "Hagar solution" to help God to keep His word (Gen. 16:1). But

---

[20] Alter, *Genesis: Translation and Commentary*, 176.

while we have the privilege of knowing how things turned out, Jacob did not. We know that no planning was needed, that Esau was coming to meet his brother in peace. But Jacob did not know this. He acted responsibly in having a "plan B."

Public Repentance

We read in Genesis 32:4-6 that Jacob, upon his approach to Seir, the country of Edom where Esau now lived, sends his messengers ahead of him as part of his elaborate plan:

וַיְצַו אֹתָם לֵאמֹר כֹּה תֹאמְרוּן לַאדֹנִי לְעֵשָׂו כֹּה אָמַר עַבְדְּךָ יַעֲקֹב עִם־לָבָן גַּרְתִּי וָאֵחַר עַד־עָתָּה

"And instructed them as follows, thus shall you say, 'To my lord Esau, thus says your servant Jacob: I stayed with Laban and remained until now'." (Gen. 32:4/5)

Jacob is between a rock and a hard place, i.e., Laban and Esau! He cannot return to Laban because of the agreement with him, and he cannot yet return home – he must meet Esau first. He continues:

וַיְהִי־לִי שׁוֹר וַחֲמוֹר צֹאן וְעֶבֶד וְשִׁפְחָה וָאֶשְׁלְחָה לְהַגִּיד לַאדֹנִי לִמְצֹא־חֵן בְּעֵינֶיךָ

"I have acquired cattle, asses, sheep, and male and female slaves; and I send this message to my lord in the hope of gaining your favor." (Gen. 32:5/6)

There is one central issue of note here. The messengers (in this case human, not angelic servants) are instructed to refer to their master as עַבְדְּךָ יַעֲקֹב *(avdekha Yaakov)* "your servant Jacob" when speaking to Esau, while referring to Esau as Jacob's lord, לַאדֹנִי לְעֵשָׂו *(l-adoni le-Esav)* "to my lord Esau." This idea is repeated as Jacob approaches Esau in the hope of reconciliation. Jacob no longer wants the blessing of dominance over his brother that he stole. By these repeated symbolic actions, Jacob strives to communicate clearly that both the right and the blessings of the firstborn do indeed belong to Esau and not to him. Jacob is now a great man who is both blessed by God with the blessing of Abraham and repentant in every way toward the brother he wronged many years ago. The plan is not simply some manipulation to get what he wants and to secure a safe passage home. The central part of the plan is a ceremony of public repentance and reparation of the wrongs done. Jacob knows from his struggles with Leah, Rachel and Laban (and of course with himself) that love (even brotherly love) is not sufficient.

Jacob has learned, over time and through many struggles, to listen both to God and to the cries of those around him. As he struggled with the insecurities of both Leah and Rachel, Jacob became a different man. He would no longer "walk over corpses" to get what he needed. He now understands the deep human need for justice and righteousness. He has learned that love without justice is not sufficient. Those less-loved must be treated with honor and dignity; with sensitivity and care. Jacob has learned what Israel will later be commanded to learn – to listen (*Shema*). According to Rabbi Sacks, in Jewish tradition

> the highest spiritual gift is the ability to listen – not only to the voice of God, but also to the cry of other people, the sigh of the poor, the weak, the lonely, the neglected and, yes, sometimes the un-loved or less-loved. That is one of the meanings of the great command: *Shema Yisrael*, "Listen, O Israel." Jacob's other name, we recall, was Israel... He is the most tenacious of all the patriarchs and the only one whose children all become part of the covenant. It is rather that every virtue has a corresponding danger. Those who are courageous are often unaware of the fears of ordinary people. Those of penetrating intellect are often dismissive of lesser minds. Those who, like Jacob, have an unusual capacity to love must fight against the danger of failing to honor the feelings of those they do not love with equal passion. The antidote is the ability to listen. That is what Jacob discovered in the course of his life, and why he, above all, is the role model for the Jewish people the nation commanded to listen.[21]

But there is something else of great importance in Jacob's response to the messenger's news. We read in Genesis 32:7/8:

וַיִּירָא יַעֲקֹב מְאֹד וַיֵּצֶר לוֹ

Jacob was greatly afraid and distressed. (Gen. 32:7/8)

Normally we understand this as Jacob being afraid for his life and the lives of his loved ones, but this may have not been the case, given the repetitive

---

[21] Sacks, *Covenant & Conversation*, 209.

wording. Jewish sages have speculated that Jacob was not only afraid that he will be killed, but that he will kill also. Remember the fear of Rebekah, Jacob and Esau's mother, that if they were to meet they may kill each other! (Gen. 27:45) Israelite theology sees any human killing as problematic and Jewish theologians spend massive amounts of time thinking about the ethical implications of all imaginable life situations. Even when there is clarity about a situation, such as a thief who is killed during a night intrusion (Ex.22:2-3), the killing of the thief is a justified but still regrettable thing. "In a conflict between two rights or two wrongs, there may be a proper way to act – the lesser of two evils, or the greater of two goods – but this does not cancel out all emotional pain."[22] We read in an early Midrash about the following discussion:

> "Rabbi Judah bar Ilai said: Are not fear and distress identical? The meaning, however, is that "he was afraid" that he might be killed; "he was distressed" that he might kill. For Jacob thought: If he prevails against me, will he not kill me; while if I prevail against him, will I not kill him? That is the meaning of "he was afraid" – lest he should be killed; "and distressed" – lest he should kill." (Bereshit Rabbah 76:2).

Only people who know how to experience "not only the physical fear of defeat but the moral distress of victory... and are capable of feeling both, can defend their bodies without endangering their souls."[23]

Jacob's Prayer

The messengers returned to Jacob with disturbing news. Esau himself, in the company of four hundred men, was now approaching. Jacob was truly afraid, and he had every good reason. After following through with his plan to divide his household into two camps, he did what all great men of faith do when met with an enormous challenge, he prayed humbly, but boldly.

> Oh God of my father Abraham and God of my father Isaac, O LORD, who said to me, "Return to your native land and I will deal bountifully with you"! I am unworthy of all the kindness that You have so steadfastly shown Your servant: with my staff alone I crossed this Jordan, and now I have become two camps. Deliver me, I pray, from the hand of my

---

[22] Ibid., 217.
[23] Ibid., 218.

brother, from the hand of Esau; else, I fear, he may come and strike me down, mothers and children alike. Yet You have said, "I will deal bountifully with you and make your offspring as the sands of the sea, which are too numerous to count." (Gen. 32:10/11-12/13)

First, Jacob appeals to the LORD God based upon his connection to his fathers – Abraham and Isaac. Second, he appeals to God's direct command to leave Haran and return home. Third, he confesses that he is unworthy of any goodness that the LORD has demonstrated to him so far. Fourth, he asks for God's deliverance from the hand of Esau, being afraid also for the lives of all those with him. And fifth, Jacob holds the LORD God to his own promise that he will be treated well by Him and that his descendants would become abundantly numerous. If Jacob and his family do not survive this day, clearly God's words cannot be trusted. Jacob, ending with a recital of God's promise and holding God up to this promise, shows that, in the end, he did not count on his own smart "kissing-up-to-Esau" plan. In the end he trusted in God, who has kept His word and whose promises one can truly rely upon. In this, his faith resembled that of his grandfather Abraham. A faith like this is best seen in the story of the "binding of Isaac." There, as well, God's promises and the God-arranged events in Abraham's life seemed to be at odds with each other. Jacob not only had the blessing of Abraham, he now also had his faith and his ability to trust God.

Restitution and Confession

After a sleepless night, Jacob organized the reconciliation gifts intended for his older brother. In Genesis 32:14/15-15/16 we are given an exact description of his gifts: "200 she-goats and 20 he-goats; 200 ewes and 20 rams; 30 milch (milk) camels with their colts; 40 cows and 10 bulls; 20 she-asses and 10 he-asses." The proportions of male and female animals here are not coincidental. Jacob sought to communicate that with this balance Esau is set for exponential growth of his livestock. When the number of males and females is about the same, the growth would be a lot slower, but when the percentage of males and females is such as we see here, prolific increase is almost guaranteed.

Walking separated from each other in groups, Jacob's plan was to gradually soften the heart of his brother Esau and thus receive his forgiveness. Each group was to give Esau exactly the same message: "Your servant Jacob's gift sent to my lord Esau… and he (Jacob) himself is right behind us." (Gen. 32:18/19) We read in Genesis 32:20/21:

וְאָמַרְתֶּם גַּם הִנֵּה עַבְדְּךָ יַעֲקֹב אַחֲרֵינוּ כִּי־אָמַר אֲכַפְּרָה פָנָיו בַּמִּנְחָה הַהֹלֶכֶת לְפָנָי וְאַחֲרֵי־כֵן אֶרְאֶה פָנָיו אוּלַי יִשָּׂא פָנָי

And you shall add, 'And your servant Jacob himself is right behind us.'" For he reasoned, "If I propitiate him with presents in advance, and then face him, perhaps he will show me favor." (Gen. 32:20/21)

The Hebrew word פָּנִים (*panim*), which literally means "face," occurs seven times in this passage (Gen. 32:17-21). If we don't regard that fact as coincidental, it might indicate the idea of completion. This (especially vs. 21) builds a case and connects with the place being called פְּנִיאֵל (*Penuel*), which means "face of God" (Gen. 32:31/32). This all underscores the association of Esau with the mysterious figure with whom Jacob is about to wrestle. This same concept of "face-to-face" encounters is used in the case of Moses (Ex. 33:11, Deut. 34:10) and Gideon (Jud. 6:22). As the gifts slowly make their way to Esau, Jacob remains in the camp, giving enough time for his reconciliation offerings to be received. That night, taking his family, "he crossed the ford" of the Jabbok וַיַּעֲבֹר אֵת מַעֲבַר (*va-yaavor et maavar*). The word for "ford" here is מַעֲבַר (*maavar*). It is connected with the verb עָבַר (*avar*) "to cross over." The Jabbok is an offshoot spring of the Jordan River, running from East to West. Jacob has been traveling south from the high country of Gilead. Esau is heading north from Edom to meet him. Once Jacob's family reached the other side, he sent over all his remaining possessions. Jacob, however, stayed behind.

The text says that he was now left alone. His next surprise encounter will confirm all that was already true of Jacob. Jacob is all about struggle. "Both his names – *Jacob*, 'he who grasps by the heel,' and *Israel*, 'he who struggles with G-d and man and prevails' – convey a sense of conflict… The gifts he has, he has fought for. None have come naturally. Jacob is the supreme figure of persistence."[24] The name change to Israel resembles that given to Sarai – Sarah (Gen. 17:15), since both involve the same root שַׂר (*sar*). The association of Sarah's new name with royalty is explicitly made in Gen.

---

[24] Jonathan Sacks, *Covenant & Conversation*, http://rabbisacks.org/covenant-conversation-5768-vayetse-leahs-tears/

17:16. Jacob's name will be changed to reflect the obvious reality in his life – he was a man born to overcome.

Two Meetings

In Genesis 32:24-25 we are told that when Jacob sent his family over the river he was left alone. He had done all he could – he sent reconciliatory gifts, he prayed to the LORD, he even prepared his household for a military confrontation. Now he was alone. And this is what took place that night in Genesis 32:25-26:

וַיִּוָּתֵר יַעֲקֹב לְבַדּוֹ וַיֵּאָבֵק אִישׁ עִמּוֹ עַד עֲלוֹת הַשָּׁחַר

Jacob was left alone. And a man wrestled with him until the break of dawn. (Gen. 32:24/25)

וַיַּרְא כִּי לֹא יָכֹל לוֹ וַיִּגַּע בְּכַף־יְרֵכוֹ וַתֵּקַע כַּף־יֶרֶךְ יַעֲקֹב בְּהֵאָבְקוֹ עִמּוֹ

When he saw that he had not prevailed against him, he wrenched Jacob's hip at its socket, so that the socket of his hip was strained as he wrestled with him. (Gen. 32:25/26)

This root אָבַק *(avak)* "to wrestle" is found only here in these two Bible verses and apparently plays on the similar-sounding names of the river Jabbok יַבֹּק *(Yavok)* and of Jacob himself יַעֲקֹב *(Yaakov)*. The geographical locale and the events that take place there are punned together. So the river becomes associated with "the place of the supplanter's struggle." It is not clear from the text who it was that wrestled with Jacob, nor why. What is clear is that Jacob himself did not expect this meeting and this fight. His mind was naturally preoccupied with meeting Esau. The text states that it was אִישׁ *(ish)* "a man" that wrestled with Jacob. Later, the prophet Hosea depicts him as "angel/messenger of God" (Hosea 12:4). Some Rabbinic sages thought it was Esau's guardian angel who came to oppose him, while others thought it was Satan himself. In the end, Jacob was convinced beyond a shadow of a doubt that he had wrestled with God. "And he took leave of him there. So Jacob named the place Penuel, meaning, "I have seen a divine being face to face, yet my life has been preserved" (Gen. 32:31).

Why Now?

A truly intriguing and original interpretation was suggested by an 11th-century Jewish commentator, Rashbam. He suggested that this event must be connected with other events in which great people, called by God to something important, suddenly doubted their mission and, perhaps, were tempted to reconsider the validity of God's call and in some way to disobey it. A truly puzzling, but very important event in the life of Moses when the LORD Himself (similar to this meeting with Jacob) came to Moses and sought his death, must be mentioned. Only the quick action of Zipporah in circumcising their son saved Moses from sure death (Ex. 4:24-25). Joshua, before confronting Jericho's tall walls was also met by "a man," who turned out to be the Commander of the LORD's armies, his sword already drawn.

What was curious about Joshua's meeting is that, just as with Jacob, "the man" also seemed to be God Himself. Joshua "fell on his face to the earth and worshipped him," and was commanded to take off his shoes because of the holiness of the ground upon which he stood (Josh. 5:13-15). This particular encounter parallels exactly the one between Moses and God at the burning bush. Both removed their shoes because of the holiness of the place (Ex. 3:5). "The confrontation" is one of the common factors in each encounter. As a result, God's struggle with His own chosen people appears to be a major theme. We can recall other times when God just would not let something happen. For example, Jonah tried to evade the Nineveh mission, but God pursued him and compelled him to accomplish the task. Balaam, on the way to cursing Israel was literally stopped by the Angel of the LORD (Num. 22:21-35). The examples are numerous, and they seem to form a pattern. When something vitally important, in a covenantal sense, is imminent, God intervenes to ensure it happens.

A New Name

The man who fought with Jacob blessed him, and in blessing him he changed his name to Israel. We read about it in Genesis 32:28-29:

וַיֹּאמֶר אֵלָיו מַה־שְּׁמֶךָ וַיֹּאמֶר יַעֲקֹב

Said the other, "What is your name?" He replied, "Jacob." (Gen. 32:27/28)

וַיֹּאמֶר לֹא יַעֲקֹב יֵאָמֵר עוֹד שִׁמְךָ כִּי אִם־יִשְׂרָאֵל כִּי־שָׂרִיתָ עִם־אֱלֹהִים וְעִם־אֲנָשִׁים וַתּוּכָל

Said he, "Your name shall no longer be Jacob, but Israel, for you have striven with beings divine and human, and have prevailed." (Gen. 32:28/29)

Names in the ancient Jewish world were far more important than they are for many today. In the biblical culture they carried a very important weight. A name spoke of a person's character, his deeds and his identity. For a person to be given a new name, meant a change in their identity. That Jacob's name was "Jacob" (the heel-grabber) was, of course, known to the one who attacked him. This divine being (whoever he may have been) probably asked Jacob's name as a part of the name-changing process. But before he could assign Jacob a new name, Jacob himself had understood the name he was now leaving behind. After this "heel-grabbing" acknowledgement Jacob's name changed to Israel. As discussed previously, the word "Israel" most likely comes from the root שַׂר *(sar)*, which in biblical Hebrew means "to struggle" and "to exercise influence," "to rule as a prince."

Jacob became Israel precisely because he struggled with and overcame both Heaven and Earth, both God and humanity. There is "some question about its meaning, though an educated guess about the original sense of the name would be: 'God will rule,' or perhaps, 'God will prevail.'"[25] Another important observation should also be mentioned. While this אִישׁ *(ish)* "man" changes Jacob's name to Israel, in Genesis 35:9-10 it is clear that God does so. It is worth noting that Genesis 32:31/32 states that: "The sun rose upon him as he passed Penuel, limping because of his hip." We might recall that in Genesis 28:11 we read "And he came to a certain place and stayed there that night, because the sun had set." The sun "setting" at the beginning of Jacob's journey and in its end, seems to bracket the transformation journey of Jacob becoming Israel. God appears to Jacob when he reaches home and blesses him there, telling him that from then on, his name will no longer be Jacob, but Israel.[26] God identifies

---

[25] Alter, *Genesis: Translation and Commentary*, 182.
[26] What is striking is that in contrast to Abram/Abraham, the Torah continues to use Jacob/Israel interchangeably.

himself as *El Shaddai* and confirms the blessing of Abraham upon him (Gen. 35:11-13).

Father of the Nation Israel

It is only much later, after the fall of the Northern Kingdom of Israel that the people of Israel as a whole would begin to be called "Judeans" or "Jews." This is not a biblical injunction, but merely a historical reality identifying survivors with the Southern Kingdom of Judah and its lands. In biblical terms, the true name of the covenantal descendants of Abraham, Isaac and Jacob is not "Jews," but "Israelites" – the children of the man whose name was changed by this very encounter with the divine. The modern term "Jews" came to be because those who returned from Babylon lived in Judea and so all (regardless of original tribe) were called "Judeans." Over time even those living in diaspora were identified with Judea and called "Jews."

But why did this unexpected meeting happen right before the meeting with Esau? The basic answer in my view is that the founder of Israel as a nation could not have been a thief, a liar and a coward. We must remember that the Book of Genesis is a prelude to the Book of Exodus, which was written for Israelites who departed from Egypt and were on their way to Canaan. Jacob needed to become Israel. It took twenty-two years of exile to accomplish this. He had now changed and was ready. He possessed the blessing of Abraham (land and children), but he needed to return the blessing he had stolen which was not his own (power and wealth). This reconciliation with Esau was not simply a personal family affair, as it must surely have seemed to Jacob and Esau. It was an event of global significance, for the very identity of the future nation of Israel was at stake.

Their father, called by the same name as they, was in fact the rightful owner of the covenant blessing of Abraham and Isaac. When he learned the truth he acted upon it courageously, being willing to face Esau and return to him that which was rightly his. Once that was accomplished, everything that Jacob/Israel had would legitimately belong to him and his children. Israelites were not thieves and robbers, but the legitimate custodians of the divinely promised land. This is bigger than Jacob and Esau. If Rashbam is right, it was God, in the moment of Jacob's weakness, who was determined to stop Jacob from running away from this fundamentally important meeting. The stakes were too high for Jacob to fail. He was not simply Jacob, he was the founder of the nation of Israel – a people who would be blessed by the LORD God, and a people who existed in order to bless all others (Gen. 32:32-33; Gen. 12:1-3).

Unexpected Grace

After the encounter with the mysterious man, Jacob crossed the Jabbok, where his family was waiting for him. Jacob saw Esau and his delegation from afar. He told both wives and both concubines to stand with their children. The two concubines were to go first, followed by Leah and her children, and Rachel and her son Joseph followed last. (Gen.33:1-3). As Esau approached, Jacob went to the front of his family procession and bowed down seven times as he came closer. This tradition of bowing down or prostrating seven times is attested to in ancient documents as a sign of homage that a vassal king shows to his suzerain master (Tel El Amarna Letters). This scene reverses the dominance of Jacob over Esau prophesied in Genesis 25:23 and 27:29, 37.[27]

Much later, when the Israelites who left Egypt heard this story, they were probably shocked at how things developed. We read in Genesis 33:4:

וַיָּרָץ עֵשָׂו לִקְרָאתוֹ וַיְחַבְּקֵהוּ וַיִּפֹּל עַל־צַוָּארָו וַיִּשָּׁקֵהוּ וַיִּבְכּוּ

Esau ran to greet him. He embraced him and, falling on his neck, he kissed him; and they wept. (Gen. 33:4)

Perhaps Esau's rage and swearing to kill his brother was nothing more than a manifestation of his impulsive personality. The same personality which we saw displayed when he so carelessly sold his birthright for food. Esau was fully prepared to formally forgive his brother. When people are hesitant about their offer of forgiveness they don't run towards the one who offended them. Esau ran to Jacob. Esau had probably forgiven Jacob

---

[27] Jon D. Levenson, "Genesis Introductions and Annotations," in *The Jewish Study Bible. Tanakh Translation,* eds. Adele Berlin and Marc Zvi Brettler (New York: Oxford University Press, 2014), 63.

a long time ago, and now, at the opportunity of their meeting, Esau's healed emotions could be expressed to show how much he truly loved his younger brother after all. As the brothers continued to greet one another, Esau looked up and saw the women and children. He then asked about who they were, to which Jacob responded:

$$\text{הַיְלָדִים אֲשֶׁר־חָנַן אֱלֹהִים אֶת־עַבְדֶּךָ}$$

"The children with whom God has favored your servant." (Gen. 33:5)

The emphasis here is upon God's grace in giving him many children, and also upon him being Esau's humble and submissive servant. Everything that Jacob says and does speaks of his servitude to his brother, not the other way around. It was not only Jacob himself, but also his wives and children, who were said to be Esau's servants as they too approached and bowed before Jacob's older brother (Gen. 33:6-7).

Esau then asked about the meaning of all the animal groups that he met one after another on the way to greet Jacob. Jacob responded that he sent those "to find grace in your eyes, my lord" לִמְצֹא־חֵן בְּעֵינֵי אֲדֹנִי *(limtso chen be-eyne adoni)*. This phraseology is still in use today. In Modern Hebrew, one way to ask someone if they liked something is to ask them literally if it "found grace in their eyes."[28] Esau's response is:

$$\text{יֶשׁ־לִי רָב אָחִי יְהִי לְךָ אֲשֶׁר־לָךְ}$$

I have plenty, my brother. Let what you have remain yours. (Gen. 33:9)

Jacob then said to Esau:

$$\text{אַל־נָא אִם־נָא מָצָאתִי חֵן בְּעֵינֶיךָ וְלָקַחְתָּ מִנְחָתִי מִיָּדִי כִּי עַל־כֵּן רָאִיתִי פָנֶיךָ}$$
$$\text{כִּרְאֹת פְּנֵי אֱלֹהִים וַתִּרְצֵנִי}$$

---

[28] This reconciliation between "Edom" and Jacob/Israel is perhaps another harbinger of the future when both will be part of the same inheritance (Amos 9:12, Obadiah 19-21). The name "Edom" is used explicitly in Gen. 32:4.

No, I pray you; if you would do me this favor, accept from me this gift; for to see your face is like seeing the face of God, and you have received me favorably. (Gen. 33:10)

קַח־נָא אֶת־בִּרְכָתִי אֲשֶׁר הֻבָאת לָךְ כִּי־חַנַּנִי אֱלֹהִים וְכִי יֶשׁ־לִי־כֹל וַיִּפְצַר־בּוֹ וַיִּקָּח

Please accept my present which has been brought to you, for God has favored me and I have plenty." And when he urged him, he accepted. (Gen. 33:11)

Jacob and Esau's assessment of what they own is not the same. This is a point most Bible translations miss. While Esau says יֶשׁ־לִי רָב (*yesh li rav*), which means "I have plenty," Jacob states יֶשׁ־לִי־כֹל (*yesh li kol*), which means "I have everything." One speaks of a large quantity, while the other speaks of sufficiency. The verb פָּצַר (*patsar*) in this Hebrew sentence implies a very forceful insistence by Jacob: Jacob "urged" his brother. A crucial point not to be overlooked in this passage is that Jacob has frequently been using the word מִנְחָה (*minchah*), commonly translated "gift," as he does in verse 10, but in verse 11 this suddenly changes. Instead of מִנְחָתִי (*minchati*) "my gift," Jacob asks Esau to take בִּרְכָתִי (*birkhati*) "my blessing." Jacob is not simply "kissing up" to Esau, he is "returning" the blessing he stole.

We would be remiss if we did not pay attention to verse 10 where Jacob explains that to see the forgiving and welcoming face of Esau was "like seeing the face of God" כִּרְאֹת פְּנֵי אֱלֹהִים (*ki-reot pene Elohim*). We have noted before how the idea of פָּנִים (*panim*), variously translated as "face" or "presence" (among other things), is certainly a common and possibly key word in the Jacob narratives. Of course this will not only be limited to Jacob, because the stories about the nation of Israel and her dealings with the God of Abraham, Isaac and Jacob will continue this same trajectory. Here, suffice it to say, Jacob himself clearly connected these two encounters. For him, the confrontation with "the man" of Penuel (meaning "the *face* of God") and the meeting with Esau, were clearly connected (vs. 10b). The various uses of פָּנִים (*panim*) in Hebrew abound in chapters 32-33, but most instances simply cannot be seen in our English translations. Rabbi Sacks writes:

> To take one example, Genesis 32: 21 is translated: [Jacob said to his servants,] "You shall say, 'Your servant Jacob is coming behind us,'" for he thought, "I will pacify him with these gifts I am sending on ahead; later, when I see him, perhaps he will receive me." There is nothing in the

English translation to suggest that the word פָּנִים *(panim)* actually appears four times in this verse alone. But the second half of the verse could be literally translated: "for he thought, 'I will wipe [the anger from] his face with the gift that goes ahead of my face; afterward, when I see his face perhaps he will lift up my face....'" There is a drama here and it has to do with faces: the face of Esau, of Jacob, and of God Himself.[29]

---

[29] Sacks, *Covenant & Conversation*, 223.

CHAPTER SIX: THE LIFE OF JOSEPH

The "Joseph story" picks up in Genesis 37:1 with the statement that Jacob dwelled in the land of Canaan, the land where Abraham sojourned before him. This should not be glossed over. The story that the narrator is about to tell takes place at a particular point in time, a significant moment. Jacob firmly settled in the very land where Abraham was only a guest. Joseph assisted his older brothers (Dan, Naphtali, Gad and Asher) in shepherding the flock. One possible way to interpret the Hebrew text is as literally saying something like "he was being their young man" וְהוּא נַעַר אֶת־בְּנֵי בִלְהָה וְאֶת־בְּנֵי זִלְפָּה *(ve-hu naar et bene Vilhah ve-et bene Zilpah)*. In other words, he did the jobs of an errand boy that his older brothers did not want to do. (Gen. 37:2).

Most of the things that happen to Joseph give an impression of him being passive, i.e. things were usually done *to* him by someone else. This would only be true until his brothers' arrival to his residence in Egypt. Like Jacob his father, Joseph had character flaws. The text speaks of him bringing "evil reports" to his father regarding his brothers (Gen. 37:2). One may understand this in various senses. Joseph is perhaps accused of habitual tale-bearing on his brothers. But we may also understand that there were legitimate evils to be reported and dealt with. Joseph might have simply reported or carried what his brothers said to him. In the end, his brothers were guilty of wanting to kill him, so perhaps the reports were indeed justified.

וְיִשְׂרָאֵל אָהַב אֶת־יוֹסֵף מִכָּל־בָּנָיו כִּי־בֶן־זְקֻנִים הוּא לוֹ וְעָשָׂה לוֹ כְּתֹנֶת פַּסִּים:

Now Israel loved Joseph more than all his sons because he was a son born to him late in life, and he made a special tunic for him. (Gen. 37:3)

We are told that Israel loved Joseph more than his brothers because he was born to him in his old age. We cannot help but wonder why the narrator does not mention that Joseph was the son of Rachel, Jacob's special love. Be that as it may, *Israel* openly expressed his favoritism by giving Joseph a very special tunic. In Hebrew it is called כְּתֹנֶת פַּסִּים *(ketonet passim),* which clearly showed him to be loved above his brothers. The traditional idea seen in many English translations and folklore is that this was some sort of multi-colored outer garment. But the meaning of the Hebrew is not completely clear and there is no way to know for sure. Alter comments, "We are told that the *ketonet pasim* was worn by virgin princesses. It is thus a unisex garment and a product of ancient haute couture."[30]

This was most likely the kind of robe worn by royalty. In Genesis 37:8 his brothers asked him rhetorically if Joseph is going to be a king over them. We read in 37:4 that the older brothers became so filled with envy and hatred towards Joseph that they could not even say "shalom" to him וְלֹא יָכְלוּ דַּבְּרוֹ לְשָׁלֹם *(ve-lo yakhlu dabro le-shalom)*. But how do they move from truly disliking Joseph to harboring resentment which leads to his kidnapping and attempted murder?

The Fateful Dreams

What seemed to push the brothers over the line (although of course their murderous violence towards Joseph was inexcusable) is that he began to dream dreams. In one dream that he relates to his brothers, he saw himself as an upright sheaf while the sheaves of his brothers were bowing before him (Gen. 37:5-8). In another dream, which Joseph naively relayed to his brothers and his father, he saw the moon and the sun, along with eleven stars bowing before him. His father rebuked him. But, while his brothers' jealousy grew only more intense, Jacob kept this matter in his thoughts, wondering exactly what it might mean given the clear interpretation of the second dream (Gen. 37:9-11).

It is interesting to note that the brothers were so obsessed with disdain towards Joseph that they ignored the meaning of the dreams entirely. They dismissed the prophetic nature and focused only on the suggestions of subservience to their younger brother. Moreover, "as has often been noted, the dreams in the Joseph story reflect its more secular orientation in comparison with the preceding narratives in Genesis. They are not direct messages from God, like His appearance in the dream-visions to Abimelech and to Jacob."[31]

---

[30] Alter, *Genesis: Translation and Commentary*, 209.
[31] Ibid., 209.

Joseph's account of his dreams shows a young man who is self-absorbed, naively assuming that all involved will be equally fascinated by the content of his dreams. The text repeats the Hebrew word הִנֵּה (*hineh*) "behold" three times in the space of only one verse, perhaps highlighting Joseph's fascination with the dream (Gen. 37:7; then twice in vs. 9). Alter notes further:

> It should also be observed that doublets are a recurrent principle of organization in the Joseph story, just as binary divisions are an organizing principle in the Jacob story. Joseph and Pharaoh have double dreams; the chief butler and the chief baker dream their pair of seemingly parallel, actually antithetical dreams. Joseph is first flung into a pit and later into the prison-house. The brothers make two trips down to Egypt, with one of their number seemingly at risk on each occasion. And their descent to Egypt with goods and silver mirrors the descent of the merchant caravan, bearing the same items that first brought Joseph down to Egypt.[32]

The Plot to Kill

It is not clear what Israel was thinking when he sent a 17-year-old Joseph, too well-dressed for what seems to be a job, on a fairly long errand from Hebron all the way to Shechem where his brothers were tending the livestock. When Joseph arrived near Shechem, he found out that his brothers had gone even further away to Dothan. When his brothers saw him from afar, they immediately began to conspire how to get rid of him once and for all. Even their opening words are chilling, anticipating the violence that is to follow. In English Joseph is often labeled simply as a "dreamer," but the Hebrew term בַּעַל הַחֲלֹמוֹת (*baal ha-chalomot*) is stronger and, in the Hebrew context, likely more sarcastic. The term בַּעַל (*baal*) "master" suggests someone who has a special "proprietary relation to, or mastery of, the noun that follows it."[33] This means that the brothers (probably mockingly) described Joseph as a "master of dreams."

Ancient texts are often hard to read. This terminology could be showing that in the minds of the brothers, Joseph's dreams were something he himself is responsible for – that they are of his own doing. Or, it could be pointing out that he simply had an abundance of colorful dreams. Again, the hate-filled, conspiring brothers completely miss the point of Joseph's

---

[32] *Ibid.*, 210.
[33] *Ibid.*, 212.

dreaming. It has been said, "When you are holding a hammer, everything begins to look like a nail."

Speculatively, perhaps Joseph's brothers even went further from home with the flocks in the expectation that he would come and could be lured further away from home (though we don't know that for sure). Maybe they were already lying in wait for Joseph.

Of course, not all the brothers were a part of the plot to kill him. We learn that Joseph had "the bad judgment to wear on his errand the garment that was the extravagant token of his father's favoritism."[34]

וְעַתָּה לְכוּ וְנַהַרְגֵהוּ וְנַשְׁלִכֵהוּ בְּאַחַד הַבֹּרוֹת וְאָמַרְנוּ חַיָּה רָעָה אֲכָלָתְהוּ וְנִרְאֶה מַה־יִּהְיוּ

Come now, let's kill him, throw him into one of the cisterns, and then say that a wild animal ate him. Then we'll see how his dreams turn out! (Gen. 37:20)

וַיְהִי כַּאֲשֶׁר־בָּא יוֹסֵף אֶל־אֶחָיו וַיַּפְשִׁיטוּ אֶת־יוֹסֵף אֶת־כֻּתָּנְתּוֹ אֶת־כְּתֹנֶת הַפַּסִּים אֲשֶׁר עָלָיו: וַיִּקָּחֻהוּ וַיַּשְׁלִכוּ אֹתוֹ הַבֹּרָה

When Joseph reached his brothers, they stripped him of his tunic, the special tunic that he wore. Then they took him and threw him into the cistern. (Gen. 37:23–24)

We read in Genesis 37:22 that Reuben tried to save Joseph by tricking the brothers. "Reuben tries not to contradict the violence of his brothers' feelings toward Joseph and uses the same phrase, to fling him[35] into a pit, with the crucial difference that in his proposal it is a live Joseph who will be cast into the pit."[36]

Sacks comments as follows:

> It is a confusing episode. Who pulled Joseph from the pit? Who sold him to the Ishmaelites? Was it the brothers or the Midianites? The subject, "they," is ambiguous. Commentators offer many interpretations. Of

---

[34] *Ibid.*, 213.
[35] Alter notes in a footnote here: "This is precisely the verb used for Hagar (21:15) when she flings Ishmael under a bush in the wilderness."
[36] Alter, *Genesis: Translation and Commentary*, 212.

these, the simplest is given by Rashbam, who reads it as follows: The brothers, having thrown Joseph into the pit, sat down some distance away to eat. Reuben sneaked back to rescue Joseph, but found the pit empty and cried, "The boy is not! And I, where can I go? Rashbam points out that the brothers did not calm him down by telling him that they had sold Joseph. They seem as surprised as he was. It follows that the brothers, having seen the Ishmaelites in the distance, decided to sell Joseph to them, but before they had the chance to do so, a second group of travelers, the Midianites, heard Joseph's cries, saw the possibility of selling him to the Ishmaelites, and did so.[37]

There is also a simpler explanation. Judges 8:22, 24 seems to equate Midianites with Ishmaelites, so the Torah was probably speaking here of a single group, not two distinct ones.

A particularly chilling detail is highlighted in this narrative. Once they had stripped Joseph of his clothes and thrown him into the pit, they calmly sat down to break bread and to have a meal. The Hebrew וַיֵּשְׁבוּ לֶאֱכָל־לֶחֶם (*va-yeshvu le-ekhal lechem*) literally means "and they sat down to eat bread" (vs. 25). When the brothers go to Egypt many years later, they will do so to buy *grain for bread* from none other than Joseph. When Reuben returned and realized that his plan had failed and that his young brother had already been sent off, he grieved, but joined his brothers in their conspiracy of keeping secret what had really happened to Joseph (Gen. 37:29-31).

Deceiving Jacob

וַיִּקְחוּ אֶת־כְּתֹנֶת יוֹסֵף וַיִּשְׁחֲטוּ שְׂעִיר עִזִּים וַיִּטְבְּלוּ אֶת־הַכֻּתֹּנֶת בַּדָּם: וַיְשַׁלְּחוּ אֶת־כְּתֹנֶת הַפַּסִּים וַיָּבִיאוּ אֶל־אֲבִיהֶם וַיֹּאמְרוּ זֹאת מָצָאנוּ הַכֶּר־נָא הַכְּתֹנֶת בִּנְךָ הִוא אִם־לֹא:

So they took Joseph's tunic, killed a young goat, and dipped the tunic in the blood. Then they brought the special tunic to their father and said, "We found this. Determine now whether it is your son's tunic or not." (Gen. 37:31-32)

Jacob, once the master of trickery and manipulation, becomes the deceived in this story. He falsely concludes exactly what the conspiring brothers hoped he would think. We read in Hebrew that חַיָּה רָעָה אֲכָלָתְהוּ טָרֹף טֹרַף

---

[37] Sacks, *Covenant & Conversation*, 275.

יוֹסֵף *(chayah raah akhalathu tarof taraf Yosef)*, which literally translated means "a wicked animal ate him; Joseph was truly torn up." The story underscores the irony of being deceived in a very similar way as one has deceived in the past. First Laban substituted sisters to trick Jacob at the moment he lowered his guard. Now, just as Jacob had used a slaughtered kid and his brother's clothes in the deception of his father many years earlier, so do his sons in implying the fate of Joseph. Thus Genesis 37 ends with Jacob's inconsolable grief over the loss of Joseph. He is so convinced that Joseph is dead and his body fully devoured, that he does not even order a search for his remains. All the years that Joseph was in Egyptian exile, Jacob suffered from tremendous emotional pain such that his life was defined by grief over the loss of Joseph. As Israel wailed over Joseph, the merchants sold him to Potiphar in Egypt.

The Judah Interruption

Highlighting that the so-called "Joseph story" is not only about Joseph, the text is suddenly interrupted by a story about Judah's moral failure in withholding from Tamar the benefit of a levirate marriage (Deut. 25:5-6). It is as if Judah's story was later inserted into the text to break up the drama. The custom of levirate marriage was simple. If a man died without any heirs, his brother was obligated to marry his widow, and her firstborn son would be considered as the offspring of the deceased brother. Thus his line lives on. After the death of his first son, Judah's second son married Tamar, but he refused to produce a son for his dead brother. As a result, the LORD took his life as a punishment. Why such a harsh punishment? We read about it in Genesis 38. Judah's second son Onan, after each intercourse with Tamar, deliberately spilled his seed on the ground. Onan seems to have reasoned that if a child was born as a result of his sexual union with Tamar, not only would he have to spend his family resources on a child that did not legally belong to him, but he would also forfeit the right to his brother's inheritance as next in line.

He failed to act responsibly and righteously towards this community of faith that God was forming from the children of Jacob/Israel. When Onan died, Judah promised Tamar that when his third son was old enough to marry he would become her husband. But Judah did not honor his promise and did not act righteously as well. Judah's concern is understandable. Two of his sons already died while they were married to Tamar. Maybe something is wrong with her? He was afraid that the same fate would befall his youngest child. Even though the chapter seems oddly placed, Judah's moral failure in withholding his youngest son from Tamar ties back in some important ways to the Abraham, Isaac and Jacob narratives, as well as to the main drama of Joseph and his brothers. Joseph was the youngest (except Benjamin) and most treasured.

Tamar was desperate and took matters into her own hands. She determined that her father-in-law's unfaithfulness will not stop her from having children and being a part of God's family. Tamar pretends to be a prostitute. Judah, after a period of mourning (his wife had died some time ago), seeks a one-time sexual service from a (presumed) prostitute who unknown to him, is actually Tamar in disguise. Tamar becomes pregnant and when the news of Tamar's extra-marital pregnancy became known to Judah, he harshly condemned her to death. When he was presented with his personal items, given to the prostitute as a pledge, he had a change of heart. (Gen. 38:24-26).

When Tamar showed Judah's personal items to him she said in Hebrew הַכֶּר־נָא *(haker na)* "please examine" (vs. 25). Ironically these are the exact same words Judah and the brothers said to Israel, הַכֶּר־נָא *(haker na)* "please examine" (Gen 37:32), while showing him Joseph's torn clothes. Judah's deception returned to him in his own words.

What is striking to most modern readers is that Tamar's action of pretending to be a prostitute is not exactly condemned in any way. There is no condemnation of Judah's use of a prostitute either. Rather, the focus of Torah's text is on Judah's sin of mistreating Tamar. One interpretation is that this demonstrates that the overall concern of the chapter (and probably by extension the entire story of Jacob's children) is focused not on individual purity of life, but on communal responsibility towards the well-being of a group. What was asked of Judah was "that he risk his son for the sake of the community, that he make his son, even his last son, available for the solidarity and future of the community now focused in the person of this defenseless widow."[38]

---

[38] Brueggemann, *Genesis: Interpretation*, 310.

Unrighteous/unjust behaviors are not viewed as merely personal failings, but communal issues. "What is taken most seriously is not a violation of sexual convention, but damage to the community which includes a poor, diminished female."[39] The story of Tamar and Judah seems to operate according to the principle: "From one to whom much is given, much is required." Tamar had the right to a child by the nearest of kin of her dead husband. The right was deliberately withheld from her. Judah later repented of his action:

צָדְקָה מִמֶּנִּי כִּי־עַל־כֵּן לֹא־נְתַתִּיהָ לְשֵׁלָה בְנִי וְלֹא־יָסַף עוֹד לְדַעְתָּהּ

"She is more in the right than I, inasmuch as I did not give her to my son Shelah." And he was not intimate with her again. (Gen. 38:26b).

After Tamar became pregnant with the twin children of Judah (Perez and Zerah), Judah does not approach her sexually again. This is a very important observation and a point that the writer/compiler(s) of Torah narrative seek(s) to communicate. Yes, Judah is a man of flawed character. Like others, he sometimes does things that are both unwise and plainly wrong. But he is Jacob/Israel's true son. Like Jacob, Judah is a man who is able to "own" his guilt, thereby chartering a new repentant course for his future. Judah's destiny will soon become clear. It is his family that will lead Israel, bringing forth the quintessential Israelite King (Gen. 49:8-10) in the person of David, who himself will exhibit both Judah's vices and his virtues.

While the story of Ruth (the great-grandmother of David) occurs much later in history, there are a number of very strong connections between Tamar and Ruth. They are both widows who bear children to older relatives. Another important point to note is that both are found in the genealogy of King David, the Israelite King, who was a descendant of the tribe of Judah. The medieval Jewish Kabbalistic work called the Zohar observes this similarity in the following summary:

> There were two women – Tamar and Ruth – from whom the line of Judah was built, and from whom issued King David, King Solomon, and the Messiah. These two women were similar: after their first husbands died, they made efforts to win their second husbands. In doing so, both of them

---

[39] *Ibid.*, 311.

acted properly for the sake of kindness to the dead [by bearing children who would perpetuate their memory]." (Zohar 1:188b)

The parallels between Tamar and Ruth are extensive and deserve more recognition than the brief reference that the Zohar affords them. The importance of their roles is clear: both are joined together and both anticipate the Lion from the Tribe of Judah who will one day rise up to govern Israel and the entire world (Gen. 49:8-12).

Potiphar's Trust

As chapter 38 ends, the story returns to Joseph in Potiphar's house. Verse 2 is a key phrase establishing the connection between the LORD God's faithfulness to Joseph with His faithfulness to Jacob in preceding narratives:

וַיְהִי יהוה אֶת־יוֹסֵף וַיְהִי אִישׁ מַצְלִיחַ

And the LORD was with Joseph, and he was a successful man (Gen. 39:2).

The personal presence of the LORD God was with Joseph. It did not matter where Joseph found himself. It did not matter if the circumstances were good or bad. God was with him. It was the "LORD being with him" that brought the preordained result – Joseph a successful man, much like Abraham, Isaac and Jacob before him. Potiphar, who himself worked in the court of the Pharaoh of Egypt knew what it was to do work with excellence. He knew success when he saw it. It was because of this excellence and success in virtually everything Joseph did, that Potiphar took favorable notice of him. He promoted Joseph, appointing him as steward over everything he owned (Gen. 39:4). We read in Genesis 39:5-6.

וַיְהִי מֵאָז הִפְקִיד אֹתוֹ בְּבֵיתוֹ וְעַל כָּל־אֲשֶׁר יֶשׁ־לוֹ וַיְבָרֶךְ יהוה אֶת־בֵּית הַמִּצְרִי בִּגְלַל יוֹסֵף וַיְהִי בִּרְכַּת יהוה בְּכָל־אֲשֶׁר יֶשׁ־לוֹ בַּבַּיִת וּבַשָּׂדֶה

And from the time that the Egyptian put him in charge of his household and of all that he owned, the LORD blessed his house for Joseph's sake, so that the blessing of the LORD was upon everything that he owned, in the house and outside. (Gen. 39:5)

The story of Joseph shows one thing very clearly. The LORD of the covenant is committed to being faithful to Jacob's children also. The blessing of Abraham that was confirmed upon Jacob included his children, whether or not they resided in the Promised Land. Just as God said that the nations that bless Abraham will themselves be blessed, so we see the outworking of this blessing in the life of Joseph, the descendant of Abraham, Isaac and Jacob. The Hebrew says וַיְבָרֶךְ יהוה אֶת־בֵּית הַמִּצְרִי בִּגְלַל יוֹסֵף *(va-yevarekh YHWH et bet ha-mitsri biglal Yosef)*, which translated means that "the LORD blessed the house of the Egyptian because of Joseph." Using the Hebrew parallelism technique of stating the same thought differently and expanding it a little, the text continues וַיְהִי בִּרְכַּת יהוה בְּכָל־אֲשֶׁר יֶשׁ־לוֹ בַּבַּיִת וּבַשָּׂדֶה *(va-yhi birkat YHWH be-khol asher yesh lo ba-bayit u-va-sadeh)*, which translated means that "the LORD blessed everything that belonged to him, (whether) in the house or in the field." The blessing of God that came to this Egyptian household was overwhelming, and it was all because of Joseph.

A very similar situation had occurred in the life of Jacob while he was living and working with Laban. In Genesis 30:27 we read that God blessed Laban because of Jacob's presence in his house. This is a deliberate parallel between Israel and Joseph. To state it more precisely, the blessings were all because of God's promise to Abraham, Isaac and Jacob and their posterity.

וַיַּעֲזֹב כָּל־אֲשֶׁר־לוֹ בְּיַד־יוֹסֵף וְלֹא־יָדַע אִתּוֹ מְאוּמָה כִּי אִם־הַלֶּחֶם אֲשֶׁר־הוּא אוֹכֵל וַיְהִי יוֹסֵף יְפֵה־תֹאַר וִיפֵה מַרְאֶה

He left all that he had in Joseph's hands and, with him there, he paid attention to nothing save the food that he ate. Now Joseph was well built and handsome. (Gen. 39:6)

Potiphar entrusted everything to Joseph with the exception of just one thing – the food he ate. While Potiphar saw that Joseph was extremely successful in everything he did, Joseph was still a foreign slave and someone who was, according to Egyptian religious customs, ceremonially unclean and therefore could not be involved in the preparation of food. At the end of the narrative when Joseph's brothers are not allowed to eat together with the Egyptians, we will clearly see why (Gen. 43:32). Egyptians, like the Israelites, did not view the matters of food consumption as mundane – they belonged to the realm of the sacred. The thought that such economic refugees or migrants could have anything to do with the realm of the sacred, no matter how mundane this encounter seemed to everyone around, never entered his mind.

However, there may have been another reason as well. Potiphar is called שַׂר הַטַּבָּחִים (*sar ha-tabachim*), which could be translated as "the chief of the cooks" or also "the chief of the bodyguards" – or literally even "executioners" (Gen. 37:36). If the job of Potiphar was to provide security to the Pharaoh of Egypt, then it would have included security over the food he consumed. A primary way to remove any unwanted king from his throne throughout history has been to poison him. So, in this case, Potiphar's job would have predisposed him to put Joseph in charge of everything in the household except the matters of food. This job could not be entrusted into the hands of a foreign national. It was just too dangerous. It is, of course, ironic that years later Pharaoh will appoint Joseph to be his right-hand man in all Egypt. Joseph will then administer the matters of food on behalf of the entire nation of Egypt as well as the surrounding world that will come to find bread in Egypt.

Joseph's Temptation

Potiphar was not the only one who took a liking to Joseph. His wife was also attracted to him. He was young, handsome, and incredibly successful. Perhaps she saw far more of him than she did of her own husband. As the text testifies, one of the character traits of Joseph was his loyalty. Acting as a true Israelite, he guarded Potiphar's *honor* just as he guarded everything else in Potiphar's house. Everything that belonged to Potiphar, was Potiphar's, and that included his unfaithful wife. When Joseph spoke to Potiphar's wife attempting to dissuade her from her continual sexual harassment, among other things, he said the following about Potiphar:

אֵינֶנּוּ גָדוֹל בַּבַּיִת הַזֶּה מִמֶּנִּי וְלֹא־חָשַׂךְ מִמֶּנִּי מְאוּמָה כִּי אִם־אוֹתָךְ בַּאֲשֶׁר אַתְּ־אִשְׁתּוֹ וְאֵיךְ אֶעֱשֶׂה הָרָעָה הַגְּדֹלָה הַזֹּאת וְחָטָאתִי לֵאלֹהִים

He wields no more authority in this house than I, and he has withheld nothing from me except yourself, since you are his wife. How then could I do this most wicked thing, and sin before God?" (Gen. 39:9).

There are two reasons that held Joseph back from succumbing to the temptations of Potiphar's wife. First, Joseph's gratitude to Potiphar for the trust he placed in him. Literally, the Hebrew says, אֵינֶנּוּ גָדוֹל בַּבַּיִת הַזֶּה מִמֶּנִּי (*eynenu gadol ba-bayit ha-zeh mi-meni*), which means "there is no one greater than me in this house." Joseph was greatly honored by Potiphar. To use his willing wife for sexual pleasure would have violated this trusting relationship at its core. Like Adam in the Garden of Eden, there was only one thing that was strictly forbidden to Joseph in Potiphar's house. Adam failed by eating from the only tree that was forbidden to him; whereas Joseph succeeded by avoiding sexual contact with the one woman who was forbidden to him. Joseph, as a true son of Abraham, Isaac and Jacob, must not fail where their ancestor Adam did.

The second reason was based upon Joseph's awareness of God's presence with him. The God of Abraham, Isaac and Jacob was not merely a territorial god like many others in the minds of ancient people. He supervised the affairs of the entire world. This meant that Joseph (who was no doubt taught by Jacob/Israel about his God), was convinced that whether he was in the Land of Canaan or in Egypt, or whether he was in a public place or in the locked chambers of Potiphar, God was present there as well. God was with him, not only in his success and prosperity, but also in moments of great temptation and responsibility. God being with him was not simply Joseph's magic power to be righteous, but also his moral compass that provided guidance.

Joseph's Faithfulness

Joseph resisted the temptation. Unlike Judah in Chapter 38, Joseph is praised for upholding community values and seeking its greater good at the expense of his own discomfort (the opposite to Judah's actions towards Tamar). Joseph does so in a foreign land, in a community to which he does not really belong. One intent in these stories is simple – community is of utmost importance in the sight of God. Jacob's covenant children must learn to behave in selfless ways. God is building not just a family, but a nation. The nation of Israel which will emerge from Jacob's children cannot follow the path of Cain. It must become a holy people, a kingdom of priests. In Exodus 19:5-6 we read: "Now then, if you will obey Me faithfully and keep My covenant, you shall be My treasured possession among all the peoples. Indeed, all the earth is Mine, but you shall be to Me a kingdom of priests and a holy nation. These are the words that you shall speak to the children of Israel." (Ex. 19:5-6)

After repeated unsuccessful attempts to persuade Joseph to sleep with her, Potiphar's wife accused the innocent Joseph of attempted rape – apparently out of a sense of disappointment, anger and vengeance. He denied the charges, but Potiphar just could not overlook his own wife's accusation.[40] So, ignoring the plea of Joseph and taking the accuser's circumstantial evidence as sufficient, Potiphar placed Joseph in the prison where Egyptians sentenced by the Pharaoh himself were held indefinitely (Gen. 39:11-20). It is possible that Potiphar suspected something and did not believe his wife either. He did not want to kill Joseph, just in case he was innocent. And at the same time he wanted to remove Joseph from his wife, and so Joseph was imprisoned. It should not come as a surprise to us that the LORD's presence could not be held back by the prison doors. We read in Genesis 39:21 that "the LORD was with Joseph" וַיְהִי יהוה אֶת־יוֹסֵף *(va-yehi YHWH et Yosef)*.

Interpreting Dreams

The next section of the narrative begins with Pharaoh's displeasure with his מַשְׁקֶה *(mishkeh)* "cup bearer" and אֹפֶה *(ofeh)* "baker" who served in his royal court. Pharaoh puts both of these main servants into jail, probably pending an investigation about what really took place on their watch. They end up in the same prison as Joseph. Just as Joseph quickly found favor with Potiphar, he also found favor with the jailer. Joseph was given duties in the jail house and the jailer trusted him with taking care of prisoners because he was successful in everything he did. Multiple times we read that the Lord was with Joseph and he is the one who gave him favor with people and success.

As providence would have it, given their high status as the king's servants, Joseph was assigned to take care of them. Both of Pharaoh's servants dreamt disturbing dreams at night. Because they were in prison, they had

---

[40] There is one other point that should be made. There existed in Egypt a tale of two brothers who lived and worked together - "The Tale of the two Brothers Anpu and Bata". The wife of one of the brothers sought to seduce him, but the other brother refused, remaining faithful. She accused him of rape and the brother, believing her to be a victim, sought his brother's death. God helped the fleeing brother, who eventually died, and after series of what seems to our modern ear of bizarre events, is resurrected and is able to impregnate his wife, producing posterity. It is likely that both Potiphar and Joseph, and especially Israelites that left the land of Egypt, were very familiar with this story. What connection (if any) may have existed between this story and the story of Joseph and Potiphar is not clear.

no access to priests. There were no professional dream interpreters around for them to seek explanations. The logic of ancient people was simple: if the gods are trying to tell them something, but they don't understand, they could end up displeasing the gods further by their actions. This is a very undesirable result for men who are already in jail. In the morning Joseph finds them perplexed and they share their problem with Joseph. Joseph assures them that his all-present God is certainly capable to interpret their dreams.

הֲלוֹא לֵאלֹהִים פִּתְרֹנִים סַפְּרוּ-נָא לִי:

"Surely God can interpret! Tell me." (Gen. 40:8)

Alter explains, "In Egypt, the interpretation of dreams was regarded as a science, and formal instruction in techniques of dream interpretation was given in schools called 'houses of life.'"[41] Joseph tells these men that the Egyptian idea about dreams is wrong. God is perfectly capable to interpret dreams and give the interpretation to those not considered "experts." The chief cupbearer tells Joseph the details of his dream. Joseph interprets it to mean that in three days the Pharaoh will free him and he will be restored to his service in the same honorable position. The chief baker tells Joseph the details of his dream. Joseph interprets it to mean that in three days the chief baker will be executed by hanging. Both interpretations of the dreams come true exactly in the way Joseph interpreted them. (Gen. 40:9-13). Interestingly, when Joseph told his dreams to his family there was no need to interpret them. Jacob and his sons understood the dreams perfectly. But Egyptians needed interpretation.

Joseph is Forgotten

After Joseph interpreted the meaning of the dream to the chief cupbearer, he asked him something that at the time the cupbearer probably did not pay much attention to. Joseph asked that when the cupbearer finds himself free again in the service of the king, that he would tell Pharaoh about Joseph's fate (Gen. 40:14-15). Understandably or, perhaps, even conveniently, the cupbearer forgot about Joseph when he was freed. As readers or hearers of the story grow in their sympathy towards Joseph, it

---

[41] Alter, *Genesis: Translation and Commentary*, 230.

is with great pain that they hear about the cupbearer's forgetfulness. We read in Gen. 40:23:

וְלֹא־זָכַר שַׂר־הַמַּשְׁקִים אֶת־יוֹסֵף וַיִּשְׁכָּחֵהוּ

Yet the chief cupbearer did not think of Joseph; he forgot him. (Gen. 40:23)

The Torah uses phrases like לֹא־זָכַר *(lo zakhar)*, which means "did not remember" and יִּשְׁכָּחֵהוּ *(yishkachehu)*, which means "forgot about him." Both phrases restate and reinforce the same exact concept – Joseph was not remembered. This concept is set in opposition to the familiar idea of God's remembrance of Noah, Lot and Rachel. When Noah, his family and his animals were drifting in the boat amidst the flood, the Hebrew texts states that יִזְכֹּר אֱלֹהִים אֶת־נֹחַ *(yizkor Elohim et Noach)* "God remembered Noah." God spared Lot from being judged together with the evil inhabitants of Sodom and Gomorrah because He remembered Abraham (Gen. 19:29). The Hebrew phraseology in that case is remarkably similar to the case of God remembering Noah: יִזְכֹּר אֱלֹהִים אֶת־אַבְרָהָם *(yizkor Elohim et Avraham)*. When Leah bore Jacob six sons and one daughter while Rachel remained barren in utter distress, we are told in Hebrew יִזְכֹּר אֱלֹהִים אֶת־רָחֵל *(yizkor Elohim et Rachel)* - "God remembered Rachel."

In all the scenarios, Noah, Lot and Rachel, whom God remembered, were very much in need of God's salvation. They were in need of a relief from their misfortunes. This particular phraseology also looks forward to God remembering the children of Abraham, Isaac and Jacob in Egyptian captivity and being willing to act on their behalf, leading them out of the land of their slavery (Ex. 2:24; 6:5). The "God remembered" phraseology in reality functions as a synonym for "God acted on behalf of someone." When God remembered Noah, the waters of the flood receded. When God remembered Abraham, his nephew Lot was taken to safety. When God remembered Rachel, he opened up her womb. By the same token, when the chief cupbearer "forgot" and "did not remember," the statements simply signified his inaction.

This does not necessarily mean that the cupbearer literally forgot Joseph or his request. The chief cupbearer most likely remembered Joseph's request, but for some reason he chose not to act upon it. The cupbearer never told Pharaoh about Joseph. Perhaps it was too risky, considering how close he came to death the last time when Pharaoh was displeased with his servants. This lack of action on the part of the cupbearer would cost Joseph two more full years of life in jail. The emphasis is on the length of the wait in Torah. This is probably why the emphatic Hebrew phrase שְׁנָתַיִם יָמִים (*shenatayim yamim*), which literally means "two years of days," was used. It expressed the fullness of time. When God directs the events in people's lives they happen exactly when they need to occur.

Pharaoh's Dreams

The Pharaoh dreamed two dreams. They were strange and Pharaoh, just like the chief cupbearer and chief baker, was truly distressed about their meaning (Gen. 41:8). It was the duty of the Pharaoh of Egypt to ensure the tranquility and prosperity of the Land. So obviously the contents of the dreams got Pharaoh really worried. The next morning his spirit was agitated and he sent for all the magicians of Egypt, and all its wise men. Pharaoh told them his dreams, but none could interpret them for Pharaoh. The chief cupbearer and chief baker were distressed in the previous story because there was no professional interpreter of dreams around in the jail house, but Pharaoh had them at his disposal.

The ineptness of the Egyptian priesthood becomes obvious. Everyone was called in but no one was capable to provide a certain answer. Pharaoh was at a loss. "The monopoly of knowledge in the empire is broken. Pharaoh knows many things. He knows how to manage and administer and control. As we may see in the Exodus narrative, he knows how to prosper and how to oppress. But he does not know how to discern the movement of God's way within his realm. Only God knows that."[42] Only then does the chief cupbearer find the courage to speak to the Pharaoh about a Hebrew slave locked up in his prison (Gen. 41:9-13). The suggestion is still risky, but now it seems fully justified since everyone has failed to interpret the dreams and Pharaoh is still upset. Without much delay Pharaoh orders Joseph to be brought from the dungeon into his presence. The dungeon in Genesis 41:14 is called בּוֹר (*bor*) "pit." This is the exact same word as used in Genesis 37: 24 to describe the dried-up well that Joseph's brothers used to confine him.

---

[42] Brueggemann, *Genesis: Interpretation*, 322.

Once Joseph was cleaned up and prepared to enter the King's presence he was ushered in without much delay. His head was shaved and new clothes were given to him (Gen.41:14). "In the ancient Near East, only the Egyptians were clean-shaven, and the verb used here can equally refer to shaving the head, or close-cropping it, another distinctive Egyptian practice."[43] The new garments on Joseph were probably necessary, but the listeners of the story are probably meant to remember also all the stories of Joseph's garments. His special garment got him into trouble with his brothers. It was taken from him and dipped in blood to deceive his father. Joseph's garment was used by Potiphar's wife to accuse him. Each time Joseph was mistreated and thrown into a dark place his garment was taken from him. Now a garment is restored to him. When Pharaoh elevates him (later in the story), Joseph will receive another special garment worthy of an Egyptian aristocrat and ruler.

The story moves quickly and the next scene begins with the Pharaoh himself retelling Joseph the content of his first dream. We read in Genesis 41:15-16 that Pharaoh said to Joseph:

חֲלוֹם חָלַמְתִּי וּפֹתֵר אֵין אֹתוֹ וַאֲנִי שָׁמַעְתִּי עָלֶיךָ לֵאמֹר תִּשְׁמַע חֲלוֹם לִפְתֹּר אֹתוֹ

"I have had a dream, but no one can interpret it. Now I have heard it said of you that for you to hear a dream is to tell its meaning." (Gen. 41:15)

וַיַּעַן יוֹסֵף אֶת־פַּרְעֹה לֵאמֹר בִּלְעָדָי אֱלֹהִים יַעֲנֶה אֶת־שְׁלוֹם פַּרְעֹה

Joseph answered Pharaoh, saying, "Not I! God will see to Pharaoh's welfare." (Gen. 41:16)

Pharaoh received a report that Joseph possesses an extraordinary ability to interpret dreams. Joseph, however, responds that "only God himself" בִּלְעָדָי אֱלֹהִים *(biladay Elohim)* will answer regarding the שָׁלוֹם *(shalom)* "well-being" of Pharaoh. It is possible that Joseph's refusal to claim that he interprets dreams himself has to do with the divinity claims of the Pharaoh himself. For Joseph, the Pharaoh was not divine. It would be God who will answer Pharaoh. So Joseph says that he is not the source of interpretation.

---

[43] Alter, *Genesis: Translation and Commentary*, 236.

When Pharaoh told Joseph that exact content of both dreams, Joseph told him that the two dreams are really the same one dream repeated. The meaning of the dreams is that God has decided to show Pharaoh His plans for the next 14 years. The double dreaming confirms the irreversibility of this message and that it is imminent. It will surely come to pass (Gen. 41:25-32). The dream, in fact, was a sign of God's favor upon Pharaoh and upon Egypt. Now that the Pharaoh has been informed of God's plans, preparations could be made to avoid an economic catastrophe. While providing the interpretation, Joseph also suggested a plan to Pharaoh – the purposeful and consistent saving of extra grain that will be received in the next seven coming harvest seasons to insure future prosperity (Gen. 41:33-36).

Joseph is Elevated

When Pharaoh took council with his royal advisors, all agreed that Joseph can be put in charge of this project effective immediately (Gen. 41:37-38). Pharaoh made Joseph the second man in Egypt, stating that only Pharaoh's throne will separate the authority of Joseph from that of Pharaoh. We read in Genesis 41:40:

אַתָּה תִּהְיֶה עַל־בֵּיתִי וְעַל־פִּיךָ יִשַּׁק כָּל־עַמִּי רַק הַכִּסֵּא אֶגְדַּל מִמֶּךָּ

You shall be in charge of my court, and by your command shall all my people be directed; only with respect to the throne shall I be superior to you." (Gen. 41:40)

The Hebrew אַתָּה תִּהְיֶה עַל־בֵּיתִי *(atah tihyeh al beti)* literally means "you will be over my house" and עַל־פִּיךָ יִשַּׁק כָּל־עַמִּי *(al pikha yishek kol ami)*, which is very difficult to translate literally, perhaps means something like "over your mouth/according to you will all people kiss [i.e., be ruled]." Pharaoh's words were not empty. He proceeded to grant Joseph formal authority in Egypt. Joseph will govern Egypt in every way but just coming short of being Pharaoh. These words reflect the state of things that had been at Potiphar's house. Joseph had had responsibility over almost all of Potiphar's affairs (Gen. 49:4).

וַיֹּאמֶר פַּרְעֹה אֶל־יוֹסֵף רְאֵה נָתַתִּי אֹתְךָ עַל כָּל־אֶרֶץ מִצְרָיִם

Pharaoh further said to Joseph, "See, I put you in charge of all the land of Egypt." (Gen. 41:41)

וַיָּסַר פַּרְעֹה אֶת־טַבַּעְתּוֹ מֵעַל יָדוֹ וַיִּתֵּן אֹתָהּ עַל־יַד יוֹסֵף וַיַּלְבֵּשׁ אֹתוֹ בִּגְדֵי־שֵׁשׁ וַיָּשֶׂם רְבִד הַזָּהָב עַל־צַוָּארוֹ

And removing his signet ring from his hand, Pharaoh put it on Joseph's hand; and he had him dressed in robes of fine linen, and put a gold chain about his neck. (Gen. 41:42)

This time Pharaoh not only speaks but acts. He officially confers the high office upon Joseph and confirms this by adorning the Hebrew slave with the regal insignia. Joseph receives the signet ring, the golden collar, and the fine linen dress. Based on Egyptian frescos the "golden chain" should be understood as an Egyptian ornamental collar instead.[44] Pharaoh had Joseph ride in the chariot of his second-in-command, and they cried before him, "Abrek!" Thus he placed him over all the land of Egypt. "The narrative reflects the firm authority of Joseph. He is clearly in charge. None may resist or question… As the story develops, there is a ruthlessness which makes survival possible. There is also remarkable technical "know-how" put at the service of imperial well-being."[45]

Pharaoh summarized the level of authority that he granted to Joseph by stating in Genesis 41:44:

אֲנִי פַרְעֹה וּבִלְעָדֶיךָ לֹא־יָרִים אִישׁ אֶת־יָדוֹ וְאֶת־רַגְלוֹ בְּכָל־אֶרֶץ מִצְרָיִם

"I am Pharaoh; (yet) without you, no one shall lift up hand or foot in all the land of Egypt." (Gen. 41:44)

Alter writes, "Most commentators and translators have construed this as an implied antithesis: though I am Pharaoh, without you no man shall raise hand or foot… But this is unnecessary because we know that royal decrees in the ancient Near East regularly began with the formula: I am King X. The sense here would thus be: By the authority of the Pharaoh, I declare

---

[44] Alter, *Genesis: Translation and Commentary*, 240.
[45] Brueggemann, *Genesis: Interpretation*, 328.

that without you…"⁴⁶ It is interesting that the same phraseology בִּלְעָדֶיךָ *(biladekha)* "without you" that is used in reference to Joseph by Pharaoh, was used by Joseph to say that "only God" could interpreted Pharaoh's dreams בִּלְעָדָי אֱלֹהִים *(biladi Elohim)*. It is possible that the use of this phrase is intentional. The Torah writer may be drawing a connection here between Joseph's complete reliance and honor of God and Pharaoh honoring of Joseph with great authority in Egypt.

Another commentator adds: "Joseph will indeed rule, just as his brothers feared (Gen. 37.8, 10 - 11), but with this crucial qualification: His rule will be rooted not in sheer power, but in the benefit he provides to the less fortunate. This corresponds to an ideal of kingship widespread in the ancient Near East, in which the king is the rescuer and servant of the people."⁴⁷ As a sign of Joseph's new identity Pharaoh gave Joseph a new name. He called him Zaphenath-Paneah (צָפְנַת פַּעְנֵחַ). Although there is no agreement among Egyptologists as to what this name may actually mean, one fitting, but only possible suggestion is that צָפְנַת פַּעְנֵחַ is a Hebrew transliteration of Egyptian for "God speaks, he lives." In Gen. 42:6 Joseph's brothers bowed to him, and Hebrew uses the same verb for this act as in Gen. 37:9-10 where Joseph's dreams are described.

Pharaoh also gives him Asenath אָסְנַת *(Osnat)*, a daughter of Poti-Phera priest of On, as a wife. The association of Poti-Phera, a priest of the city of On with Potiphar of Pharaoh's court is unlikely. While Asenath's name translated from Egyptian means "the one belonging to Neith (goddess)," in Jewish tradition we witness the transformation of Asenath into a faithful convert to Judaism. Of course, only in prototype, since the peculiar Jewish way of life, national identity and tradition for conversion itself would be developed much later in history. Suffice it to say that Asenath is regarded as having accepted the faith and the ways of her husband, and Joseph's children were deemed true descendants of Jacob. This of course follows the biblical patrilineal pattern of heritage (vs. the later rabbinic matrilineal system). Moses, by the way, also married a daughter of a Gentile priest. He was also rejected by his own, but became a great leader and redeemer of

---

46   Alter, *Genesis: Translation and Commentary*, 240.
47   Levenson, "Genesis Introductions and Annotations," *The Jewish Study Bible*, ed. Berlin and Brettler, 77.

his people. In the case of Joseph, it is clear that the covenant of Abraham, Isaac and Jacob was continued through Manasseh and Ephraim, Asenath's children.

Asenath's story would later be told in a Jewish book from the Hellenistic era called *Joseph and Asenath*. This book attempted to resolve the unspoken tension of Asenath in Joseph's life. Authored probably sometime around the first century CE, the twenty-some chapter work speaks about the transformation of Asenath the idol-worshiper to a worshiper of Israel's God. The imaginative story provides a window into the world of Jewish thinking about conversion at the time of its composition. Of course, the book was written many centuries after Torah and adds no real historical value to the understanding of the original story of Joseph and Asenath.
Joseph was roughly thirty years old when all of these things took place (Gen. 41:26). His new job involved a lot of traveling. He was supervising the entirety of Egypt to reach a very important point – enough provisions saved to survive a regional famine. Just as everything prior that Joseph put his hand to, this nationwide project was also destined for great success. In Genesis 41:38 Pharaoh asks a rhetorical question:

הֲנִמְצָא כָזֶה אִישׁ אֲשֶׁר רוּחַ אֱלֹהִים בּוֹ

"Could we find another like him, a man in whom is the spirit of God?" (Gen. 41:38)

Almost identical words were said about a craftsman named Bezalel in Exodus 31:2. It is ironic that Joseph's family did not recognize (or admit) these traits in him, but Pharaoh did. "The Egyptian monarch has not been turned into a monotheist by Joseph, but he has gone along with Joseph's idea that human wisdom is a gift of God, or the gods, and the expression he uses could have the rather general force of 'divine spirit.'"[48] The ancient Egyptians and many other people of the Near East worshipped forces of nature, which they also personified as gods and depicted visually. Israel's neighbors were known to refer to the divine as El, or Eloah. But the word El often meant a personified force, a power connected to the element of nature. "There is a fundamental difference between those belief-systems and Israelite faith. It held that the forces of nature were not independent

---

[48] Alter, *Genesis: Translation and Commentary*, 239.

and autonomous. They represented a single totality, one creative will, the author of all being.[49]

During the first seven years, Joseph's Egyptian wife Asenath bore him two sons. He called the firstborn son "Manasseh" מְנַשֶּׁה *(Menasheh)*, which translated means "(God) has caused me to forget" – כִּי־נַשַּׁנִי אֱלֹהִים *(ki nashani Elohim)* – the hardship of the past and my parental home. The second son's name has a more positive meaning, described in the text as "God made me fruitful." The meaning of Joseph's sons' names has to do with his awareness that it was God who set him free and made him fruitful in Egypt (Gen. 41:51-52). The fertility of all Israelites in the land of Egypt will eventually prove to be a mixed blessing, because it is precisely when the Israelites were very fertile that a new king arose over Egypt who did not know Joseph, and he enslaved the Israelites (Ex. 1:7- 8).

Joseph Governs Egypt

As seven fruitful harvest years came to an end, it became obvious that Joseph was not a lunatic and that Pharaoh was right in appointing him to the task of setting aside massive quantities of food. When the whole region began to experience starvation, Egypt still had bread. At some point, however, Egyptians too began to experience a famine just like the other nations around them. When that took place, Pharaoh directed people to ask Joseph, by telling them to "do whatever he tells you" אֲשֶׁר־יֹאמַר לָכֶם תַּעֲשׂוּ *(asher yomar la-khem taasu)*. Joseph rationed out the previously collected grain to the Egyptians. The world around Egypt also entered the time of severe famine. Not only did Egyptians come to Joseph, but the rest of the Mediterranean world did, too. The hunger becomes unbearable for Joseph's family in Canaan. Everything was set in motion for the eventual meeting of Joseph with his brothers as well as of Joseph and his beloved father.

Time to Go to Egypt

When it became clear that Egypt had a significant surplus of food that could be acquired by others, Jacob said to his sons to stop wasting time by looking at one another: "Just go and get us what our family needs, so that

---

[49] Sacks, *Covenant & Conversation*, 287.

we may live and not die!" (Gen. 42:1-3). The language is ironic. Many years ago some brothers were ready to lead Joseph into a path of death and eventually send him to Egypt as a slave to live and not die. Now Joseph's father is sending them to Egypt so that the entirety of Jacob's family will live and not die. (Other than the irony of meaning, these words – live and not die – of course show the high urgency that Jacob placed on his words to his ten sons). Jacob did not send his youngest son Benjamin, Joseph's full brother, with them out of fear that he would lose the only son he still has from Rachel, so the first trip to Egypt they make without him. Once they arrived, the sons of Israel got into a long line of those who had also come to Egypt to get food (Gen. 42:5).

The Brothers Bow Down to Joseph

The text reminds us, as if we had the chance to forget, that it was Joseph who was appointed a vizier of Egypt and that when the brothers came to pay homage they had to bow down to him personally. We read in Genesis 42:6, 8:

וְיוֹסֵף הוּא הַשַּׁלִּיט עַל־הָאָרֶץ הוּא הַמַּשְׁבִּיר לְכָל־עַם הָאָרֶץ וַיָּבֹאוּ אֲחֵי יוֹסֵף וַיִּשְׁתַּחֲווּ־לוֹ אַפַּיִם אָרְצָה:

Now Joseph was the vizier of the land; it was he who dispensed rations to all the people of the land. And Joseph's brothers came and bowed low to him, with their faces to the ground. (Gen. 42:6).

וַיַּרְא יוֹסֵף אֶת־אֶחָיו וַיַּכִּרֵם וַיִּתְנַכֵּר אֲלֵיהֶם וַיְדַבֵּר אִתָּם קָשׁוֹת וַיֹּאמֶר אֲלֵהֶם מֵאַיִן בָּאתֶם וַיֹּאמְרוּ מֵאֶרֶץ כְּנַעַן לִשְׁבָּר־אֹכֶל:

When Joseph saw his brothers, he recognized them; but he acted like a stranger toward them and spoke harshly to them. He asked them, "Where do you come from?" And they said, "From the land of Canaan, to procure food." (Gen. 42:7).

וַיַּכֵּר יוֹסֵף אֶת־אֶחָיו וְהֵם לֹא הִכִּרֻהוּ:

For though Joseph recognized his brothers, they did not recognize him. (Gen. 42:8).

The English expression "to bow down" does not clearly communicate the idea of full prostration practiced in the Ancient Near East and inferred here by the use of the Hebrew וַיִּשְׁתַּחֲווּ־לוֹ *(va-yishtachavu lo)*, which basically means "and they prostrated themselves to him." "The verb for "recognize" (וַיַּכִּרֵם) and the verb for 'play the stranger' (וַיִּתְנַכֵּר אֲלֵיהֶם) are derived from the same root (the latter being a reflexive form of the root). Both uses pick up the thematically prominent repetition of the same root earlier in the story: Jacob was asked to 'recognize' Joseph's blood-soaked tunic and Tamar invited Judah to 'recognize' the tokens he had left with her as a security for payment for her sexual services."[50]

We will see later how the story of Judah and Tamar is intricately connected to the story of Joseph, but for now we see the linguistic hints here and there. The story simply mentions that he acted as a stranger towards them and spoke harshly to them: וַיְדַבֵּר אִתָּם קָשׁוֹת *(va-yedaber itam kashot)*. It is unlikely that at this time Joseph was already overwhelmed by a well-thought-through and appropriated sense of God's providential purposes and grace towards Israel's family and the world-at-large. This will certainly happen, but later. At this point Joseph is most likely rightfully angry with his flesh and blood about what they did to him, but his anger is, nevertheless, constrained by a sense of God's presence with Joseph at all times and His goodness towards him.

Joseph in Need of Grace

There is surely an element of sweet triumph for Joseph in seeing his grandiose dreams fulfilled so precisely, though it would be darkened by his recollection of what the report of his dreams led his brothers to do. As the brothers failed to recognize him, he certainly did not forget the looks of his offenders, even though they were now twenty years older. He only recalled the dreams that he had dreamt about them bowing down to him, that he was, no doubt, forced to reconsider many times over by the circumstances of his unfortunate captivity. "In chapter 37, he is a naive and guileless boy. In chapters 39-41, he is a noble and effective man of integrity who is not intimidated by the royal woman (39), the royal officers (40), nor even the Pharaoh (41). But in 42-44, he is now a ruthless and calculating governor. He understands the potential of his enormous office

---

50 Alter, *Genesis: Translation and Commentary*, 245.

and exploits his capacity fully. He not only manipulates the scene but seems to relish his power to intimidate and threaten."[51]

In Genesis 42:9b we read of Joseph's accusation towards them as he sought to hide his identity from them:

וַיֹּאמֶר אֲלֵהֶם מְרַגְּלִים אַתֶּם לִרְאוֹת אֶת־עֶרְוַת הָאָרֶץ בָּאתֶם׃

He said to them, "You are spies, you have come to see the land in its nakedness." (Gen. 42:9b).

The idiom refers to that which should be hidden from an outsider's eyes, as the nakedness of a human should be hidden from all but the legitimate sexual partner. The vizier is accusing the brothers of wanting to take advantage of Egypt's vulnerability, in some sense comparing it to a woman who can be overpowered and raped by a foreign evil-doer. The brothers argued that the assumptions of the vizier are baseless for the simple reason that all of them were brothers, the sons of the same father. The idea here being that the work of spies was a highly dangerous enterprise and it was unheard-of that the team of spies will be formed from an entire family. In the case of failure, the entire family will be dead. When they denied Joseph's accusations by stating that they were honest men, he restated his statement about their suspicious identity.

A Demand to See the Brother

They said that they were once twelve brothers. They stated in Genesis 42:13b that:

וְהִנֵּה הַקָּטֹן אֶת־אָבִינוּ הַיּוֹם וְהָאֶחָד אֵינֶנּוּ׃

Behold, the youngest is now with our father, and one is no more. (Gen. 42:13b).

It is probably at this point in the story that, while Joseph still put up a harsh front, things in his heart may have begun very slowly to change from bitter hurt to eventual forgiveness, however far it was still from his heart. He told the brothers that in order to verify their story one of them would be allowed to go back to their father's house to bring their youngest brother to the Pharaoh, while all others would remain under arrest. He sent them

---

[51] Brueggemann, *Genesis: Interpretation*, 336-7.

into a jail house for three days to make sure that they saw how serious he was. On the third day he said to them something very interesting. We read in Genesis 42:18:

זֹאת עֲשׂוּ וִחְיוּ אֶת־הָאֱלֹהִים אֲנִי יָרֵא:

"Do this and you shall live, for I am a God-fearing man. (Gen. 42:18).

He then told them that he was willing to change his previous verification test by allowing for only one to be kept captive with him and for the rest of them to go back to get their youngest brother. This made perfect sense. (Later on we will see a similar dynamic at play when Benjamin will be found riding with Joseph's silver cup in his sack). If the men were spies, they would not come back (after all they would not then be brothers but, rather, co-workers taking their own risks); but, if they were in Egypt on their stated business, they would certainly be able to do what was asked, especially now that the vizier was able to show them some leniency (Gen. 42:19-21).

The vizier's argument seemed believable to brothers. Joseph spoke to them through an interpreter and his incredible emotional self-control did not allow his brothers to know that he understood their every word. This sense of self-control will be lost completely when Judah, later in the narrative, begs Joseph to allow him to become a slave instead of Benjamin, Rachel's second son. It is at this point that Joseph will reveal himself to his brothers and weep out loud for all the neighbors to hear.

Already at this point in the narrative, a moment of truth has arrived. God has called them to an account. The brothers were convinced that they were being punished for their actions against Joseph many years earlier. We read in Genesis 42:21:

וַיֹּאמְרוּ אִישׁ אֶל־אָחִיו אֲבָל אֲשֵׁמִים אֲנַחְנוּ עַל־אָחִינוּ אֲשֶׁר רָאִינוּ צָרַת נַפְשׁוֹ
בְּהִתְחַנְנוֹ אֵלֵינוּ וְלֹא שָׁמָעְנוּ עַל־כֵּן בָּאָה אֵלֵינוּ הַצָּרָה הַזֹּאת:

"Alas, we are being punished on account of our brother, because we looked on at his anguish, yet paid no heed as he pleaded with us. That is why this distress has come upon us." (Gen. 42:21).

וַיַּעַן רְאוּבֵן אֹתָם לֵאמֹר הֲלוֹא אָמַרְתִּי אֲלֵיכֶם לֵאמֹר אַל־תֶּחֶטְאוּ בַיֶּלֶד וְלֹא שְׁמַעְתֶּם וְגַם־דָּמוֹ הִנֵּה נִדְרָשׁ:

Then Reuben spoke up and said to them, "Did I not tell you, 'Do no wrong to the boy'? But you paid no heed. Now comes the reckoning for his blood." (Gen. 42:22).

Upon hearing these words, Joseph turned away, walked and wept in secret. In what seems almost like a fit of rage, Joseph came back to his brothers with his guards and arrested Simeon before their eyes. He then gave orders to fill their bags with grain, reimburse them the money paid and to give them enough food for their journey. When the brothers later discovered that on the top of the grain the money that each one of them brought to Egypt to pay for the grain had been returned, their hearts sank.

Bending under Pressure

An important series of disqualifying behaviors are recorded here to show that Reuben, in spite of being the firstborn son, would not be the leader of the future nation of Israel. It would be Judah who would take his role, and the later incorporation of Joseph's sons into the tribal count will further destabilize Reuben's communal standing. Reuben was too weak then to be a real leader, and he is too weak now. All he can do is to blame ("I told you so"), something that Joseph would not do in the end. This will be clearly contrasted with the responsible and brave actions of Judah (but more about that a bit later). Returning to their dismay at finding money in the grain sacks, Genesis 42:28b tells us of their words:

וַיֵּצֵא לִבָּם וַיֶּחֶרְדוּ אִישׁ אֶל־אָחִיו לֵאמֹר מַה־זֹּאת עָשָׂה אֱלֹהִים לָנוּ:

Their hearts sank; and, trembling, they turned to one another, saying, "What is this that God has done to us?" (Gen. 42:28b).

The Hebrew וַיֵּצֵא לִבָּם *(va-yetse libam)* literally means "and their hearts went out." They were truly afraid. They were no longer in control. When they arrived home, they told Jacob the entire truth about what had occurred during their journey (Gen. 42:29-35). "Because they could not believe the dream, they are forced to treat father Jacob as though he were the last generation who must be kept alive and unharmed for perpetuity. They cannot see themselves as a generation of promise-bearers."[52]

"The dream is happening. The future is at work toward life. But in their fearfulness, the brothers do not notice it."[53] The news was too much for Jacob to bear. Jacob's highly charged emotional response makes clear that he still blamed the brothers for Joseph's death, which was the reason he was so upset that they wanted to take the second child of Rachel with them on a perilous return journey to Egypt. One of the clear faults of Jacob is his unashamed and obtuse favoritism of Rachel's children. Yet these scandalously faulty character traits are an important part of the story.

None of the wrong sentiments of Jacob excuse the murderous passion towards Joseph by his brothers. In fact, later on we will see Judah accepting his father "as he is" and not "as he should be." This favoritism of Jacob is clearly wrongdoing, but one that will be graciously understood by Judah as he recalls his own wrongdoing towards Tamar due to his own favoritism toward his youngest son from a wife who had also died. (The story of Tamar claiming Judah's seed for her own by pretending to be a prostitute and Judah's failure to treat her justly suddenly becomes important, which finally explains why this seemingly unrelated story was inserted into the Joseph-related narrative. It had everything to do with it).

We read in Genesis 42:36:

וַיֹּאמֶר אֲלֵהֶם יַעֲקֹב אֲבִיהֶם אֹתִי שִׁכַּלְתֶּם יוֹסֵף אֵינֶנּוּ וְשִׁמְעוֹן אֵינֶנּוּ וְאֶת־בִּנְיָמִן תִּקָּחוּ עָלַי הָיוּ כֻלָּנָה:

Their father Jacob said to them, "It is always me that you bereave: Joseph is no more and Simeon is no more, and now you would take away Benjamin. These things always happen to me!" (Gen. 42:36).

Reuben tells his father that he can kill both of his sons if Benjamin does not return – a morally questionable and economically unsound business deal that once again shows Reuben as someone lacking wisdom to lead, in spite of him being the eldest of the brothers and having some sense of

---

[52] *Ibid.*, 338.
[53] *Ibid.*

conscience. Jacob rejects the request to allow Benjamin to go with the brothers to Egypt, preferring the comfort of knowing that Benjamin is safe, even though Simeon remains in an Egyptian jail (Gen. 42:36-38).

In this story salvation for Benjamin – and also for entire family of Israel – will come from Judah. He will turn the situation around by his self-sacrifice on behalf of Benjamin and, without realizing it, will forever establish his own tribe as a royal leader of the future nation of Israel. A possible reason Simeon was chosen to remain incarcerated in Egypt is because as Leah's second son (Gen.29:31-33), he could be an appropriate hostage for Benjamin, Rachel's second son. Simeon's name שִׁמְעוֹן *(Shimon)* is connected with the verb שָׁמַע *(shamah)*, which means "to hear." In the context of the narrative, this meaning probably brings a hint of the brothers not paying heed to the cries of Joseph from the pit before he was auctioned off to Egypt. (Gen. 42:21-22). We read in Genesis 42:38:

וַיֹּאמֶר לֹא־יֵרֵד בְּנִי עִמָּכֶם כִּי־אָחִיו מֵת וְהוּא לְבַדּוֹ נִשְׁאָר וּקְרָאָהוּ אָסוֹן בַּדֶּרֶךְ אֲשֶׁר תֵּלְכוּ־בָהּ וְהוֹרַדְתֶּם אֶת־שֵׂיבָתִי בְּיָגוֹן שְׁאוֹלָה׃

"My son must not go down with you, for his brother is dead and he alone is left. (Gen. 42:38).

It is interesting that in this verse Jacob spoke of the second son of Rachel – Benjamin – as "my son," while failing to make any additional mention as to the second son of Leah – Simeon, who now was kept in captivity in Egypt (and who was mentioned in vs. 36). By stating that "only" Benjamin was left, he presumably meant of the sons of Rachel. Jacob betrays once again his parental shortcoming that first nurtured in the hearts of the brothers the sense of inferiority in his, their father's, house in comparison to the beloved and honored first son of Rachel. This theme is emphasized in the narrative over and over again. This is so because the brothers will, in the end, be tested as to whether or not they can now live with this unjustified favoritism of Jacob towards Rachel's children. Joseph will make sure that this is tested before reveals himself to them.

Jacob refuses to speak to his sons again about this matter. It is only after some time, when the supply of food brought from Egypt was almost gone, that the father again told the sons to go back to Egypt (not to save Simeon, but) to bring more food. It is also possible of course that Jacob here does not display any lack of care for the misfortune of Simeon, but instead is simply overwhelmed with fear and grief, thinking that Simeon, just as Joseph, is now as good as dead (the earlier mention in Gen. 42:36 may support this supposition). However, given everything we are told about Jacob's preferential treatment and his unfairness with love distribution in his family, it is likely that Jacob viewed the loss of Simeon as truly unfortunate "collateral damage," but what he really fears more than that is the loss of the last child of Rachel.

Judah Steps Up

What follows is the intense interaction between Jacob and one of his sons – Judah, who will eventually be trusted by Jacob with the leadership of his family and, thereby, the future nation of Israel. In Genesis 43:8-9 we read:

וַיֹּאמֶר יְהוּדָה אֶל־יִשְׂרָאֵל אָבִיו שִׁלְחָה הַנַּעַר אִתִּי וְנָקוּמָה וְנֵלֵכָה וְנִחְיֶה וְלֹא נָמוּת גַּם־אֲנַחְנוּ גַם־אַתָּה גַּם־טַפֵּנוּ:

Then Judah said to his father Israel, "Send the boy in my care, and let us be on our way, that we may live and not die – you and we and our children. (Gen. 43:8).

אָנֹכִי אֶעֶרְבֶנּוּ מִיָּדִי תְּבַקְשֶׁנּוּ אִם־לֹא הֲבִיאֹתִיו אֵלֶיךָ וְהִצַּגְתִּיו לְפָנֶיךָ וְחָטָאתִי לְךָ כָּל־הַיָּמִים:

I myself will be surety for him; you may hold me responsible: if I do not bring him back to you and set him before you, I shall stand guilty before you forever. (Gen. 43:9).

כִּי לוּלֵא הִתְמַהְמָהְנוּ כִּי־עַתָּה שַׁבְנוּ זֶה פַעֲמָיִם:

For we could have been there and back twice if we had not delayed." (Gen. 43:10).

When Jacob tells his sons to get more food from Egypt, Judah – on behalf of all the brothers – refuses, citing the Egyptian vizier's condition to return only with their youngest brother accompanying them. Jacob then accuses Judah and the brothers of making a mistake by volunteering information about Benjamin. Judah defended their actions, stating that the vizier asked pointed and precise questions about their father and any more children, so they had no choice but to tell him the truth.

Jacob as a Son of Abraham

Jacob reluctantly agrees. He instructs the sons to take gifts for the vizier, return the money the sons found in the bags and to also pay the expected price for grain. He then extends his blessing upon the children, trusting that *El Shaddai* will have mercy towards them and that both brothers will be released. This shows that, in the end, Jacob is a son of Abraham. In this moment of great personal challenge (the feared loss of yet another beloved son) he was willing to trust *El Shaddai* with his most treasured Benjamin. Jacob is willing to stake everything on the God he has gotten to know through his rocky but redemptive sojourns. "The father invokes this old name for God and hopes for mercy. Everything is staked on that one name. Injured Jacob believes more than his sons. He dares to think of a new possibility. In his boldness, he breaks the cycle of his own grief and loss. And at the same time, he breaks the sons' spiral of betrayal and deception. Jacob is a picture of faithfulness that permits newness. He is able to care and grieve and therefore to hope."[54]

Joseph Meets Benjamin

When the brothers arrived in Egypt, Joseph, upon the sight of Benjamin (probably from behind the scenes), instructed his steward to welcome the men into his own house and to prepare a festive meal. The first thing that the brothers hurried to tell Joseph's steward was that somehow the last time when they were in Egypt their money was returned to them, so they had brought that silver back. The silver will continue to follow them throughout the story, echoing the silver they received as a payment for their brother Joseph when he was sold into slavery. We read in Genesis 43:23 a telling explanation (even if contrived):

שָׁלוֹם לָכֶם אַל־תִּירָאוּ אֱלֹהֵיכֶם וֵאלֹהֵי אֲבִיכֶם נָתַן לָכֶם מַטְמוֹן בְּאַמְתְּחֹתֵיכֶם כַּסְפְּכֶם בָּא אֵלָי וַיּוֹצֵא אֲלֵהֶם אֶת־שִׁמְעוֹן׃

"All is well with you; do not be afraid. Your God, the God of your father, must have put treasure in your bags for you. I got your payment." And he brought out Simeon to them. (Gen. 43:23).

---

[54] *Ibid.*, 339.

The steward welcomed them in, washed their feet and took care of their donkeys as well. The brothers laid out all the gifts they brought for the vizier, expecting him to arrive at some point later, since they understood from the steward that the vizier was planning to dine with them. When Joseph arrived, the brothers again bowed themselves to the ground before him. Just like Jacob before Esau when he returned the stolen blessing of the first-born and made a rightful restitution payment to Esau, the brothers, too, continue to bow down before Joseph, not once as the dream described, but many times over.

The first thing the vizier said to them upon his arrival was in the form of a question. We read about it in Genesis 43:27-28:

וַיִּשְׁאַל לָהֶם לְשָׁלוֹם וַיֹּאמֶר הֲשָׁלוֹם אֲבִיכֶם הַזָּקֵן אֲשֶׁר אֲמַרְתֶּם הַעוֹדֶנּוּ חָי:

He greeted them, and he said, "How is your aged father of whom you spoke? Is he still in good health?" (Gen. 43:27).

וַיֹּאמְרוּ שָׁלוֹם לְעַבְדְּךָ לְאָבִינוּ עוֹדֶנּוּ חָי וַיִּקְּדוּ וַיִּשְׁתַּחֲוּוּ:

They replied, "It is well with your servant our father; he is still in good health." And they bowed and made obeisance. (Gen.43:28).

As we will learn at the moment of Joseph's revelation of himself to the brothers, the issue of his father still being alive (something of which Joseph is not sure) is of utmost importance to him. It was not only that Joseph was violently taken from Jacob, but it was also Jacob who was violently taken from Joseph. What follows is an amazing display of Joseph's emotions as he first confirms with the brothers that the young boy standing with them is really Benjamin. He then proceeds, to the surprise of the brothers, to address the child in the kindest words possible. We read in Genesis 43:29b אֱלֹהִים יָחְנְךָ בְּנִי *(Elohim yachnekha beni)*, which literally means, "God be gracious to you, my son." One can almost feel the choking in Joseph's throat when he pronounced the appropriate words "my son," while in all reality he was desperately wanting to call him "my (full) brother." The time for that, however, has not yet come. The narrator then explains that once Joseph greeted Benjamin, he was overcome with emotion to such a degree that he was about to cry but, holding back his tears, he went to a different room and wept there. When he regained control of himself he ordered his servants to serve the meal.

Joseph Tests His Brothers

He directed the steward to seat everyone in accordance to their age. The brothers were astonished at this, but complied. Their astonishment likely had to do with the steward's knowledge of the order of births. To their further amazement, the youngest brother Benjamin received a portion that far exceeded the portions of food received by all the others, irrespective of their seniority. We read in Genesis 43:34:

וַיִּשָּׂא מַשְׂאֹת מֵאֵת פָּנָיו אֲלֵהֶם וַתֵּרֶב מַשְׂאַת בִּנְיָמִן מִמַּשְׂאֹת כֻּלָּם חָמֵשׁ יָדוֹת וַיִּשְׁתּוּ וַיִּשְׁכְּרוּ עִמּוֹ:

Portions were served them from his table; but Benjamin's portion was five times larger than that of anyone else. And they drank their fill with him. (Gen. 43:34).

It appears that Joseph leveled against his brothers a series of tests. First, will they come back for one of their own (Simeon)? Second, will they display an envy-based reaction to Benjamin getting five times more food? The next and the ultimate test was to follow. Will the brothers defend at all cost the life the second son of Rachel (Benjamin)?

Joseph's Ultimate Test for His Brothers

Joseph instructed his stewards to give as much grain to the brothers as they could carry, give back all the money they had brought, and to place Joseph's silver cup into the sack of Benjamin as they departed, seemingly with the vizier's mighty blessing and favor. As soon as they left the city, Joseph told the steward to stop the brothers and to accuse them of stealing his property. We read in Genesis 44:4b, 5b Joseph's precise instructions. The steward with accompanying guards were instructed to say to the brothers:

לָמָּה שִׁלַּמְתֶּם רָעָה תַּחַת טוֹבָה:

'Why did you repay good with evil? (Gen. 44:4b).

הֲלוֹא זֶה אֲשֶׁר יִשְׁתֶּה אֲדֹנִי בּוֹ וְהוּא נַחֵשׁ יְנַחֵשׁ בּוֹ הֲרֵעֹתֶם אֲשֶׁר עֲשִׂיתֶם:

It is the very one from which my master drinks and which he uses for divination. It was a wicked thing for you to do! (Gen. 44:5b).

It is likely that the brothers knew exactly what cup the steward thought they had stolen as Joseph most likely used, or at least on purpose paraded it before them, perhaps even explaining his great abilities and connection with the divine. After all, Joseph's staff seemed to know things they simply could not have known naturally. Alter writes:

> The probable mechanism of divination in a goblet would be to interpret patterns on the surface of the liquid it contained or in drops running down its sides. Divination would have been a plausible activity on the part of a member of the high Egyptian bureaucracy, with its technology of soothsaying, but the emphasis it is given here is also linked with Joseph's demonstrated ability to predict the future and his superiority of knowledge in relation to his brothers.[55]

The brothers, unsuspecting of any set-up, defend themselves and foolishly proclaim that whoever is found with the cup in their sack should be put to death and the rest stay in Egyptian captivity indefinitely (Gen. 44:6-8). Though the proposed punishment sounded extreme, it is very much possible that the theft of a sacred item (like this divination cap) was traditionally understood in the Ancient Near East to deserve capital punishment. Interestingly enough, the brothers' words sound very similar to the exchange between Laban and Jacob (Gen. 31:32), and this is one of the ways we can see that these seemingly unconnected stories are actually connected. Laban does not find what he is looking for, but it is presumed that the price of the theft of Laban's gods is exacted in the early death of Rachel later in the story when she gave birth to Benjamin.

Here, however, the divination cup is found, though it was not stolen by the brothers. They will, of course, be forgiven in the end, but only after they understand that this was somehow related to the great sin they had committed together 20 years prior against Joseph. When the brothers claimed that whoever stole the cup should die and the rest become slaves, the steward replied that though the proposed punishment fit the crime, a

---

[55] Alter, *Genesis: Translation and Commentary*, 260.

far more merciful option would be executed – only the guilty one will be held as a slave, the rest will go free. We read in Genesis 44:17:

חָלִילָה לִּי מֵעֲשׂוֹת זֹאת הָאִישׁ אֲשֶׁר נִמְצָא הַגָּבִיעַ בְּיָדוֹ הוּא יִהְיֶה־לִּי עָבֶד וְאַתֶּם עֲלוּ לְשָׁלוֹם אֶל־אֲבִיכֶם׃

"Far be it from me to act thus! Only he in whose possession the goblet was found shall be my slave: the rest of you go back in peace to your father." (Gen. 44:17).

The language and role-playing are striking. Long ago, the brothers were probably upset not so much by Joseph but by Jacob, because of his preferential treatment of Joseph as Rachel's son. They turned their anger, however, not against their father, choosing to deal directly not with him but, predictably, with the object of Jacob's intense love – Joseph. In this brilliant scene, the steward echoes the words of Joseph's instructions to him and utters the words, "Far be it from me to act like that!" We have got to see the irony here. An Egyptian worshiper of pagan divinities has a sense of justice, while the children of Jacob, the members of the Covenant with Israel's God, do not. They were not in any way prepared for this turn of events and that was exactly Joseph's plan.

Benjamin is Arrested

All the brothers were searched and the last bag to be checked was that belonging to Benjamin, Rachel's second son and Joseph's full brother. Seeing that the cup was in fact found in Benjamin's sack, the brothers tore their clothes as a sign of grief and mounted their donkeys to return to the city with the steward. "Joseph's scheme, after all, is to make the brothers feel they are trapped in a network of uncanny circumstances they can neither control nor explain."[56] As all who want revenge, Joseph too wanted them, at least for a short time, to feel exactly what he had felt when he was thrown into the pit and sold to Egypt – perplexed, lost and alone. Thankfully by now revenge was not the center of Joseph's plan; rather, testing of the brothers was. Did the brothers remain the same? Did they change? Will they allow for the other son of Rachel, Benjamin, to be given over to slavery and possible death too? Will they abandon him as they had Joseph?

---

[56] *Ibid.*, 259.

Judah Acts Sacrificially

Judah, the one who originally conceived the plan to sell Joseph to Egypt, spoke up on behalf of the brothers, addressing the grand vizier. As Judah retells the entire drama (Gen. 44:18-30) he, without realizing it, speaks to his brother who is presumed dead (the fate of most slaves in Egypt after 20 years of intense labor). He tells him that "the father of Benjamin does not see meaning in life without his youngest son." The very issue that caused the negative feelings towards Joseph in the past is now accepted by a much older and more mature Judah. Judah still disagrees with Jacob, his father, but he now clearly understands him. He cannot bear seeing his father go through the pain of losing another son of Rachel and dying a depressed man who felt that he had completely failed in life. There is nothing that Judah fears more than his father's eternal disappointment and disapproval. Judah begs the vizier to allow him to exchange places with Benjamin. It is he who will remain a slave in Egypt and it is Benjamin that is to return to his father, Jacob (Gen. 44:30-34). Judah's tone of voice betrayed full determination. He was ready and willing to save Benjamin even at the cost of his own freedom (or even life).

Joseph Reveals Himself

Now is the moment that Joseph was waiting and hoping for with all of his heart. He wanted to reconcile with his brothers, but he wisely did not want to do that apart from seeing their truly repentant hearts. Joseph could hardly keep back his tears as he shouted for everyone to leave them alone in that room. Joseph's sobbing was so intense that the Egyptians heard it, and the news quickly was reported to the Pharaoh himself (Gen. 45:1-2). We read in Genesis 45:3 the words of Joseph's self-disclosure:

אֲנִי יוֹסֵף הַעוֹד אָבִי חָי וְלֹא־יָכְלוּ אֶחָיו לַעֲנוֹת אֹתוֹ כִּי נִבְהֲלוּ מִפָּנָיו:

I am Joseph. Is my father still alive? But his brothers could not answer him, so dumfounded were they on account of him. (Gen. 45:3).

The revelation אֲנִי יוֹסֵף *(ani Yosef)* "I am Joseph!" is quick and stunning. Joseph's very first question after this, הַעוֹד אָבִי חָי *(ha-od avi chai)* "Is my father still alive?" shows that, up until now, he had not really trusted anything that the brothers had said. That is, Joseph was not sure that the brothers had a living father. Now that he saw Judah's action in being willing to be left as a slave in Egypt forever, the hope of his father still being alive was suddenly resurrected in full force. Hence, his quick question to the brothers about his father. What was revealed here was not for the eyes and ears of the Egyptian empire. The listening community of the children of Israel, however, were not asked by the narrator to leave the room together with the Egyptians (45:1), but were in fact invited to stay with the family. Think about it. The reader is permitted to witness a disclosure of the good news for Israel: The dead one is alive! The abandoned one has returned in power! The dream has had its way![57] Our God reigns.

Joseph's Assurance

We read in Genesis 45:4b-8 Joseph's statement to his brothers:

אֲנִי יוֹסֵף אֲחִיכֶם אֲשֶׁר־מְכַרְתֶּם אֹתִי מִצְרָיְמָה׃

"I am your brother Joseph, he whom you sold into Egypt. (Gen. 45:4b).

וְעַתָּה אַל־תֵּעָצְבוּ וְאַל־יִחַר בְּעֵינֵיכֶם כִּי־מְכַרְתֶּם אֹתִי הֵנָּה כִּי לְמִחְיָה שְׁלָחַנִי אֱלֹהִים לִפְנֵיכֶם׃

Now, do not be distressed or reproach yourselves because you sold me hither; it was to save life that God sent me ahead of you. (Gen. 45:5).

וַיִּשְׁלָחֵנִי אֱלֹהִים לִפְנֵיכֶם לָשׂוּם לָכֶם שְׁאֵרִית בָּאָרֶץ וּלְהַחֲיוֹת לָכֶם לִפְלֵיטָה גְּדֹלָה׃

God has sent me ahead of you to ensure your survival on earth, and to save your lives in an extraordinary deliverance. (Gen. 45:7).

וְעַתָּה לֹא־אַתֶּם שְׁלַחְתֶּם אֹתִי הֵנָּה כִּי הָאֱלֹהִים

So, it was not you who sent me here, but God. (Gen. 45:8).

---

[57] Brueggemann, *Genesis: Interpretation*, 343.

Joseph told the brothers to go back to Jacob as quickly as they were able to tell him about Joseph and to bring everyone back with them so that the prophecy once given to Joseph in a dream would be fulfilled. Joseph will provide bread and sustenance to his entire family during these difficult times of famine in the entire Middle East. Two years of famine were over, but five more were still to come. The brothers needed to hurry. The good news for the house of Israel need not be kept secret any more. It needed to be told now.

It is interesting that Joseph does not demand from his brothers that they confess to their father the whole truth, realizing that the truth would probably be too traumatic for him to hear. The Torah leaves this to the imagination of the listening community of the children of Israel. He only instructs them to tell him of the good things that now await the family of Israel in Egypt.

The Graciousness of Pharaoh

Pharaoh was very pleased when the report came to him that Joseph's brothers had come. The phraseology used points us to the possibility that Joseph had shared with Pharaoh the bitter, intimate details of his life and suffering, and perhaps both of them knew or suspected that sooner or later the brothers of Joseph would have to come to Egypt for bread. Joseph was prepared and so was Pharaoh as he extended his personal guarantees of well-being and prosperity to Joseph's family as soon as they reach Egypt (Gen. 45:16-20).

In Brueggemann's words: "The revelation breaks as news upon the entire family. The news is abrupt in a narrative that has been shaped in a quite secular way. This speech completely redefines the situation for all parties. Now the guilty fear of the brothers is superseded. The grief of the father is resolved. He had grieved unnecessarily, for what seemed death was God's way to life. The revengeful cunning of the successful brother is superseded. He has no need to triumph over his family. The guilt of the brothers, the grief of the father, and the revenge of Joseph are all used as means for this disclosure of the hidden call of God. None of that matters now, for the whole family is now brought to a new moment."[58]

---

[58] Brueggemann, *Genesis: Interpretation*, 345-6.

The story does read like a drama with a very moving conclusion. The Torah's portrayal of Jacob and his emotion at hearing, and at first disbelieving, that Joseph was still alive is highlighted. That which could have been stated in one summarized sentence (as was almost always the case in Genesis earlier) is opened up and savored by the storyteller (Gen. 45:25-28) to be truly felt by its original hearers – the Israelites who had left Egypt and were on the way to the Promised Land, meeting all the struggles of this perilous journey.

The story does not end here, but goes on. There is so much more that could be said about the Book of Genesis, but perhaps it should be left for another time. After all, this story was never meant to be read, considered and understood only once, but rather lived and relived from year to year by all children of the scandalous but truly remarkable man who struggled with God.

BIBLIOGRAPHY

Alter, Robert. 1998. *Genesis*. New York: W.W. Norton.

Berlin, Adele, and Marc Zvi Brettler. 2014. *The Jewish Study Bible: Torah, Nevi'im, Kethuvim*, 2nd edition. New York: Oxford University Press.

Brueggemann, Walter. 2010. *Genesis*. Louisville: Westminster John Knox Press.

Levenson, Ron D. "Genesis Introductions and Annotations." In *The Jewish Study Bible. Tanakh Translation,* edited by Adele Berlin and Marc Zvi Brettler, New York: Oxford University Press, 2014.

Sacks, Jonathan. 2009. *Covenant & Conversation: a Weekly Reading of the Jewish Bible*. Genesis: The Book of Beginnings. New Milford, CT: Maggid Books & The Orthodox Union.

Sacks, Jonathan. 2015. *Not In God's Name*. New York: Schocken Books.

Made in the USA
Columbia, SC
20 September 2021